The History of India
for Children

FROM THE MUGHALS TO THE PRESENT

VOLUME 2

Archana Garodia Gupta

Shruti Garodia

hachette
INDIA

With a lifelong passion for books, languages, travel and history, **Archana Garodia Gupta** has a knack for weaving delightful nuggets of information into engaging tales. A leading national quizzer, she has won the 'Champion of Champions' title from BBC *Mastermind India*. She regularly writes articles on history and business for magazines, and was seen as a member of the expert panel on *Kaun Banega Crorepati*. She was the national president of the FICCI Ladies Organization (FLO) in 2015–16, where she set up many programmes for the empowerment of Indian women. Archana was raised in New Delhi and holds an MBA from IIM, Ahmedabad. She lives in Delhi where she and her husband run a jewellery business under the Touchstone brand.

An incurable reader and writer, **Shruti Garodia** has an abiding love of history, especially through storytelling. She is a keen traveller, and loves new places and experiences. When not exploring historic sites and museums around the world, she can often be found trying new adventures – scuba-diving in Egypt, trekking to Machu Picchu, skiing in the Alps, or learning to sail a yacht in Greece.

Shruti is passionate about retaining the natural curiosity of children, and is developing modules to make history and complicated concepts accessible to young minds by crafting them into simple, fun stories.

From New Delhi, Shruti graduated from Cornell University, USA, with a degree in statistics and engineering, and has a Certificate in Quantitative Finance. She has lived in New York and London during her career in investment banking.

In memory of our mother Chandra Garodia for her unflinching belief in her daughters.

You made us believe too.

First published in 2018 by Hachette India
(Registered name: Hachette Book Publishing India Pvt. Ltd)
An Hachette UK company
www.hachetteindia.com

2

ISBN 978-93-5195-253-4

Hachette Book Publishing India Pvt. Ltd
4th & 5th Floors, Corporate Centre,
Plot No. 94, Sector 44, Gurugram - 122003, India

Typeset in Sabon Lt Std 11/14
by Manmohan Kumar, Delhi

Printed and bound in India
by Manipal Technologies Limited, Manipal

Contents

Introduction   1

1. Foundation of the Mughal Empire   5
   AN ACCIDENTAL EMPEROR
2. Akbar the Great   27
   CONQUEROR AND MYSTIC
3. The Great Mughals   53
   AN AGE OF SPLENDOUR
4. Decline of the Mughal Empire   81
   AN EMPIRE SPLINTERS
   INTO A THOUSAND PIECES
   Peek into the Past   109
   HISTORY IN A BOWL OF PANEER MAKHANI
5. Lifestyle in Mughal India   111
   TALES OF OPULENCE AND DECADENCE
6. The Europeans Arrive   133
   THE FORTUNE HUNTERS
7. The Uprising of 1857   157
   TALES OF HORROR AND COURAGE
8. Reform and Renaissance   181
   A NATION AWAKENS

Peek into the Past   205
CALENDARS, INDIAN STYLE

9. Impact of the British Raj   207
PLUCKING THE GOLDEN BIRD

10. The Raj in India   225
MEMSAHIBS AND BOX-WALLAHS

11. The Rise of Nationalism   243
A PEOPLE FIND THEIR VOICE

12. Independence at Last   265
A NEW PATH FOR THE WORLD

Peek into the Past   293
COINS AND CURRENCY

13. Sweeping Changes   295
EAST AND WEST: THE TWAIN DO MEET

14. Forging of a Nation   311
THE MAKING OF A COUNTRY

15. The Nehru Years   327
A PHOENIX RISES FROM THE ASHES

16. The Indira Years   347
A SHARP TURN LEFT

Peek into the Past   365
INDIAN SCRIPTS

17. Liberalization   367
BREAKING THE SHACKLES

Photo Acknowledgements   385
Timeline   386
Index   388
Acknowledgements   394

Introduction

In this volume of *The History of India for Children*, we will track India's journey from the peak of Mughal splendour to her fall into abject poverty and degradation as Britain's captive golden goose, and then on to her hard fight for independence and beyond.

Today, Indians are eagerly waiting for India to finally join the club of rich countries. In fact, for most of her long history, India *was* the First World. It was the fabled land where it seemed the streets were paved with gold; it was the golden bird (waiting to be plucked…!).

A thousand years ago, greater India, with only 3 per cent of the world's land, was earning a full one-fourth of the entire world's income! Countries around the globe looked to India for trade and Indian religions like Buddhism and Hinduism were spreading rapidly across Asia (which had half the people in the world).

Jump ahead to the 1940s, and India was tragically poor… where most people did not even have enough food to eat, and starvation and famine were always round the corner. India now earned a measly 4 per cent of the world's income. After centuries of colonial suppression, Indians had little confidence in themselves and looked to Europe for most things.

India: Rise and Fall (and Rise!)

How did India become so rich in the first place? Even China, with its similar population and wealth, was two-and-a-half times larger in size.

The main reason is that India has very, very fertile land, with enough sun and water. Most countries of the world can grow a crop a year. India has usually produced at least two crops a year if not three (and sometimes sneaked in even four!). This means that there has simply been much more food available, and this 3 per cent of the world's land easily supported 25 per cent of the world's population through the ages. India could also grow and harvest many different things, like spices, cotton, sugar, pearls and coral that other people always wanted. This abundance of food and materials allowed many Indians to stop farming and start making products like fabric, cloth and steel that were in demand across the world.

In return, India had a never-ending thirst for gold and silver! As the French traveller Francois Bernier put it: 'It should not escape notice that gold and silver, after circulating in every other quarter of the globe, come at length to be absorbed in Hindustan…' In fact, the only way gold left India was when invaders like Timur Lang and Nadir Shah forcibly took it away. But as most invaders ended up settling in India, their conquests did not affect India's overall wealth.

It was only with the British that India's true decline started, as they steadily took away the wealth back to England. At the same time, the rest of the world became much richer with the Industrial Revolution, while India was left further and further behind.

See how India's wealth compared with the world's over the last 2,000 years:

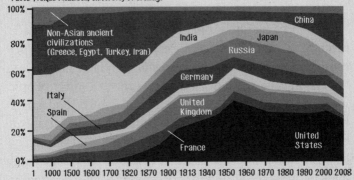

Graphics based on: 'Satistics on World Population, GDP and Per Capita... GDP, 1-2008', Angus Maddison, University of Groninge

Above: Share of the world's Gross Domestic Product (GDP); below: Share of the world's per capita income

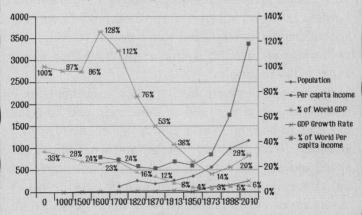

India was quite rich until 1700 CE, and at our relative poorest (per person) in the 1970s. Since then, we are getting richer surely but (very) slowly. China has raced ahead and is already five times richer than India, which still has a way to go before it reaches even the world

average, much less the richest countries. The average American earns 15 times as much as an Indian today!

The Indian subcontinent still packs a hefty punch though. Across all its countries, it still makes up 25 per cent of humanity. It has all types of climates, mountains, rivers, deserts, animals and plants. Four billion people watch Indian movies, more than even Hollywood (three billion)! Indic religions like Hinduism and Buddhism still influence 25 per cent of the world population. The Republic of India has more than 2,000 languages and dialects, all races and shades of mankind, all the religions you can think of and people living lifestyles from all ages: from prehistoric hunter-gatherers, to neolithic farmers, medieval villagers to the most modern cutting-age technologists who send space probes to Mars. We are a noisy and bustling democracy with a billion voices and a million mutinies.

The story of how all this happened is in this book – how India got so rich and so influential, and how she lost it all to become so poor and wretched; her diversity and unity; what held her together and what forced her apart; and who were the men and women who starred in India's very own historical *Kathasaritsagara* – the 'ocean of streams of stories'. These are some of the questions we have tried to answer.

Foundation of the Mughal Empire

[1526–56 CE]

'Like us, many have spoken over this spring, but they were gone in the twinkling of an eye... We conquered the world with bravery and might, but we did not take it with us to the grave...'
— Babur in Baburnama

1

An Accidental Emperor

By 1526, north India had been ruled by the sultanates based out of Delhi for more than 300 years, the area controlled varying from nearly the whole of India under Muhammad Bin Tughlaq in the 1330s, to just about Delhi under the Sayyids in the early 1400s. After Timur Lang's invasion in 1398, many different independent sultanates had come up in the east, west, and south. The Lodis, who were ruling Delhi currently, had managed to reconquer some territory in the Indo-Gangetic plains.

Now it was the turn of another sort of Persianized Central Asian to sweep in – the Turko-Mongols. For the next 300 years, one single family would dominate the fortunes of India and rule one of the most magnificent empires in the world, uniting almost all of India for the third time in her history.

They came to be known as the Mughals (from Mongols). Though their founder Babur (r. 1526–1530) came to India reluctantly, his sons and grandsons made it their own land, and brought about a deep Indo-Islamic social and cultural fusion. They appointed Hindus to high positions in their government and army. They were mostly (with a few infamous exceptions) tolerant and inclusive. They married Hindus, had Jain spiritual advisers and kept pictures of the Virgin Mary in their bedrooms. This spirit was first introduced by the greatest Mughal emperor, Babur's grandson Akbar.

But where did Babur come from? Genghis (or Chinggis) Khan's mighty Mongol Empire had been divided into four '*khanates*'. Over time, the Ilkhanate, which included Central Asia, adopted both the religion and culture of Islamic Persia. In the mid-14th century, a prince of the Turko-Mongol Barlas tribe, called Timur, formed a short-lived empire of his own, taking over the Ilkhanate and expanding even further, including a truly brutal sack of Delhi.

After Timur's death, his sons and grandsons started squabbling, and his empire quickly crumbled into small regional territories perpetually at war. As one writer puts it, 'there were too many kings and not enough kingdoms'.

In one such small fiefdom was born Prince Babur.

Political History
Babur (r. 1526–30 ce)

Babur (a nickname meaning 'lion') led an action-packed life full of dramatic turns. He was born in 1483 ce as Zahiruddin Muhammad in Ferghana in Uzbekistan, to a minor regional chieftain, with famous ancestors on both sides – Timur Lang and Genghis Khan himself!

Babur was crowned when he was just twelve, after his father died in a bizarre accident when his royal dovecote collapsed (with him in it) into a steep ravine. Young Babur yearned to conquer the city of Samarkand, Timur Lang's dazzling imperial capital, which was coveted by all the Timurid cousins. While he went off to capture it, jealous rivals put his younger brother on the throne of Ferghana. In a twist of fate, Babur was left with neither Samarkand nor Ferghana and at 15 years, became a landless fugitive with few supporters. He wrote in his diary: 'I could not help crying a good deal.'

He struggled to regain some land, but failed. With just 200–300 followers, he roamed the hills of Central Asia, taking refuge with local tribes. During his stay with his maternal uncle in Tashkent, he 'endured much poverty and humiliation... No country, or hope of one!' He even thought of going to China to stay with his maternal cousins, but ironically, considered the eastern 'pure' Mongols to be uncivilized barbarians, unlike his tribe, the Persianized 'Timuri Turks'. How appalled he would have been to know that his dynasty would be named after those same Mongols!

Babur finally had a stroke of luck in 1504 CE, when he captured Kabul and Ghazni. He ruled there for 22 years, making periodic attempts to capture Samarkand, and dealing with minor rebellions by his brothers, cousins and Afghan tribesmen. He built a merry court in Kabul, where he indulged in gardening, feasting, poetry and (a lot of) wine.

Still, Babur was ambitious. He had heard many tales of the enormous bounty his ancestor Timur had carried back from India and decided to try his luck.

By 1523, he pretty much controlled Lahore and made a series of forays further inward, which succeeded only on his fifth try (patience pays!). Delhi now beckoned. Because it had been once conquered by his great-grandfather Timur, Babur felt that he had a right to it (much as he felt Samarkand was his!). He wrote to Delhi's sultan,

Ibrahim Lodi, and asked him to step aside, but the sultan, unsurprisingly, ignored him.

THE BATTLE OF PANIPAT

Babur marched towards Delhi, and met Lodi on 20 April 1526 in the First Battle of Panipat. A low-lying plain 80 km north-west of Delhi, not far from Kurukshetra (the site of the Mahabharata war), Panipat would see two more key battles in future, each of which would dramatically change the course of Indian history.

Babur writes in his memoirs that his 12,000 troops met Ibrahim Lodi with his 100,000 men and 1,000 elephants (probably exaggerated). Still, it was a very unequal fight. Babur claimed he was not nervous, because Lodi 'knew

The Battle of Panipat, 1526, was where Babur first introduced field guns to his style of warfare; detail from a miniature painting

neither when to stand, nor move, nor fight'. Babur used the artillery (gun) tactics he had learnt from the Ottoman Empire very successfully. He got 700 carts tied together as a shield, with gaps from which his cannons could fire.

Though they were used for besieging forts, this was the very first time cannons were used on an open battlefield in India. Lodi's elephants panicked, while his forces could not penetrate Babur's solid shield. Babur got his men to swiftly encircle Lodi's humungous army, who were unable to retreat or move, their large numbers working disastrously against them. In half a day, Sultan Ibrahim Lodi and 15,000–16,000 of his troops lay dead. Babur took over Delhi's throne, and got many treasures as booty, including the famed Koh-i-noor diamond.

Now Babur really disliked India with a passion, and longed for the cool, green valleys of his lost homeland of Uzbekistan. Even Kabul seemed like a dream in comparison. He wrote in his *Baburnama*: 'India is a country of few charms... The people lack good looks and good manners...' Everything about India was wrong: The people were ugly, they had no manners, no culture, no good horses or dogs. It was hot and dusty, and there was no cool water or ice. Worst of all, there were no melons nor grapes!

Babur's troops too longed to escape the fierce Indian summer and return to cooler Kabul, laden with their wealth and jewels, and eventually try and recapture Samarkand (yet again).

The one thing that Babur liked about India, though, was the 'abundance of gold and silver'. For all his private grumblings into his diary, Babur was made of stern stuff and 'after long years of struggle... they had at last obtained broad lands, infinite wealth and innumerable subjects...

who would seriously abandon such plenty for the harsh poverty of Kabul?' He convinced most of his soldiers to stay on, though some left. One soldier's parting couplet shows his relief: 'If safe and sound I cross the Sind/ Blacken my face before I wish for Hind'.

Rana Sanga, ruler of Mewar. He was defeated by Babur in the battle of Khanua, 1527

Babur soon faced a significant threat from the Rajput king Rana Sanga of Mewar, who had come to power in 1508 CE and became one of the most powerful rulers in north India, as well as a constant thorn in Ibrahim Lodi's side through his regular raids. In 1527, Rana Sanga went to see off this new foreign invader – joined by many of the defeated Afghan nobles who threw in their lot with him. An early skirmish at Bayana ended in disaster for the Mughals, whose mood was grim; there had been many desertions by Indian recruits.

To motivate his dispirited men, Babur declared the battle a holy jihad against the Rajput infidels, elevating it to a noble religious war. Babur tells us that the 'plan' worked perfectly as he too made a noble sacrifice... promising to give up his beloved alcohol forever. All the fine wine, decanters and goblets in the Mughal camp were ostentatiously smashed. Fortified by this high drama, his men met their enemies near Fatehpur Sikri in Khanua.

Emperor Babur's Thoughts on India

'The peasants parade around stark naked with something like a loincloth tied around themselves and hanging down two spans below their navels. Under this rag is another piece of cloth, which they pass between their legs and fasten to the loincloth string. Women fasten around themselves one long piece of cloth, half of which they tie to their waists and the other half of which they throw over their heads.'

***

'Most of the inhabitants of India are infidels, called Hindus, believing mainly in the transmigration of souls; all artisans, wage-earners, and officials are Hindus. Every artisan follows the trade handed down to him from his forefathers.'

***

'Another nice thing is the unlimited numbers of craftsmen and practitioners of every trade... in Agra alone there were 680 stonemasons at work on my building every day. Aside from that, in Agra, Sikri, Bayana, Dholpur, Gwalior and Koil, 1,491 stonemasons were labouring on my buildings. There are similar vast numbers of every type of craftsman and labourers of every description in Hindustan.'

The battle of Khanua was more evenly matched as some Lodi generals had joined Babur, who again applied the same military strategies. The Rajputs fought with valour but were ultimately defeated, helped by treachery and defection. Rana Sanga died the next year.

Babur moved south and laid siege to Chanderi fort in Malwa, which committed *jauhar* after some days. Meanwhile, Ibrahim Lodi's brother had gathered a large army along with the sultan of Bengal. In his last major battle, Babur defeated them at the Battle of Ghaghra near Benares in 1529 CE.

Soon, his eldest (and favourite) son and heir, Humayun fell perilously ill. The legend goes that as Babur prayed for Humayun's recovery, he was told to offer God his most precious possession. When later asked whether he had offered the Koh-i-noor or his kingdom, he replied simply that he had offered his own life in exchange for his son's. Humayun recovered and within a few months, Babur fell ill and died at the age of forty-seven. He was buried at Agra, but his remains were later shifted to a green hillside in his beloved Kabul.

Babur the Man

Babur's diary, the *Baburnama*, is one of the oldest autobiographies in India, and an entertaining read that brings out his personality nicely. Babur was honest and human, and his frank discussion of his disappointments, emotions, pride and inner demons let us connect with him even 500 years later. It was written in his native Chagatai, a now extinct Turkic language.

Babur was a city man, well educated and fluent in Chagatai Turki, Persian and Arabic. He prized literature, science, arts and music, and even wrote some (not very good) poetry. He often chided the writing style of his son Humayun, urging him to write plainly and not confuse the reader!

Babur loved nature and developed a passion for gardening in Kabul. He had many gardens built there and in Delhi, but lamented that 'flowers do not do as well here as in the crisp air of Kabul'.

> **FUN FACT!**
> Babur thought that melons from his Uzbek homeland were far superior to the much-praised mangoes that all Indians seemed to love!

Another obsession was fruits, especially melons. He wistfully mentions how excellent the melons were in Ferghana, how he did not get any in India, and how he could not understand why Indians preferred mangoes!

His great-grandson Jahangir later wrote that no fruit had the flavour of the Indian mango, showing us that the 'Indianization' of the Mughals was complete in a few generations!

Like others of his time, Babur's notion of justice was rather different from today. He mentions matter-of-factly how he had thousands of people killed while subduing rebellions, and in Mongol fashion, had towers built of their skulls. He writes frankly that the heavy tax he levied on Kabul after conquering it 'was excessive and the country suffered badly'. In general, he was a liberal ruler, and felt that 'defeated enemies must be conciliated, not antagonized'; and 'one's own followers must be prevented by discipline from victimizing the local populations'.

His soldiers loved Babur, because he ate and drank and suffered alongside them. Once when travelling at the height of winter, the snow was too deep for the horses and his soldiers had to trample it down. Babur got down and started helping his men, and it was only on seeing him that his nobles rushed to follow.

Babur missed Ferghana, Samarkand, and especially Kabul most terribly, longing for the jovial court atmosphere and his old friends. He kept planning to return to Kabul as soon as he had set his affairs in order in India, but he never made it back.

Humayun (r. 1530–56 ce)

Humayun became king at the rather more mature age of twenty-two. Though father and son were close, Humayun and Babur had very different personalities. While he had many of Babur's virtues like his intellect, bravery and formidable military planning skills, Humayun lacked

Babur's iron will and determination. He was a charming and witty man, indolent and pleasure-seeking. Humayun was also extremely superstitious and apparently assigned his nobles to posts based on their sun signs rather than their suitability! His sentimentality and overly forgiving nature would prove to be his downfall again and again.

Humayun obeyed his father Babur's request to treat his brothers generously a little too well, even when they kept rebelling and betraying him – like when his brother Kamran, in charge of Kandahar and Kabul, got greedy and took over Lahore and Multan as well!

Humayun's empire was surrounded by enemies on all sides – the rebellious Afghans in the east and the sultanate of Gujarat in the west.

Humayun defeated the Afghan forces in 1532 at Dadrah, besieged Chunar in eastern Uttar Pradesh, and was able to sign a peace treaty with its ruler, Sher Khan Suri, a rising Afghan chieftain. He then returned to Agra and whiled away the next year building a new city in Delhi called Dinpanah (Purana Qila), spending his time on wine, feasting and opium, a nasty drug habit common in those days. In 1535, Humayun defeated Sultan Bahadur Shah and conquered Gujarat and then Malwa, showing sound military skills and great personal bravery, while almost doubling the size of his empire.

A Persian painting depicting Babur and Humayun

However, Humayun appointed his brother Askari as governor, who quickly lost both provinces and was forced to flee back to Humayun at Agra. Humayun immediately forgave him and busied himself with the pleasures of court life. Meanwhile, Sher Khan Suri had spent his time building up his forces and many regional chiefs started throwing in their lot with him. In 1537, Humayun once again marched to Chunar, but after a long siege, realized that Sher Khan was not even there, but had been busy consolidating his newly won territories in Bihar and Bengal!

In 1539, Humayun met Sher Shah (as he now called himself) between Benares and Patna at the Battle of Chausa. Humayun was badly defeated, and barely escaped with his life. Meanwhile, his younger brother Hindal had been trying to grab the throne at Agra (his brothers were clearly not the most loyal). Humayun returned to Agra, and forgave his brothers... again! In 1540, Humayun and Sher Shah Suri met again at the Battle of Kannauj.

FUN FACT! Humayun was so superstitious that even the colour of the clothes he wore was determined every day by the 'movement of the planets'!

Humayun was again roundly defeated, despite his larger army. He had to retreat in humiliation, flee to Agra and then to Lahore.

Sher Shah followed at a leisurely pace. Humayun even sent him a dramatic message, exclaiming, 'I have left you all of Hindustan! Why can't you leave Lahore for me?' Sher Shah wrote back, saying, 'I leave you Kabul.' Now, Kabul was under his rebellious brother Kamran, who was not about to give any of 'his' lands to his brother (the emperor!), and even plotted to betray him.

Humayun and the Water Carrier – A Tale

Emperor Humayun was locked in terrible battle against his fierce enemy, the Afghan chieftain Sher Shah, at Chausa, near Benares. Humayun and his forces were losing badly. His brothers Kamran and Hindal had joined forces and were trying to topple him. As his army scattered and retreated, Humayun's horse slipped and he fell into the river.

Humayun was badly hurt as he was tossed around in the churning water. A humble *bhishti* (water carrier) named Nizam came to his aid, inflating his buffalo-skin water bag with air. He managed to rescue the wounded emperor and get him to safety.

When a grateful Humayun tried to thank Nizam, he cried out, 'You are a just and great emperor! Your subjects adore you! I was doing my duty, your safety is my only reward!' Overwhelmed, Humayun asked him what he would like.

Nizam thought for a minute and said, 'Well, I would like to sit on your throne for a day and be king.'

Humayun agreed, and so Nizam the Water Carrier was emperor for a day.

Humayun once again had to flee while Sher Shah Suri became supremo of northern India. Like his father before him, Humayun became a fugitive king without any lands to rule. With a dwindling band of courtiers, he wandered in the merciless desert heat of Rajasthan. Here he married a young Persian girl called Hamida Banu. It was in a desert oasis in Sindh, that Humayun's son Jalaluddin was born. He would go on to become the greatest Mughal emperor, Akbar.

Humayun eventually went to Persia in 1543 and took refuge with the Safavid emperor, Shah Tahmasp. Here he was finally reintroduced to the finer side of courtly life after many years of living rough.

The Persian Shah instructed his governor of Herat in Afghanistan, 'Each day let 500 dishes of varied food be

Rani Karnavati and the Rakhi

The story of how Rani Karnavati of Chittor sent a rakhi to Emperor Humayun to claim him as her brother still thrives in Rajasthani folklore as an unlikely bond between a chivalrous Mughal emperor and a brave Rajput queen.

The legend goes that when the sultan of Gujarat attacked Chittor in 1534, Rani Karnavati, who was ruling as regent for her young son, sent a rakhi to Emperor Humayun, appealing to him to come and rescue her, his 'sister'. Though Humayun rushed over, the sultan of Gujarat had breached Chittor fort, which committed its second *jauhar* with 13,000 women throwing themselves into a funeral pyre, and all the men going out to fight to their deaths. A grief-stricken Humayun defeated Bahadur Shah and restored young Rana Vikramaditya (who had been sent away) to Chittor's throne.

However, written histories tell a different story altogether!

Humayun was in Agra when Bahadur Shah besieged Chittor. He left Agra months later, and dawdled 250 km from Chittor for months, waiting for it to fall! Bahadur Shah did not retreat because his ministers assured him that Humayun would not attack a fellow Muslim who was fighting an infidel. They were wrong, and once Chittor had fallen, Humayun besieged Bahadur Shah's forces. He had to flee, shedding bitter tears when his favourite elephants, Sharzah and Pat-Singar, and his chief cannons (called Laila and Majnu!), were destroyed. Humayun was awestruck at Bahadur Shah's large, lavish camp, draped with velvet, silk and brocade, with pegs made of gold and silver. Humayun pursued the fleeing army and conquered Gujarat and Malwa. Bahadur Shah, meanwhile, was unceremoniously dumped in the sea from a Portuguese ship in 1537 CE and killed!

Chittorgarh fort is central to the story of Rani Karnavati and the rakhi

Humayun's tomb in Delhi, built by a Persian architect, Mirak Mirza Ghiyas, and commissioned by his first wife, Bega Begum

presented. The total of the food, sweetmeats and liquids should not be less than 1,500 dishes, and should be served on plates of porcelain, gold and silver, placing covers of gold and silver on them.' The Shah gave Humayun both Persian troops and money, in exchange for the promise that Humayun would promote the Shia sect of Islam favoured by the Safavids.

With these reinforcements, Humayun took Kandahar from Askari and Kabul from Kamran, but found himself unable to order his brothers' executions. When his troops rebelled due to his softness, he finally had Kamran blinded, and sent him off on pilgrimage to Mecca, where he died in the Arabian Desert. Askari was sent off to Mecca separately (though with his eyes intact) and also died on the way.

Meanwhile, after Sher Shah's accidental death, his son Islam Shah Suri had started ruling. When he too died after some years, the new Sur Empire was thrown into disarray without a strong leader. A resurgent Humayun now defeated them and on 23 July 1555, fifteen long years after having been chased out of kingdom and country,

Humayun once again sat on his father Babur's throne in India. What a comeback story! However, Humayun's life was always dramatic, and just a few months later, he fell down the steep steps of his library and died shortly after.

As an unforgiving historian puts it, he 'stumbled out of this life as he had stumbled through it'. At the time of his death, the Mughal Empire spanned almost a million square kilometres. Young Akbar was just thirteen, and rivals were snapping greedily at his heels.

SHER SHAH SURI (R. 1540–45 CE)

The life and times of Sher Shah Suri were as remarkable as that of Babur's or Humayun's, perhaps even more.

Sher Shah was born as Farid Khan in Bihar. His father was a small-time *jagirdar* in Bihar from the Afghan Sur tribe and his mother was a Kayamkhani Rajput. Farid rebelled against parental authority and left home at an early age, taking up service under the chieftain Bahar Khan Lohani, who ruled southern Bihar. When he courageously slew a tiger while hunting, Bahar Khan gave him the title of 'Sher' Khan.

He joined Babur's army in Agra in 1527 for a year and studied the Mughal military set-up very closely.

When Bahar Khan declared himself independent, he appointed Sher Khan as his deputy and tutor to his young son. After his mentor's death, Sher Khan became the de facto ruler of south Bihar.

Babur's death in 1530 CE caused a general revolt by Afghan chieftains in the east, who wanted to expel the 'new' Mughal invaders, but Sher Khan was compelled to sign a treaty of submission with Humayun.

Meanwhile, his rapid rise made his fellow Afghan nobles in the area jealous (or nervous?) of him. They ganged up with the king of Bengal and attacked him. Sher Khan inflicted a crushing defeat on the allies in 1536 at Surajgarh, making him the undisputed master of Bihar, and later, Bengal. In 1537, Humayun also became alarmed at Sher Khan's rapid rise and attacked him.

This time, Sher Khan soundly defeated the Mughal forces despite having a smaller army, and forced Humayun to keep retreating towards Lahore and Kandahar.

Sher Khan declared himself ruler of India with the title of Sher Shah Suri in 1539 after Chausa. He then basically hounded Humayun out of India and occupied Punjab. Malwa and Ranthambore followed, after which he was very nearly defeated in a hard war against the desert kingdom of Marwar. He wryly commented that '… for a handful of bajra (grain), I almost lost all Hindustan!' He then conquered Sindh and Multan.

In just a few years, Sher Shah was master of most of north India. However, in 1545, while besieging Kalinjar fort, some ammunition caught fire and burned him badly. The fort was taken, but Sher Shah died that evening.

Despite his tremendous military victories, Sher Shah is best remembered for his many government reforms. Despite his constant conquests, in his short, action-packed five years, Sher Shah set up the government systems that the Mughal emperors would use for the next 300 years!

Sher Shah divided his empire into large regions called *sarkar*s, which were divided into provinces called parganas. Each pargana had a governor, judge, treasurer, both Hindu and Persian accountants, and so on. He fixed the tax rate at one-fourth the annual food each area could grow. He asked his officials to be lenient while fixing how much food the lands could grow, but very

The first rupee: The silver rupiya of Sher Shah Suri

strict in revenue collection after the assessment.

Sher Shah also started systems to reduce corruption in the government and military. He restarted branding all the army's horses, so that they could not be switched for inferior breeds and made official lists of all the soldiers in his army.

It was said that a helpless old woman could set off on a long journey with a basket of gold ornaments on her head, and no robber would come near her for fear of Sher Shah's harsh justice.

He also introduced the ingenious system of *kabuliyat* and *patta*. These were unique legal contracts between the government and each tenant-farmer. The *kabuliyat* was taken from the tenant and outlined his rights and obligations. The *patta* was the corresponding title deed given to the tenant. This seems normal today, where everything from employment to house rentals is confirmed through legal documentation, but it was a novel and revolutionary concept back then!

Sher Shah also rebuilt and extended the Grand Trunk Road (the ancient 'Uttarapath') which ran from Peshawar in Pakistan to Pataliputra in Bihar. Trees were planted for shade along the highway, and caravanserais (inns) were started for travellers.

It was Sher Shah who introduced the currency system used by the Mughals and until the 20th century! He issued the first standard silver *rupiya* with a weight of 178 grains or 11.6 g. Countries still using the 'rupee' as their currency include India, Pakistan, Nepal, Sri Lanka,

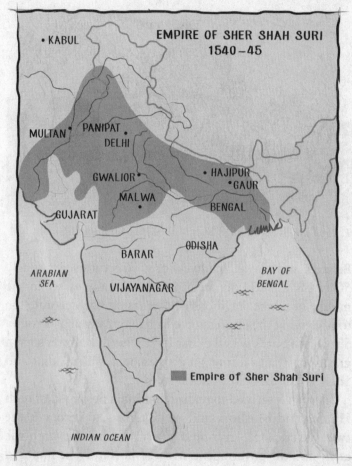

EMPIRE OF SHER SHAH SURI
1540–45

- KABUL
MULTAN • PANIPAT •
DELHI
GWALIOR • • HAJIPUR
MALWA • GAUR
GUJARAT BENGAL

ARABIAN
SEA
BARAR ODISHA
VIJAYANAGAR BAY OF
BENGAL

▮ Empire of Sher Shah Suri

INDIAN OCEAN

Sher Shah Suri's vast empire laid the foundations for the later Mughal emperors

Indonesia, Mauritius, Maldives and the Seychelles. He also introduced gold coins called mohur, weighing 169 grains, and copper coins called *dam*.

As a keen patron of architecture, Sher Shah built a magnificent tomb for himself at Sasaram, between

The red sandstone tomb of Sher Shah Suri in Sasaram, Bihar

Benares and Gaya. The five-storey structure soars nearly 50 m high. The Lodi-style octagonal tomb is set in the middle of a lake. Pavilions of decreasing size decorate the tomb, giving the impression of a palace as well as a tomb. Sher Shah Suri's was the first Indian tomb built on such a grand scale, and future Mughal emperors like Akbar and Shah Jahan drew inspiration from it.

Sher Shah seemed to realize that India belonged to both Hindus and Muslims, and made efforts to reconcile the two societies. He recruited many Hindus for both the army and the government. Most importantly, he imposed the law impartially, regardless of faith.

What in the World Was Happening!
(1500–50 CE)

Europe

- Age of European expansion launches as ships from different countries start sailing all around the world.
- The Portuguese explorer Ferdinand Magellan captains the first expedition from Europe to Asia by the west, rounding the Americas, and crossing the Pacific Ocean in the first circumnavigation of the Earth.
- Protestant Reformation takes place in Europe with German Martin Luther, and Swiss Zwingli. In England, in the 1530s, Henry VIII breaks away from the Pope.
- The Italian Renaissance is in full swing. Leonardo da Vinci and Michelangelo are creating their masterpieces. St Peter's Cathedral is built in Rome.
- Copernicus, the Renaissance astronomer, claims that the earth revolves around the sun and not the other way round.
- The first watches are made in Nuremberg: they are small spherical clocks worn on a ribbon around the neck.

Asia

- The Safavid Dynasty is founded in Iran.
- Suleiman extends the Turkish empire to Egypt, Hungary.
- The Portuguese come to dominate the profitable Indian Ocean trade routes between Asia and the Middle East.

Americas

- Spanish occupation destroys the Aztec and Inca Empires.
- European diseases bring death on a massive scale to the Native Americans.

Africa

- The shameful Atlantic slave trade begins, with the first African slaves taken to the Americas.

Explore More

* FIND out more about Rohtas Fort, a UNESCO World Heritage Site, located near the city of Jhelum in the Pakistani province of Punjab. The fortress was built during the reign of Sher Shah Suri between 1541 and 1548 in order to block the return of Mughal emperor Humayun, who had been exiled to Persia following his defeat at the Battle of Kannauj, and also to help control the rebellious tribes of the Potohar region of northern Punjab, who were loyal to the Mughal emperors.

* VISIT Sher Shah's tomb at Sasaram and the Purana Qila in Delhi to explore various aspects of the architecture of the times.

Akbar the Great

2

'Indeed he was a great king, for he knew that the good ruler is he who can command, simultaneously, the obedience, the respect, the love and the fear of his subjects. He was a prince beloved of all, firm with the great, kind to those of low estate and just to all men... so that every man believed the king was on their side.'
– Pierre du Jarric, French Jesuit, about Akbar

2
Conqueror and Mystic

Although it was under the reluctant Babur that the Central Asian Turkic Mongols set up shop in India, it was his grandson Akbar who was the true founder of the Mughal Empire over his long rule of 50 years. He placed his stamp on many different facets of Indian life. He was the first Muslim ruler in India to practise religious harmony as we know it.

His idea of a state with a ruling class drawn from all ethnic backgrounds and religions, equal justice for all regardless of religion or class, and his championship of human rights, were modern and far ahead of anything practised in Europe at the time. Though Akbar had not one drop of Indian blood in him, he considered himself to be truly Indian.

Early Life

Abu'l-Fath Jalaluddin Muhammad Akbar was born in uncertain times on 15 October 1542 in the remote Sindhi outpost of Umarkot. His father Humayun was a fugitive king without a kingdom. His mother was Humayun's young Persian wife, Hamida. Upon his birth, Humayun distributed a simple pod of musk, saying, '... my son's fame, I trust, will one day expand all over the world, as the perfume of the musk now fills this room.'

By 1545, Humayun had reconquered Kandahar and Kabul but was faced with various rivals including his two brothers and regional kings. He would lose and recapture Kabul again and again. As a child Akbar was even taken hostage and used as a human shield by the enemy, held up in front of the guns and arrows of his own father's army!

Through Akbar's childhood dramas (or traumas), his princely education progressed in Timurid style – in artillery, archery, swordsmanship, horse riding, wrestling, commanding men, and governance.

However, young Akbar probably suffered from dyslexia and seemed to have little interest in learning to read and write. He acquired many distinct personality traits perhaps due to his illiteracy: an outstanding memory and a lifelong love of manual hobbies like carpentry and stonework. As emperor, he had books read out to him every day.

In 1555, fifteen long years after losing Delhi, Humayun was able to reconquer it. When he died less than a year later, the Mughals were not yet on sure ground in India. Young Akbar was away on a military expedition, and was crowned Padshah (emperor) and Shahanshah (king of kings) in a small garden on a plain brick throne in Kalanaur (now in Haryana). Just like his father and his grandfather, Akbar became an emperor with very little land – only a precarious hold over Punjab! The Afghan nobles of India sensed a chance to recapture their lands.

Akbar was lucky to have a powerful, protective guardian in Bairam Khan, who ruled as regent in his name. Bairam was a Turki noble with the Mughals since Babur's time, and helped spirit Humayun to safety in Persia, resisting job offers from the Persian ruler Shah Tahmasp!

Meanwhile, Hemu, a Hindu general of the Sur dynasty, marched to Delhi, defeating Mughal forces all the way. Born poor and puny, he started by selling provisions to the Afghan army at a young age. He turned out to be a military and organizational genius, and rose quickly through the Sur army to become chief minister and general. He fought and won 22 battles, before finally conquering Delhi. Raja Vikramaditya, as he now styled himself, was determined to rout the Mughals.

The vastly outnumbered Mughal forces met Hemu's army at the Second Battle of Panipat on 5 November 1556, where Babur had fought *his* decisive battle 30 years earlier.

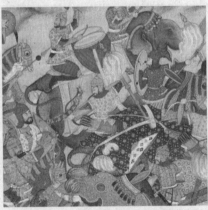

Bairam Khan faced Hemu, a valiant, inspired general. The battle seemed to be almost decided, and had an arrow not pierced Hemu's eye and killed him, causing panic among his men, it may have been the end of Mughal rule.

Detail from a painting of the Second Battle of Panipat, from the 1590s, titled 'The Defeat of Hemu'

A triumphant Mughal army then entered the gates of Delhi, and Mughal rule over Delhi was restored. Bairam Khan was the *khan-i-khana* (prime minister) and regent for four years.

As a teenager, Akbar spent his time in Agra, amusing himself with elephant fights and deer-hunting with his pet cheetahs. As he matured, Akbar started chafing at the restrictions placed by his increasingly arrogant guardian. Finally, in 1560, Khan Baba was 'persuaded' by Akbar to give up his title and go off on a pilgrimage to Mecca. He was murdered by Afghan rivals on the way.

Out of respect, Akbar married his cousin Salima, Bairam Khan's widow. Bairam Khan's son Abdur Rahim would become an important noble and *khan-i-khana* in time.

An 18-year old Akbar now got a *new* de facto regent, his former wet nurse, Maham Anga, who kept trying to grab more power for her son Adham Khan! Adham Khan was sent as general to capture Malwa in 1561 and decided to keep the war spoils, sending only a few measly elephants to the emperor. Akbar was furious and stripped him of his command, but did not banish him.

The next year, the uncontrollable Adham Khan murdered prime minister Ataga Khan, before forcing his way into the emperor's chambers. Akbar knocked him down with a blow and had him thrown down from the terrace – twice, to make sure that he was quite dead.

Maham Anga died of grief within 40 days. Akbar had a handsome tomb built for them near the Qutub Minar in Delhi. (The British later used it as a residence! It was also used as a rest house, a police station and a post office.)

And so, at nineteen, Akbar finally emerged from 'behind the veil' and began his rule proper.

Akbar's Conquests

Akbar was at war for most of his life, expanding his territories and subduing rivals and rebels – resentful

Afghan warlords, fierce Rajputs, half-hearted Uzbek tribes and sly opponents from among his own Timurid nobles!

How did the Mughals keep winning? Once again, it was the cavalry. They controlled the supply of fine-quality 'Turki' horses from Central Asia and raised bands of mercenary Mongol-style mounted foreign archers. This nimble cavalry fired arrows six times in the time it took musketeers to shoot their guns twice! Mughal cavalry could defeat 20 times the number of foot soldiers.

MALWA

Akbar's regent Bairam Khan quickly conquered Ajmer, Gwalior, Awadh and Jaunpur.

In 1561, it was Malwa's turn. Its colourful ruler Baz Bahadur indulged his passions. Surrounding himself with musicians and artists, Baz Bahadur danced away at his own court, wearing pearl anklets. His beloved Rajput wife, Roopmati, was a Persian and Hindi poet.

When their party was rudely interrupted, Baz Bahadur lost and fled in disgrace. Roopmati drank a poisonous mixture of camphor and sesame oil to escape Adham Khan's lechery. Baz Bahadur surrendered to Akbar after many years. He was appointed an imperial officer and became one of the best musicians at Akbar's court, developing a unique 'Bazkhani' style of singing.

A painting showing Baz Bahadur and Roopmati

Gondwana

In 1564, the Mughals attacked Gondwana (the 'forest of the Gonds'), ruled by the Chandel Rajput Rani Durgavati. Durgavati was a great general, and an excellent shot who enjoyed hunting. Her extensive public works had made her beloved of her people.

Though battle was futile, in typical Rajput spirit, Durgavati preferred to die fighting. The Rani personally led her ill-equipped soldiers against the mighty, modern Mughal forces. She fought bravely and when wounded, stabbed herself in the heart. Her young son, Bir Narayan, died defending the fortress of Chauragarh, which committed ritual *jauhar*.

Rajputana

Akbar used different strategies to prevail over the fierce Rajputs. Radically breaking from the Delhi Sultanate, Akbar married into Rajput families and gave them high posts!

States like Mewar chose to fight. In 1567, Akbar besieged Chittor. Rana Udai Singh retreated, but when the Mughals broke through after a brutal four-month siege, Chittor committed *jauhar* for the third time, where its noblewomen, dressed like brides, entered a fire-filled dungeon, and warriors fought to the death, clad in saffron clothes.

Akbar had statues of Chittor's valiant generals Jaimal and Patta placed at the entrance of his fort in Agra. The slaughter was so huge that 74½ maunds of *janeu*s (the sacred thread worn by brahmins, kshatriyas and vaishyas) were recovered from the dead. The number 74½ became an accursed one in the region.

Udai Singh's son, Rana Pratap, carried on the struggle, meeting Raja Man Singh in 1576 for the Battle of

Haldighati (which gets its name 'turmeric valley' from the yellow-coloured soil of the area).

Rana Pratap's horse Chetak was badly hurt, yet heroically managed to get the Rana to safety before dying. Chetak's legend passed into folklore.

Through guerilla tactics, Rana Pratap reconquered much of Mewar by the end of his lifetime.

GUJARAT

By the late 1560s, the fabulously wealthy sultanate of Gujarat was the main Mughal rival. Divided into constantly warring regions, Gujarat was rich from profitable western Asian trade, and had direct access to superb Persian horses and weaponry. The port of Surat had great strategic value.

Akbar himself went there in 1572 and 1573. It was the first time he saw the ocean! Sultan Muzaffar Shah was eventually captured and committed suicide in 1592.

EAST AND REST

In 1574, it was the turn of Bengal, Bihar and Odisha, the strongholds of unruly Afghan nobles. Eastern India had long been 'the house of revolt'. Akbar set off at his usual manic pace to deal with the Afghan Daud at Patna, who refused Akbar's usual offer of single combat. Eventually, Daud's straw-stuffed head, perfumed – so as to not 'trouble the emperor' – was brought before him.

In 1580, Akbar faced the biggest revolt of his reign, by his rebellious half-brother, Mirza Hakim, supported by conservative ulema. Hakim was defeated and died of poisoning in 1586.

By 1585, Kabul was annexed. Baluchistan, Kandahar, Kashmir and Sindh followed within ten years.

The majestic Buland Darwaza at Fatehpur Sikri was built to commemorate Akbar's victory over Gujarat

Akbar now eyed the Deccan and, in 1595, annexed Berar. In 1600, he battled the brave Chand Bibi of the sultanate of Ahmadnagar, who gave him a good fight before being killed.

AKBAR'S LAST YEARS

In 1600, Akbar's son Salim rebelled and attacked Agra. However, he found sealed gates and heavily guarded walls, and had to go off to Allahabad. Akbar rapidly returned north and started draining Salim's power by luring his supporters through money and favours. By 1604, Salim wanted to reconcile.

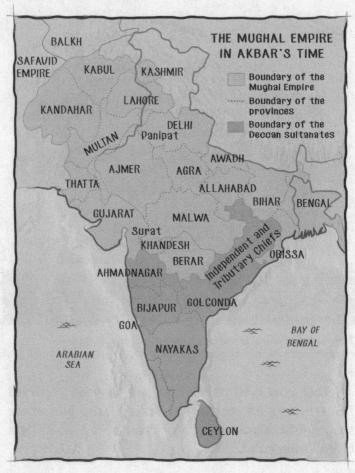

THE MUGHAL EMPIRE
IN AKBAR'S TIME

Boundary of the
Mughal Empire
Boundary of the
provinces
Boundary of the
Deccan sultanates

Through his unique methods of warfare and diplomacy, Akbar successfully extended the Mughal Empire to almost the entire Indian subcontinent north of the Godavari river

Within a year, a lonely and disillusioned Akbar was dead at 63 from a stomach infection, with whispers hinting at poisoning by Salim. He had seen his sons Murad and Daniyal die of alcoholism, while his beloved son of many prayers, Salim, was a rebellious drug addict, who had brutally murdered Akbar's confidant Abul Fazl.

AKBAR'S SPIRITUAL QUEST

A sincerely religious man, Akbar's independent thinking led to a remarkable evolution in his religious beliefs.

As he was a conventional Sunni Muslim, weekly Friday prayers were read out in Akbar's name, and he was proclaimed a 'defender of the faith' against 'infidels'. He publicly prayed five times a day, and frequently visited Sufi dargahs.

However, he married a Hindu Rajput princess and forbade the selling of prisoners of war. At just twenty-two, he abolished the *jizya* tax at a great annual cost of a million *rupiya*s.

In 1575, Akbar started the *Ibadat Khana* ('House of Worship'), where different types of Muslims debated religion in intense all-night sessions.

A major change occurred in 1578, when he went into a multi-day delirious trance and came out a changed man. His *Ibadat Khana* was expanded to include Hindus, Jains, Parsis, Christians, Jews and even Charavakas (Hindu materialistic atheists!). These different thoughts influenced him and radical changes continued.

Akbar began celebrating the Hindu festivals of Dussehra and Holi with gusto, along with the 14 Parsi festivals. He began wearing the sacred Parsi *kushti* thread. Influenced by the Jain saint Hiravijaya Suri, he gave up hunting and meat. He abolished cow slaughter upon the punishment

Akbar banned cow slaughter and declared more than 100 days every year as meat-free days throughout his empire!

FUN FACT!

of death, and banned animal slaughter for more than 100 days each year!

In 1579, the eminent cleric Shaikh Mubarak formally proclaimed that as emperor, Akbar was the supreme arbiter in all cases, including religious ones! By the 1580s, Jesuits mention that Akbar was no longer doing his daily prayers, nor keeping the Ramzan fast.

Influenced by Parsis and Hindus, Akbar became a great follower of the sun and fire. Every day, 1,001 Sanskrit names for the sun were recited in public, while Akbar publicly prostrated himself!

Akbar widely declared that 'no man should be interfered with because of his religion, and anyone could to go to whichever religion he pleased'. He allowed Christian Jesuit priests to freely preach and convert.

When conservative Islamic maulvis protested, Akbar exiled them to remote outposts, and in 1581, exchanged some for 'fine Turkish horses' in Kandahar.

He freed all slaves in 1583, claiming that all of God's creatures were free. In 1582, Akbar had invented a brand-new religion called Din-i-Ilahi, 'The Religion of God'. Without any gods, priests or prayers, it focused on social and animal welfare. It accepted widow remarriage and rejected forced sati, and marriage of children or between close relatives. Followers were to marry only once, and be vegetarian 'as far as possible'. Many courtiers adopted Din-i-Ilahi, but it did not take with the masses. After Akbar's death, everyone converted back to their original religions.

AKBAR AND THE EUROPEANS
By Akbar's time, the Portuguese had set up shop in Goa. Akbar was ambivalent about these foreigners who charged

fees for ships to pass. He considered destroying the 'feringhi infidels' and 'cleansing that road (to Mecca) from thorns and weeds', but was also quite curious about Europeans. He employed many of them, as gunners, surgeons, goldsmiths and enamellers.

In 1579, Akbar's ambassador reached Goa, with a request for 'two learned Jesuit priests'. They spent three years trying

Akbar holds a religious assembly with different faiths in the Ibadat Khana in Fatehpur Sikri

to win over Akbar in Fatehpur Sikri to Christianity, but he seemed interested only in asking endless questions. In 1591, a second mission was equally fruitless. A third Jesuit mission got permission to build churches and open a school, but still no 'Christian' Akbar. They said, 'This prince has the common fault of the atheist, who refuses to make subordinate reason to faith'.

Reforms and Government

Unlike in the past, Akbar's government was highly meritocratic. He 'judged nobility... from the personality, and not goodness from ancestors'. Talented people of all stripes were promoted and most of his Navratna ('nine gems of the court') did not come from elite backgrounds.

Akbar and Elizabeth I

The two powerful, famous monarchs, Akbar and Elizabeth I of England, lived strangely parallel lives.

Akbar became emperor at the age of 14 in 1556. Elizabeth, older by nine years, came to the throne in 1559 at the more mature age of 25. Both had very long rules by the standards of those days; Akbar ruled for 50 years, and Elizabeth for almost 45 years.

Both enjoyed hunting and riding.

Akbar had many wives, while Elizabeth never married.

Akbar ruled over a vast empire of 2,000,000 sq. km and a population of more than 100 million people, and was probably the richest emperor in the entire world. Elizabeth's small island kingdom spanned just 130,000 sq. km and had a population of four million, yet defeated the much more powerful Spanish Armada.

In India, a minority Muslim group ruled a majority Hindu population, and Akbar treated all religions equally and preached tolerance. In England, Elizabeth I became the head of the recently formed English Protestant Church, and though she was personally moderate, Catholics were persecuted in her kingdom.

Elizabeth I died in 1603 and Akbar in 1605 after stable reigns, called golden ages of their countries. The comparison may seem odd, yet, within 150 years, the queen's kingdom would conquer Akbar's land and dominate it ruthlessly for the next two centuries!

The Mughal nobility was called the *umrah*. In 1555, just before Akbar took the throne, there were 51 Muslim families of Turkish, Afghan, Uzbek or Persian origin. Indians were on the lowest social rung since the Delhi Sultanate.

By 1580, the *umrah* had swelled to 222 nobles, and nearly half were Indian, including 43 Hindu Rajput princes! Akbar's inclusiveness paid off handsomely, and he gained the loyalty of the Rajput Hindu elite, who had always been a thorn in the side of the Delhi sultans.

Akbar put into place all the major Mughal institutions, such as the *mansabdari* system. Using many ideas of Sher Shah Suri, he improved existing systems. His wide-ranging changes were followed by all later emperors.

One of Akbar's main changes was to move away from the traditional *iqtadari* system, where feudal landlords gave the emperor a fixed revenue, often leading to rebellions by overambitious regional chiefs. Instead, Akbar started the *mansabdari* system. He placed his senior military officers into *mansab*s, very precise ranks that determined their pay, how many soldiers they commanded and what their responsibilities were to the emperor. A noble's *mansab* came from his *zat* (personal ranking) and *sawar* (troop ranking). A *mansabdar* had to provide the emperor a fixed number of horsemen and troops upon request. There were 33 *mansab* grades from 10 to 5,000; ranks greater than 5,000 were reserved for the royal family. A mansabdar of 5,000 *zat* had to maintain 340 horses, 100 elephants, 140 camels, 100 mules and 160 carts, and received a salary of 30,000 *rupiya*s a month.

Akbar had 1,600 *mansabdars* directly answerable to him, of which 150 were 2,500-*mansabdar*s or higher, the most important military and government positions. *Mansab*s were not hereditary, though Akbar could reward a son his father's *mansab* if he chose.

To reduce corruption, Akbar ordered the branding of each horse (Sher Shah Suri's idea), so that dishonest *mansabdar*s could not 'borrow' horses from one another for royal inspections while misusing allocated funds!

Akbar divided his empire into 12 provinces called *suba*s. Each *suba* was made up of 100 or more districts called *sarkar*s, and each *sarkar* had sub-districts called parganas or *mahal*s. *Subadar*s had almost unlimited powers, and were responsible for the army, and overall law and order. In cities, the *kotwal* maintained public order.

There were four major ministries: revenue, headed by *wazir* or *diwan*; military headed by the *mir bakshi*; the royal household and *karkhana*s headed by the *mir saman*; and the judiciary overseen by the *sadr*.

Akbar followed the *kachcha* tax collection method, where the zamindar (revenue collectors) could keep only a fixed amount of taxes collected and sent the rest to the treasury. Later Mughals switched to the harsher *pukka* system: local tax collectors paid a fixed amount to the emperor, and extracted the maximum tax from peasants for themselves.

Akbar and Raja Todarmal changed and systemized the revenue assessment and collection, how much tax to charge and how to collect it. They introduced a method to measure the fertility of the land; then they classified the land into different categories, and finally fixed rates for each category. Revenue was fixed at about 33 per cent of the annual agricultural produce.

Economy

Akbar was perhaps the richest king in the world during his time, leaving behind treasure worth 40 million pounds of silver, worth about 1,500 billion rupees today!

New World silver amassed by the Europeans was pouring in rapidly into India. As always, India exported various goods like textiles and spices, and in return wanted only silver and gold! The number of coins struck by Mughal emperors ran into millions and vastly outnumbered those by any earlier dynasty. Akbar chose to continue with the tri-metallic (gold, silver, copper) coinage system introduced by Sher Shah Suri. One gold mohur equalled nine silver *rupiya*s, and one *rupiya* equalled 40 copper *dam*s. The coin names reflect Indian multiculturalism – 'mohur' from the Persian *muhr* (seal), *rupiya* from the Sanskrit *rupa* (silver), and *dam* from the Greek *drachma*!

The *Ain-i-Akbari* gives us many economic facts. The rate for an unskilled labourer was two *dam*s a day, which could purchase five kg of wheat. A first-class carpenter got seven *dam*s a day. Milk was a *dam* per kilo. In today's rupees, one *dam* is 13.75 rupees, as a silver *rupiya* was 11 gram, and silver is today about 50 rupees per gram. Hence, wheat cost today's five rupees per kg back then.

Personality and Hobbies

Descriptions tell us that Akbar had typical Mongol looks, and spoke with a loud, 'rich' voice. One writer mentions that 'when he looks at you, nothing escapes his notice…'. Of medium height, he was very fit. He was personally fearless, almost reckless, and even tamed wild elephants and horses himself!

Interestingly, Akbar kept only a moustache, a Rajput trait, which was odd as all adult Muslim males kept a beard. Akbar also followed the Rajput custom of gathering up his hair under a turban rather than cutting it. He wore a knee-length outer tunic embroidered with golden thread over fine trousers. His turban gleamed with pearls and gems. He enjoyed perfumes, and sometimes in private, dressed up in Portuguese suits of black silk or velvet!

All writers comment on Akbar's immense energy, vitality and curiosity. Given that he was forever at war, one wonders when he found the time for his wide variety of interests! He slept for barely three hours a night, and his courtiers were obliged to stay awake with him!

Akbar had special names for all of his intimates: Salim was *Shaikhu baba*, while Murad was *Pahadi*. His general, Raja Man Singh, became *Mirza Raja*, Rahim was *Mirza Khan* and so on. 'No sign of vanity or snobbery ever appeared on his face,' said Jahangir. Easily excited to anger and as easily calmed, he was friendly and cheerful.

However, Akbar was also very conscious of his rank as the Shahanshah, with absolute power over both the common people and his nobles. Court etiquette became much more formal, and Akbar decreed that no one other than the royal princes could remain seated in his presence, a rule followed by all future Mughal emperors. Courtiers would greet him, bending in the *kornish* or the *taslim*, or even prostrate themselves in a *sijda*.

Punishment awaited those who disobeyed. If Akbar suspected a courtier of treason, he hid his irritation, but presented the courtier with one of two gifts: either

A portrait of Akbar created by Manohar, a renowned artist of the Mughal school of painting

a 'robe of honour' with poisoned cuffs and hood, or a poisoned *paan*. The courtier would be obliged to eat or wear this, even though it meant certain death.

However, Akbar disregarded court 'etiquette' as he liked. A Persian

Detail from a Mughal miniature titled 'Akbar Hunting with Cheetahs'

merchant, who went to Agra fort to catch a glimpse of the emperor, saw Akbar alone on the palace roof, clad only in a lungi, merrily flying a kite!

Akbar liked to get the pulse of the nation, and often went out in disguise. Once he was recognized and rolled his eyes and squinted and made faces to convince people that he could not be the emperor. He then enacted the same idiotic faces to his court!

Akbar enjoyed manual pastimes like making guns and cannons, and often dropped in unannounced into the palace *karkhana*s (workshops), to offer suggestions for improvements. He also practised carpentry and stonework. He sent foreign missions to fetch the best technology and art. He sent one Haji Habibullah, armed with a big budget, to Goa to bring back European curiosities, like the organ, and copy anything worthy of imitation.

He enjoyed walking and often walked from one *city* to another, with his courtiers huffing and puffing to keep up.

Akbar revelled in hunting, animal fights and sports of all kinds. A special type of hunt that he was fond of was called *kamarga*.

Once, after a few cups of wine, a 19-year-old Akbar thought it would be 'fun' to mount his favourite bad-tempered elephant Hawai, to face off another vicious elephant called Ran Bagha ('Tiger in Battle'). The two giant mastodons battled. Ran Bagha turned to flee, with the royal rider in hot pursuit, leading to a headlong chase down the banks of the Yamuna river, and across a wildly shaking wooden bridge of boats, with people flinging themselves in the river to get out of the way!

Akbar kept more than 1,000 specially trained cheetahs to hunt. He often captured and tamed wild cheetahs himself. His pet cheetahs lived lavishly, robed with throws of embroidered velvet, gold chains around their necks, and sporting golden *zardozi* blinkers! Madan Kali, his favourite cheetah, strode along at court to a drum roll!

Akbar was a keen polo player and loved it so much that he invented a luminous ball that glowed in the dark, to enable night play, forcing his courtiers to attend!

Akbar and Food

Akbar ate only one meal a day despite being served many magnificent dishes at every meal. Due to early assassination attempts, he was paranoid about being poisoned, and his cook personally sealed each dish, breaking the seal only before the emperor. Akbar drank water only from the Ganga river. He tried periodically to become vegetarian, especially in his later years when he was influenced by Jain priests. He once said, 'It is not right that a man should make his stomach the grave of animals.' Like his grandfather Babur, Akbar loved fruit, his favourites being grapes, melons and pomegranates. He put in great effort to import and cultivate these fruits in India. He had the earliest cherry and apricot trees cultivated.

Emperor Akbar kept a great many dogs and, like any devoted dog owner, claimed that dogs have ten virtues, and 'if a man had but one of these, he would be a saint'. Akbar kept more than 20,000 pigeons, a common pastime of Central Asian nobles. Some were trained to perform manoeuvres and could perform 15 *charkh*s (wheels) and 70 *bazi*s (somersaults) at a go. Others were carrier pigeons.

Akbar had an amazing memory, and reportedly remembered the names of all his horses, elephants, dogs, cheetahs and so on. He would also name his weapons, such as his trusty musket, Sangram.

He often engaged philosophers and debaters all night long. Though unable to read, he constantly had books read out to him, and built a library of 24,000 books.

Akbar's Navratna

Akbar surrounded himself with 'nine gems' at his court, his Navratnas and renaissance men, who were his closest aides and great military commanders with many talents. Seven of these were Birbal, Man Singh, Todarmal, Faizi, Abul Fazl, Abdur Rahim and Tansen. The other two could have been Hakim Humam, Mulla Badauni, Shaikh Mubarak or Fakir Aziao-Din.

BIRBAL (D. 1586 CE)

Tales of Akbar and his trusted minister Birbal abound in Indian folklore, portraying Birbal as a righteous Hindu confidant of the emperor, who uses his wit to outsmart the emperor and other courtiers.

Birbal was a brahmin called Maheshdas from Kalpi in central Uttar Pradesh. He met Akbar in the year of

Birbal continues to be well known through stories about his wit

his coronation, and stayed at his court for the rest of his life. He was a gifted musician, poet and storyteller. He got the title of *Kavi Rai*, and was a high-ranking *mansabdar*.

He died in 1586 while fighting the Afghans in the Swat Valley. Distraught, Akbar did not eat for three days.

TANSEN (D. 1595 CE)

Tansen was a great Indian classical singer, who studied under the legendary Swami Haridas.

In 1562, Tansen shifted to Akbar's court from the court of Raja Ramchandra of Rewa. He composed many

'Words Can Kill' – An Akbar–Birbal Story

A famous astrologer once came to Agra. He was summoned by Akbar to predict the emperor's future.

The astrologer examined Akbar's palm and gravely said, 'Your Majesty, all your family members and relatives will die in front of your eyes.' Enraged, Akbar ordered the astrologer imprisoned.

The astrologer begged for Birbal's help. Birbal whispered a plan into the poor man's ear. The astrologer requested a last audience with the emperor, claiming he wanted to correct his mistakes.

After a second careful examination of Akbar's palm, the astrologer gave his verdict. 'Your Majesty, I committed a grave error. You are such a great emperor, destined to rule for many years to come. You will lead such a long and healthy life that none of your friends, family or relatives will be able to match you.'

Akbar, happy to hear the 'true and correct' prediction, set the relieved astrologer free and rewarded him handsomely.

*dhrupad*s sung even today, and also composed many ragas like 'Miyan ki Todi' and 'Miyan ki Malhar' (he was known as Miyan Tansen after he converted to Islam).

ABUL FAZL (1551–1602 CE)

Abul Fazl was the younger son of the great scholar Shaikh Mubarak of Agra. A childhood prodigy, he joined Akbar's court at the age of twenty. Akbar asked his advice on all topics, even medical treatment! Akbar entrusted him to write the *Akbarnama* and the *Ain-i-Akbari*.

Once, when the head of the ulema remarked disapprovingly at Akbar's saffron-coloured robes as un-Islamic, Abul Fazl, seeing Akbar's irritation, later taunted the shaikh for eating a saffron-flavoured dish!

Prince Salim suspected Abul Fazl of turning Akbar against him. In 1602, Raja Bir Singh Bundela of Orchha assassinated Abul Fazl and sent his head to Jahangir, who threw it in the toilet! Akbar cried for days.

Abul Fazl presents the Akbarnama *to Akbar*

FAIZI (D. 1595 CE)

Faizi was Abul Fazl's brother, appointed as tutor to the three royal princes at the age of twenty. A wit and a great poet, he composed thousands of Persian poems, but with Indian themes. A Sanskrit scholar, he translated Bhaskaracharya's *Lilavati* and parts of the Mahabharata into Persian. He composed a Persian poem on Nal–Damayanti, which was read out to Akbar each night!

Both Faizi and Abul Fazl's liberal outlooks influenced Akbar. They argued that God cannot belong to only one religion as he nourishes all, and Akbar, as a reflection of God on earth, had a duty to nourish all equally.

ABDUR RAHIM KHAN-I-KHANA (1556–1627 CE)

Rahim was the son of Bairam Khan and his Indian wife. He was appointed the *khan-i-khana* (prime minister) at 27 and wrote many Persian works. He was so good-looking, painters sold his portraits to people as pin-ups! He is most famous for his thousands of couplets in Hindi ('*doha*s'). He outlived Akbar, and his granddaughter married Shah Jahan. When battling with Rahim's son, Jahangir barbarically sent the aged Rahim a package with the son's head, saying, 'I have sent you a melon.'

MULLA BADAUNI (1540–1596 CE)

The deeply conservative Badauni was dismayed at Akbar's increasing distance from Islam and horrified when Akbar

put him to work translating Sanskrit texts like the Atharva Veda, the Mahabharata and the Ramayana into Persian! He wrote a secret, scathing history of Akbar, which came out in the time of Jahangir, who banned it.

RAJA MAN SINGH (D. 1615)

Raja Man Singh ruled Amber, and his aunt was Prince Salim's mother. His sister, Man Bai, was married to Jahangir

Raja Man Singh

with both Hindu and Muslim rituals.

He was the first noble to get a rank of 7,500-*mansabdar*. 'Mirza Raja' did not accept Din-i-Ilahi. He built the Govind Deo temple in Vrindavan, later plundered by Aurangzeb. Shaped like a European cathedral, it was built with red sandstone given by Akbar.

RAJA TODARMAL (D. 1589)

From a humble start as a writer, Raja Todarmal became the diwan (finance minister), with a genius for administration. He oversaw many of Akbar's reforms, in revenue collection and organization. A devout Hindu, he rebuilt the Kashi Vishwanath temple in Benares with funds given by Akbar.

What in the World Was Happening!
(1550–1600 CE)

Africa
- Africans are carried to America in large numbers by European slavers.

Americas
- Native population by the end of the century is one-tenth that at the beginning, due to European diseases and genocide.
- The Spanish and Portuguese occupy South America.

Asia
- The Ottoman emperor Suleiman now rules over Egypt and Hungary.
- RUSSIA: Ivan the Terrible extends the empire.
- CHINA: The Ming dynasty continues to rule.

Europe
- ENGLAND: Elizabeth I ascends the throne. The British navy expands. Shakespeare writes his plays.
- Galileo and Tycho Brahe push modern scientific methods.
- War breaks out between the Protestants and the Catholics in many countries.

Explore More

* READ Akbar–Birbal stories. They show the relationship between Akbar and his wise and witty courtier. There are many of them available as collections as books and on some websites as well. There is an animated series too.

* WATCH the movie Mughal–e–Azam, to get a glimpse of Mughal lifestyle. This historical drama, directed by K. Asif, and released in 1960, is about the legend of Prince Salim and Anarkali.

* CREATE a new faith, just as Akbar did. What would be its ideas and practices?

* VISIT Humayun's Tomb in Delhi, Fatehpur Sikri near Agra, Amber Fort in Jaipur and Akbar's tomb in Sikandra near Agra.

3

The Great Mughals

[1605–1707 CE]

'Gar Firdaus bar ruhe zamin ast
hamin asto, hamin asto, hamin asto.'

'If there is paradise on the face of this earth,
It is here, it is here, it is here.'
– Inscribed on the walls of the Diwan-i-Khas,
Red Fort, Delhi

3

An Age of Splendour

Akbar was followed by the last three Great Mughals: Jahangir, Shah Jahan and Aurangzeb.

Over this 100-year period, Jahangir and Shah Jahan created beautiful buildings and objects, and royal Mughal opulence reached new heights. Aurangzeb greatly increased Mughal territory and finally fulfilled his great-grandfather Akbar's dream of conquering the Deccan.

However, family rivalry grew nastier and nastier with intrigues, assassinations and rebellions. Aurangzeb's later rule saw conflict, less money coming in, and flourishing corruption. After his death, the million mutinies raging tore the empire apart.

Jahangir

Emperor Jahangir (r. 1605–1627) began by brutally crushing the rebellion of his eldest son, Khusrau, making him watch as his supporters were impaled or slowly suffocated inside animal skins. For Khusrau, Jahangir reserved the favoured royal method of blinding.

The fifth Sikh Guru Arjan Dev had blessed Khusrau. He was tortured and executed when he refused to pay the fine imposed by Jahangir, claiming his money was reserved for 'the poor, the friendless and the stranger'.

Despite this gory beginning, Jahangir had a largely peaceful 22-year reign.

JAHANGIR'S PERSONALITY

Jahangir was raised at Akbar's capital of Fatehpur Sikri and studied Persian, Turkish, Arabic and Hindi, and subjects ranging from arithmetic, history and geography, to music and painting. He was an enthusiastic hunter and once calculated that he had killed 28,532 animals!

Jahangir was an aesthete who loved the good life. His cultural legacy of miniature Mughal paintings, architecture and gardening all show excellent taste. He once proclaimed about his expertise in art, 'If any other person has put in the eye of a face, I can perceive whose work the original face is, and who has painted the eye.'

He invented new styles of dressing that only he was allowed to wear, including the *kurdi* (inspired by a Kurdish style) – which became the kurta! Jahangir also enjoyed dabbling in European culture and once tried, in vain, to get his entire court to dress in European clothes!

He wrote a candid memoir called the *Tuzuk-e-Jahangiri*, and filled it with tales of gifts, gossip and self-praise! He also wrote copiously about animals, trees, fruit, wine, places he visited

Jahangir often got European scientific curiosities replicated in solid gold and gemstones, including a telescope and a European–style carriage!

FUN FACT!

and his devotion to mangoes and food. The English ambassador, Thomas Roe, wrote home indignantly that the Indians must consider the English gluttons, because 'all I have ever received was eatable and drinkable' (rather than lavish gifts of gold and silver)!

Jahangir was a cheerful addict and drank 20 cups of liquor daily. Later on, under queen Nur Jahan's steadying influence, he reduced his intake to a 'mere' six cups, which he then supplemented with opium twice a day! With his love for indulgence, he weighed a hefty 110 kg and wore a new, opulent jewellery set every day of the year.

He was given to whimsical fits of great cruelty and childishness. When in a temper, he had men thrown to the lions or skinned alive. Once, when a favourite china dish broke during transportation, the noble in charge of the royal wardrobe was flogged and sent off to China with 5,000 *rupiya*s to get a new one...the original dish had cost 700 *rupiya*s! But he prided himself on being fair and had a long, golden Chain of Justice made, attached to a bell – so that anyone seeking justice could ring it and appeal directly

to him. He tried to emulate his father Akbar out of respect, declaring two vegetarian days every week, and continued the ban on cow slaughter.

Religion

Quite unlike Akbar, Jahangir was widely rumoured to be an

Detail from a Mughal miniature painting showing Jahangir hunting lions atheist. The Italian traveller Manucci says, 'This king did many things against the Mohammedan religion... the learned told him repeatedly that wine and pork were prohibited... Enraged at so many warnings, he inquired in which religions it was permissible. They replied that only the Christians had that liberty... He said publicly that he meant to become a Christian and ordered that tailors cut out European clothes. The learned men in amazement... said that the king might eat and drink whatever he liked.'

A Mughal miniature showing Jahangir holding a miniature of Akbar, his father

Jahangir did have the campaigns against Mewar and Kangra declared as jihad, and temples there destroyed, but in general, he continued Akbar's policy of *sulah-i-kul* (universal peace). He celebrated the Hindu festivals of Diwali (where he gambled for three nights), Holi, Dussehra and, of course, Akbar's favourite Parsi festival of Navroz. He also handed over to Christian Jesuit priests his brother Daniyal's three sons, who were paraded in Agra in Portuguese costumes wearing crosses, and renamed Don Felipe, Don Carlos and Don Henrique. However, they converted back to Islam after four years.

SIRHINDI THE REVIVER

Akbar's embrace of all religions, followed by Jahangir's godless merrymaking, raised a backlash from conservative Muslim ulema, especially from Shaikh Ahmad Sirhindi of the Naqshbandi Sufis. Sirhindi wanted strict sharia law

(Islamic canonical law based on the teachings of the Quran and the Prophet) and the 'cleansing' of Islam from ideas creeping in from Hinduism, Jainism and Zoroastrianism. Jahangir hated any criticism and even jailed Sirhindi briefly, whose influence increased greatly after he died. The 20th-century Urdu poet Iqbal was deeply inspired by Sirhindi and, today, both are revered in Pakistan.

Nur Jahan

Nur Jahan was Jahangir's twentieth and last wife. She had been married to an Afghan noble and upon his death moved back to Agra. In a middle-aged romance, the 42-year-old Jahangir married the 34-year old widow.

She soon effectively ruled the empire, while Jahangir claimed he was happy with a 'ser of wine and half a ser of meat'! All royal edicts started carrying her name along with Jahangir's, and even coins were struck in her name.

Her Persian father, Ghiyas Beg, and her brother, Asaf Khan, became chief ministers. She married off her brother's daughter, Mumtaz Mahal, to the heir apparent, Prince Khurram, and appointed extended family to important positions like governorships and head of the military.

Nur Jahan was beautiful, talented and piercingly intelligent. She also designed clothes, jewellery and carpets, which remained in vogue for decades afterward. For the royal kitchen, she invented new dishes, still considered the finest in Mughal cuisine. She even designed her father's Itmad-ud-Daulah's tomb, which is considered to be a 'draft' version of the Taj Mahal!

Jahangir mentions that she was an accomplished hunter who once felled four tigers with six shots. A poet herself, Nur Jahan encouraged poetry amongst other noblewomen, holding contests and even sponsoring foreign women poets like Mehri from Persia.

JAHANGIR'S WARS
Jahangir did not make any major conquests, though he effectively quelled rebellions, like in Bengal. He continued his father's liberal policy towards the Rajputs, and Rana Pratap's son, Amar Singh, finally made a treaty in 1615.

MALIK AMBAR THE HABSHI
From Delhi Sultanate times, many young non-Muslim slaves were brought into India from Abyssinia (Ethiopia), converted, trained and formed into elite military units. Habshis or Siddis, as dark-skinned Abyssinian slaves were known, became a significant political force in the Deccan Sultanates over time, marrying locally and adopting the local languages.

Malik Ambar, born 'Chapu' in Ethiopia, arrived in Ahmadnagar as a slave in the early 1570s and became an important nobleman. Ahmadnagar fell to the Mughals in 1600, but Malik Ambar prevented their occupying the kingdom. He found an obscure Nizam-Shahi boy, crowned him Sultan Murtaza Nizam Shah II, made him his son-in-law and began ruling as regent in his name!

Despite his best efforts, Jahangir was unable to defeat Ambar, a master of guerrilla warfare, who would spring surprise night attacks, destroy supply lines and draw the Mughals into hills and densely wooded areas. By 1610, all of Akbar's gains in the Deccan were lost. Ambar began recruiting many Hindu Maratha cavalrymen, going from 10,000 in 1609 to 50,000 in 1624. Ahmadnagar became a Habshi–Maratha joint venture! Jahangir detested Malik

Malik Ambar, the Ethiopian general of Ahmadnagar, stood up against the Mughals

Ambar and even had a miniature painted in which he, atop a globe, took aim at Malik Ambar's impaled head!

Until Malik Ambar died of natural causes in 1626, the Mughals made no headway in the Deccan. A Mughal historian praised Malik Ambar, 'in warfare, command, in sound judgement... in administration, Ambar had no equal...'

Finally, it was Shah Jahan who conquered Ahmadnagar. By 1636, Bijapur and Golconda also had to accept Mughal 'protection'. Due to the Mughal policy of not employing military slaves, by the 18th century, the Habshis melted into the local population.

KHURRAM'S REBELLION

Prince Khurram (Shah Jahan) was close to Nur Jahan until she married off her own daughter, Ladli Begum, to his brother Shahryar in 1620. Objecting to a faraway posting in Kandahar, Khurram revolted like a true-blooded Mughal prince. He was roundly defeated and forced to flee. An infuriated Jahangir now started calling his favourite son '*bidaulat*' (the wretch).

To add to Jahangir's fury, Khurram sought shelter with the hated Malik Ambar! Still, in 1626, Khurram was pardoned and accepted back at court. When Jahangir died the next year, Khurram forcibly retired Nur Jahan to Lahore with a 'modest' yearly allowance of 200,000 *rupiya*s until she died 20 years later.

Shah Jahan

Shah Jahan (r. 1628–1658) was the wealthiest man in the world and his reign became the byword for Mughal opulence.

Born in 1592 CE to Jahangir's Rajput wife, Jagat Gosain, Prince Khurram was taken from her and raised by Akbar's first and chief wife, Ruqaiya Sultan Begum, who was childless. As Akbar's favourite grandchild, he had refused to stir from his beloved grandfather's deathbed as a thirteen-year-old boy.

In 1628, Prince Khurram was crowned as Abu ud-Muzaffar Shihab-ud-Din Muhammad Sahib-ud-Quiran ud-Thani Shah Jahan Padshah Ghazi. He soon eliminated all possible rivals, including his brother Shahryar, his brother Khusrau's sons, and his uncle Daniyal's sons... having already killed his blind brother Khusrau in 1622.

PERSONALITY

Shah Jahan was the polar opposite of Jahangir. Courteous and controlled, he always portrayed a formal, 'royal' persona. An English traveller describes him as 'Never smiling... extreme pride and contempt of all'. Under him, courtly rituals and manners became exceedingly intricate. As a child, he had even refused to learn his ancestral Turki language, claiming it too vulgar for a prince!

Shah Jahan was intensely attached to his wife Mumtaz Mahal, whom he had married in 1612. She accompanied him everywhere, bearing 14 children. Only four boys, Dara Shikoh, Murad Bakhsh, Shah Shuja and Aurangzeb, and three girls, Jahanara, Roshanara and Gauharara lived. No children from his other wives survived.

He consulted her on all state matters, and she even placed the royal seal on his farmans (edicts). When she

Shah Jahan built the 17th-century Taj Mahal in memory of his beloved wife

died during the birth of their fourteenth child in 1631, Shah Jahan was utterly devastated and blamed himself bitterly. The Mughal court mourned for two years, dressing only in white. No music, feasting or celebrations were allowed.

The emperor was determined to build the world's most magnificent memorial for his beloved. The Taj Mahal was completed at a stupendous cost of five million *rupiya*s.

When Shah Jahan finally resumed normal life, his beloved daughter Jahanara became the chief lady at the Mughal court rather than one of his other wives.

Shah Jahan continued to display royal lavish opulence: the plush new capital of Shahjahanabad with its fancy Red Fort, Jama Masjid and Chandni Chowk, and the magnificent Peacock Throne. Shah Jahan gave us the most memorable Mughal icons we have and was perhaps the only emperor with the talent, money and sheer stubbornness needed to create such perfect masterpieces.

RELIGIOUS POLICIES

Shah Jahan was pious and far more old-fashioned than his fun-loving father. He reflected the new conservative religious sentiment popularized by the Sirhindi Naqshbandis, observed sharia personally and forbade his nobles from wearing miniature paintings of him on their turbans. In 1633, he forbade the building of any new Jain or Hindu temples.

Shah Jahan began favouring Muslims for high government positions and stopped appointing Rajputs to provincial governorships, sparking off some tensions.

It is ironic that Shah Jahan, the Mughal emperor who had three-fourths Hindu lineage was less tolerant than Jahangir, who was half-Hindu, and far less so than Akbar, who had no Hindu ancestry!

SHAH JAHAN'S WARS

Shah Jahan did not add any land, but faced rebellions by regional kings like Bir Singh Bundela of Bundelkhand. When Portuguese merchants in Bengal began raiding villages and forcibly converting locals to Christianity, he had Hooghly captured and the merchants enslaved.

Delhi's Red Fort – built by Emperor Shah Jahan

He tried and failed, again and again, to capture the Mughal ancestral city of Samarkand in Uzbekistan, which cost him another 20–30 million *rupiya*s (that's six Taj Mahals!). And his fight with the Persians over Kandahar depleted the treasury by another 120 million *rupiya*s!

GOVERNANCE

Jahangir sharply increased royal expenditure by raising the nobles' ranks across the board, reducing the hefty 70-million-*rupiya* treasury left by Akbar to just 10 million.

Shah Jahan spent recklessly. His opulent lifestyle, colossal building projects and ruinous wars, all put pressure on the Mughal treasury – the vast revenue coming in escaped even faster! He increased taxes to almost 50 per cent (further impoverishing the peasants), and reduced the salaries and ranks of his nobles. To compensate for this, he allowed them to maintain far smaller armies, which had a real impact later on in the Deccan, when the Marathas started acting up. Government bureaucracy bloated, becoming inefficient and corrupt.

SUCCESSION CONFLICTS

The conflict for succession between Shah Jahan's sons started in his lifetime, particularly between his favourite eldest son Dara Shikoh, and his third son Aurangzeb.

DARA SHIKOH: THE FAVOURED ONE

Dara Shikoh and Jahanara were Shah Jahan's favourite children. Dara Shikoh 'was courteous, quick at repartee, polite and extremely liberal'. In a lifelong quest to find common strands between Hinduism and Islam, he wrote books drawing parallels between the Quran and the

The Fabulous Peacock Throne

The legendary *Takht-e-Taus* ('Peacock Throne') was perhaps the most valuable object ever made in the world, costing one crore *rupiya*s ... twice the cost of the Taj Mahal! In today's money, that is about one billion US dollars! The throne took seven years to make.

Carried off by the Persian invader Nadir Shah in 1739, it was soon lost in tribal raids, probably melted down.

Shah Jahan's court historian, Abdul Hamid Lahori describes it: 'The Emperor decided to use the many valuable gems that had come into the Imperial jewel house... exquisite jewels of great weight, worth 86 lakh of rupees, were handed over to the goldsmith's department and one lakh *tola*s of pure gold... The outside of the canopy was of enamel work with occasional gems, the inside thickly set with rubies, garnets and other jewels, and it was supported by 12 emerald columns. On the top of each pillar there were two peacocks thickset with gems, and between each pair a tree set with rubies and diamonds, emeralds and pearls. The ascent was of three steps, set with jewels of fine water.'

Upanishads, and translated the Bhagavadgita into Persian. But Dara was also volatile and thought rather too highly of himself. While Akbar was a military man interested in spirituality, his great-grandson Dara Shikoh was a scholarly spiritual mystic who happened to be born royal.

Aurangzeb

Muhiuddin Aurangzeb, Shah Jahan's third son, grew up as a royal prince and a courageous military leader. However, from a young age he felt unloved, always referring to himself as 'this wretch' or 'this small thing'.

A deeply pious Sunni Muslim, he clung to his convictions with narrow-minded rigidity. A European visitor noted: 'He almost always carried the Quran under his arm. His prayers were frequent, and in public...'

Aurangzeb was very suspicious, thrived on intrigue and liberally used deceit to create mistrust among his enemies.

AURANGZEB'S WARS

With such contrasting personalities, it was not surprising that Dara Shikoh and Aurangzeb could not stand each other. Dara never missed an opportunity to mock Aurangzeb, whom he scorned as a religious bigot and unintelligent hypocrite. Aurangzeb resented Dara Shikoh fiercely as the privileged favourite of his father and sister, and a heretic who dabbled in un-Islamic topics.

Shah Jahan believed Dara Shikoh could do no wrong and was openly contemptuous towards Aurangzeb, often publicly undermining him. He periodically banished Aurangzeb from court, relenting only upon Jahanara's pleading. At one point, the world's richest man, the builder of the Taj Mahal and the Peacock Throne, petulantly accused his son Aurangzeb of stealing mangoes from his favourite tree in Burhanpur!

To avoid political intrigues (which he himself had done!), Shah Jahan dispatched his younger sons to different corners of the empire: Shah Shuja was made governor of Bengal, Murad Bakhsh got Gujarat and Aurangzeb, the Deccan. Dara Shikoh was promoted to official heir in 1642, the Shahzada-e-Buland Iqbal ('Prince of High

A Mughal miniature showing Dara Shikoh surrounded by his majestic army

Aurangzeb's Court

The French traveller Francois Bernier described the unimaginable opulence of the Mughal court:

'Never did I witness a more extraordinary scene. The king was seated on his throne, in the most magnificent attire. His vest was of delicately flowered satin, with the finest silk and gold embroidery. The gold turban had an aigrette (plumes of the egret) whose base was composed of diamonds of an extraordinary size and value, besides an oriental topaz exhibiting a lustre like the sun. A necklace of immense pearls reached the stomach...

The floor was covered with carpets of the richest silk. A tent pitched outside spread over half the court, and was completely enclosed by a great balustrade, covered with plates of silver, supported by pillars overlaid by silver.'

Fortune'). He was granted a higher rank and troops than the other three princes combined.

In 1657, Shah Jahan fell severely ill. As rumours of the emperor's death spread, Murad and Shuja crowned themselves in Gujarat and Bengal. Wily Aurangzeb made a secret pact with Murad, promising him the crown, publicly proclaimed Dara a heretic, and himself as the 'upholder' of Islam. All princes marched on Agra from their areas to 'free' their father Shah Jahan. Dara Shikoh met them in May 1658 in the Battle of Samugarh. Each side had about 50,000 men, but Dara was forced to flee from Aurangzeb, a far better military general.

Agra surrendered and Aurangzeb crowned himself king. Old Shah Jahan was kept under house arrest until his death eight years later. Jahanara looked after her father devotedly, but after his death became Aurangzeb's First Lady, with a handsome annual income.

Aurangzeb betrayed Murad, imprisoned him at Gwalior and executed him. He forced Shuja to retreat into Arakan in Burma (Myanmar), where he was killed by a minor chieftain. Dara kept retreating, losing battle after battle, until he was brutally betrayed by Afghan chieftain Malik Jiwan (whom he had once ironically saved from execution!).

Dara was brought to Delhi in chains, on a worn-out elephant, his son beside him, dressed in filthy coarse fabric. Bernier writes, 'The crowd... was immense; and everywhere I observed the people weeping, and lamenting the fate of Dara... ' Dara Shikoh was beheaded on charges of heresy and his headless body was paraded across Delhi. Legend has it that Aurangzeb had his head delivered to Shah Jahan in a serving dish as a 'surprise'.

AURANGZEB THE RULER

Aurangzeb accomplished Akbar's dream of winning the Deccan when he conquered Bijapur and Golconda. The Mughal Empire was now at its greatest extent. However, he spent the last 25 years of his life trying to (unsuccessfully) eliminate the Marathas in the Deccan.

Aurangzeb hastened the decline of the Mughals with his policies and attitude

THE DECLINE OF THE MUGHAL EMPIRE

The Mughal Empire splintered quickly after Aurangzeb's death, and his intolerance had a large role, as he reversed Akbar's long-standing liberal policies, and gained enemies.

He reimposed the *jizya* and pilgrimage taxes,

adding 40 million *rupiya*s of annual income. When Delhi was struck by an earthquake soon after, he was advised to retract the tax, as it was a bad omen. Aurangzeb retorted that the earth was 'trembling with joy as he was spreading Islam'. A large protest outside the Red Fort was squashed by getting imperial elephants to trample the protestors.

Sharia was strictly imposed. He discontinued the celebration of non-Muslim festivals, and banned *jharoka-i-darshan*. He once reduced the customs tax for Muslim traders to 2.5 per cent, while keeping it at 5 per cent for Hindus, but his Muslim subjects started 'fronting' for Hindu merchants to make money on the side!

According to legend, when Aurangzeb banned music, he happened across a large, wailing crowd following a richly decorated coffin... apparently the city's musicians mourning the 'Death of Lady Music'! He retorted snidely that they should 'make sure she is buried properly'.

Many temples were destroyed across the country, including the Vishwanath temple of Benares, the wealthy temple of Somnath, and temples in Odisha and Rajasthan.

Aurangezeb lived his personal life with hermit-like simplicity and spent his free time copying the Quran or sewing prayer caps.

The Mughal Empire faced severe financial problems as Shah Jahan had emptied the royal coffers. Corruption ran deep. Governors, paid to maintain armies and horses, simply pocketed the money, and revenue collection was a fraction of

Aurangzeb, whose revenue was ten times that of the King Louis XIV of France, spent his spare time sewing prayer caps and copying the Quran to earn pennies for his funeral.

FUN FACT!

what it should have been. Rebellions started springing up all across the land.

THE RAJPUTS

Rajput loyalty had been painstakingly cultivated by Akbar and Jahangir. Aurangzeb, however, discriminated against them, even annexing the kingdom of Marwar when the loyal Rana Jaswant Singh Rathore died during a (Mughal!) campaign in Peshawar. When Marwar's minister, Durgadas Rathore, took both of Jaswant Singh's infant sons to Delhi to plead with Aurangzeb, he placed them under house arrest! Durgadas escaped with Ajit Singh, while the other infant was converted and raised in the Mughal harem.

Aurangzeb declared Ajit Singh an imposter (*jali bachcha*), and the Mughal army wrecked Marwar, which built up a lot

Aurangzeb's Will

Aurangzeb's 12-point dying advice to his son is a fascinating peek into what preoccupied one of the most powerful men on earth. Some of them are:

• 'Four rupees and two annas, from the caps sewn by me, spend on the shroud of this helpless creature. Rupees 305, from the wages of copying the Quran, distribute to the faqirs.'

• 'The Turani people have ever been soldiers, expert in raids, night-attacks and arrests. They feel no despair or shame when commanded to make a retreat in the midst of a fight, unlike the crass stupidity of the Hindustanis, who would part with their heads, but not leave their positions in battle.'

• 'Never trust your sons, nor treat them in an intimate manner, because, if the Emperor Shah Jahan had not treated Dara Shikoh in this manner, his affairs would not have come to such a sorry pass.'

• 'The government should be well informed in the news of the kingdom. Negligence for a single moment becomes the cause of disgrace for long years. The escape of... Shiva [Shivaji] took place through my carelessness.'

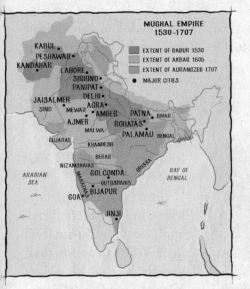

MUGHAL EMPIRE
1530-1707

EXTENT OF BABUR 1530
EXTENT OF AKBAR 1605
EXTENT OF AURANGZEB 1707
● MAJOR CITIES

KABUL
PESHAWAR
KANDAHAR
LAHORE
SIRHIND
PANIPAT
DELHI
JAISALMER
SIND
MEWAR
AGRA
AMBER
PATNA
BIHAR
AJMER
ROHATAS
MALWA
PALAMAU
BENGAL
GUJARAT
KHANDESH
BERAR
NIZAMSHAHIS
ARABIAN
SEA
GOLCONDA
QUTBSHAHIS
BIJAPUR
GOA
JINJI
ORISSA
MARATHAS
BAY OF
BENGAL

This map of the Mughal Empire shows the extent of territory captured under each emperor

of bad will. Against insurmountable odds, Durgadas kept up an unflagging resistance for the next 30 years. He combined Rajput valour, cunning, guerilla tactics and alliances with Aurangzeb's rivals. Upon Aurangzeb's death in 1707, he retook Marwar and crowned Ajit Singh. The next Mughal emperor Bahadur Shah recognized Marwar as independent. A Rajasthani folk song lauds Durgadas, 'O mother, give birth to a son like Durgadas, who stopped the flooding dam of the Mughals without any support.'

THE SIKHS

The Sikhs had conflicted with the Mughals since Jahangir's time, seemingly over trivial matters. Once, Shah Jahan's favourite hawk flew into Guru Hargobind's camp, who refused to return it. Another time, two horses intended for the Guru were seized by Mughal officials, and rescued later.

As the Sikhs became a powerful force in the Punjab, Aurangzeb allied with them. The ninth guru, Tegh Bahadur, even joined the Mughal campaign in Assam. But in 1675, Aurangzeb demanded that the guru convert to

Islam. Upon his refusal, he was beheaded in the middle of Chandni Chowk in Delhi, marked by the gurdwara Sis Ganj Sahib today.

In 1699, Guru Gobind Singh founded the Sikh Khalsa, a military brotherhood, marked by five visible badges; Kesh (hair), Kangha (comb), Kada (bangle), Kirpan (dagger), and *Kachchha* (underwear).

A fresco of Guru Gobind Singh and the Panj Pyare (the five beloved ones) in Gurdwara Bhai Than Singh

Guru Gobind Singh lost four sons in the conflicts, and was assassinated in 1708 by a Mughal governor. This troubled history caused a long aversion to Mughal rule.

ASSAM

Indomitable Assam had managed to maintain its independence over the centuries. Aurangzeb sent Ram Singh Kachhwaha to conquer it, but the Mughal forces were routed at the Battle of Saraighat on the Brahmaputra river in 1671 by the Ahom army under Lachit Borphukan.

Shivaji

From humble beginnings, Shivaji and his hardy band of Maratha warriors blazed across western India and founded the mighty Maratha Empire.

Shivaji was born in 1627 CE to Shahji Bhonsle, a Maratha general who served the Bijapur Sultanate. He was brought up by his mother Jijabai in the small hilly *jagir* of Poona (now Pune). His father lived in Bijapur with another wife. Jijabai, a proud and strong woman, regaled young Shivaji with tales of bravery and war from the Hindu epics. He was trained rigorously by his guardian-tutor Dadaji Konddev, in arms, wrestling, swimming, riding, politics and governance.

Shivaji grew up exploring every nook and cranny of the surrounding hill-country with his friends.

In 1645, the Bijapuri governors of nearby Torna and Kondana were 'persuaded' (with money) by an 18-year old Shivaji to hand over their forts. The angry sultan imprisoned his father Shahji and threatened him with death unless his son surrendered. Shahji was released in 1649 after coming to an agreement with Shivaji, who handed back Kondana. Shivaji also asked the Mughals to intercede. Shivaji truly started his career of conquest when he conquered Javli in 1656.

In 1657, Prince Aurangzeb entered Bijapur territory. Shivaji retired into the mountains and let the mighty Mughal army roll by, a large, stately (and slow) war machine. Eventually, he could not resist a quick pounce, and carried off hundreds of Mughal horses. Prince Aurangzeb would get used to the furious feeling at the news!

When Aurangzeb headed back north for the war of succession, a newly spirited Bijapur court sent 10,000 men to crush Shivaji under the well-built Afghan commander Afzal Khan, who amused himself on the way by building a cage for Shivaji!

The Marathas were ill-equipped to fight Bijapur's forces. Shivaji eventually met Afzal Khan in 1659 on a densely wooded hilltop to discuss a truce, but audaciously killed him with metal tiger claws, and launched a surprise ambush. The Bijapur army scattered in panic, leaving the Marathas an immense booty.

Shivaji finally made peace with Bijapur in 1662, retaining all the territories he had captured. Bijapur made the best of it in the hope that Shivaji would serve as a buffer from the covetous Mughals!

Raigad Fort in Raigad district, Maharashtra, the capital of Shivaji's Maratha kingdom

In 1660, Aurangzeb sent his maternal uncle Shaista Khan, who quickly captured Shivaji's Poona fort. In 1663, Shivaji and his warriors entered Poona disguised as a *baraat* (wedding party) and sneaked into the fort at night. They found Shaista Khan in his harem and Shivaji managed to chop off a few of his fingers as he jumped out of the window! Mughal forces had to leave and Shaista Khan got a 'punishment posting' as the Governor of Bengal.

Many legends sprang up about Shivaji. An English trader with the East India Company wrote: 'Report hath made him an Airy Body and added Wings, else it were impossible for him to be in so many places... at one time...' The Portuguese wrote, 'The question is still unsolved whether Sevagy is a Magician or the Devil.'

In 1664, Shivaji raided the rich, multicultural Mughal port town of Surat. The Marathas refrained from widespread killing, but carried away 10 million *rupiya*s in a matter of days, retreating speedily to their capital Raigad.

Aurangzeb began to go into a frenzy at the mention of Shivaji, whom he called 'Mountain Rat', because Shivaji was too clever and quick for him in his familiar

A portrait of Shivaji made in the 17th century, housed in the British Museum, London

hill-country. He sent high-ranking Raja Jai Singh, who forced Shivaji to the negotiating table in 1665. Shivaji was persuaded to surrender nearly 23 forts and join Mughal service (and conquer new lands alongside them). He reluctantly agreed to go and meet Aurangzeb in Agra. When an ungracious Aurangzeb made Shivaji stand with lesser nobles at court, the Maratha walked off without taking leave, and was promptly put under house arrest at Jai Singh's mansion.

Shivaji plotted his most audacious plan yet. He started sending large baskets of food as gifts every day to different nobles. One day, he went missing – legend has it he escaped in large baskets of fruit, along with his son Sambhaji!

A furious Aurangzeb set the full force of the Mughal machinery to recapture him and Shivaji became the most wanted man across the Mughal Empire. Shivaji took a long route in disguise as a Hindu hermit, reached his kingdom safely and soon recovered most of his forts.

Shivaji began charging a tax on neighbouring Mughal territories to protect them from his own invasion! The *chauth* (one-fourth) tax was 25 per cent of the revenue. An additional 10 per cent tax was called *sardeshmukhi*. The sultanate of Golconda was forced to offer two million *pagoda*s (a currency unit) as tribute.

In 1674, Shivaji crowned himself 'Chhatrapati Shivaji Maharaj' at his capital in Raigad in a grand month-long coronation celebration held in the traditional Hindu style.

A statue of Sambhaji, Shivaji's eldest son, in Pune. He succeeded Shivaji

So how did Shivaji rise with so few men and resources and come to rule a considerable empire? The main source of Maratha strength was its cavalry. Shivaji's men were kept in peak physical condition, travelled very light, could rapidly cover immense distances, and speedily retreat to their stoutly defended forts. Shivaji frequently used guerrilla warfare, using his intimate knowledge of the Western Ghats for ambushes.

In contrast, the Mughal and Bijapur armies were large but slow. English letters refer to Shivaji's 'nimble flying army of horses... his men labour and endure hardships... they fly to and fro with great dexterity.'

Shivaji resented the intolerance that the Deccan kingdoms, the Mughal governors and the Portuguese showed towards their Hindu subjects. Though a deeply devout Hindu, he did not deface any religious places during his attacks. Shivaji had an immense respect for women, and made sure his soldiers did not harm them. Once, when a captured Mughal noble lady was triumphantly presented before him, he apologized to her and returned her safely.

A charismatic leader, he had piercing eyes which 'seemed as if he was always smiling'. He had a secretive personality, and '... keeps everything to himself, trusting no one, be they his nearest and dearest'.

Shivaji died in 1680 at the young age of fifty-three. The English traders took a while to believe it because 'Sevagee had died so often that some begin to think him immortelle'! His son Sambhaji continued fighting the Mughals. He was captured and tortured to death in 1689.

Maratha resistance continued under Sambhaji's half-brother, Rajaram. Italian writer and traveller Niccolao Manucci wrote that Aurangzeb lost 100,000 soldiers and 300,000 animals every year! The constant fighting took its toll on Mughal revenues, as peasants fled, squeezed between the two warring armies.

THE END OF THE GREAT MUGHALS

The last years of Aurangzeb's life were grim and lonely on his Deccan campaign. He died of illness in Ahmadnagar at

Corruption at the Mughal Court

Corruption had reached epic proportions by Aurangzeb's time. The French visitor Tavernier describes the astonishing list of 'presents' he was obliged to give:

'No one ventures with empty hands.

Presents made to the King: A shield of bronze thoroughly well-gilt... A battle-mace of rock crystal, covered with rubies and emeralds, inlaid in gold... A Turkish saddle embroidered with small rubies, pearls and emeralds, another horse saddle covered with gold and silver embroidery... Presents made to uncle of the Great Mogul: a table with precious stones representing flowers and birds from Florence, a ring with a perfect ruby... To the Grand Treasurer, a watch having a golden case covered with small emeralds... To the attendants of the treasury of the king, 300 livres.

To the eunuch of the Grand Begum, a watch costing 260 livres.

All the presents which I made amounted to 23,187 livres.

...Those who desire to do business at the court... should not commence, until they have considerable presents... an open purse for diverse officers.'

the age of 88 in 1707. As Manucci said, Aurangzeb was 'a man born to trouble others and to be troubled by them'.

Europeans at the Mughal Court

The earliest Europeans like Portuguese sailors and Jesuit priests had come to the Mughal court from Akbar's time. William Hawkins, representative of the British East India Company, arrived in 1609 at Jahangir's court. Sir Thomas Roe was the first official British ambassador, in 1615 CE.

Jahangir liked the British, especially when they started defeating the Portuguese at sea, who had greatly annoyed him by illegally seizing a cargo-laden Mughal ship. After Jahangir arrested some Portuguese and besieged Daman, the Portuguese left him well alone. By Aurangzeb's time, revenue from British trade had become very important to the cash-strapped Mughal Empire.

Early European travellers wrote fascinating eyewitness accounts of the Mughals – from Italian gunner Niccolao Manucci to Thomas Coryat, the English budget tourist, to the French gem trader Jean-Baptiste Tavernier and doctor Francois Bernier. They took back tales of incredible opulence and, in Europe, the word Mughal became 'mogul', meaning people with great power and wealth.

What in the World Was Happening! (1600-1700 CE)

Asia
- CHINA: Manchus conquer China. End of Ming dynasty.
- JAPAN: Shogunate founded. Japan is closed off to foreigners.
- The Safavids in Iran and the Ottomans in Turkey stay strong.
- INDONESIA: Colonized by the Dutch, who dominate the spice trade.
- RUSSIA: Peter the Great becomes Tsar and modernizes Russia.

Europe
- ENGLAND: The English East India Company is founded. Establishes a factory at Surat.
- English Civil War and the increased role of the Parliament even after the restoration of the Crown.
- The Scientific Revolution is underway. Napier invents the logarithms, Newton states his theories on gravity, optics and mechanics and Leibniz invents Calculus.

America
- British settlers cross over to North America on the *Mayflower*.

Africa
- Denuded by slavers for the Americas (North and South).
- SOUTH AFRICA: Dutch settlement begins.

Explore More

* READ about Shalimar and Nishat Gardens in Kashmir, the conceptual model of the Mughal garden and what the layout and design principles were.

* VISIT the Taj Mahal and Agra Fort in Agra, Uttar Pradesh, and the Red Fort in Delhi.

* COLLECT information about the architectural elements of Jahangir's mausoleum in Lahore, Pakistan, and compare it to the other Mughal mausoleums you may have seen

Decline of the Mughal Empire

4

[1707–1820 CE]

'Dilli jo aik shehar tha aalam mein intekhaab,
Rehte the muntakhib hi jahan rozgaar ke;
Jisko falak ne loot ke viraan kar diya...'

'Delhi, the unique city in the world,
Where only the best in each field lived;
Fate looted it and laid it waste...'

– Mir Taqi Mir (1723–1810),
the poet of Delhi,
famous for *Dil aur Dilli ke
Marsiye* (Laments for the
Heart and for Delhi)

4

An Empire Splinters into a Thousand Pieces

The glorious Mughal Empire fell apart with dizzying speed after Aurangzeb's death. The Peacock Throne became a game of musical chairs as rival groups at court propped up increasingly weak and incapable emperors with vicious infighting at each round. Provinces started breaking away and new kingdoms emerged – ruled either by former Mughal governors, subordinate kings who had once been Mughal allies, or even entirely new players, like the Sikhs, the Jats and the Marathas. As the empire's weakness became clear, India was ravaged by treasure-seeking marauders from Afghanistan and Persia. Meanwhile, the British and French transformed from traders to military rulers. Within 50 years, the Mughal emperor was reduced to controlling just the city of Delhi!

This disintegration was terrible for India. Ravaged by war, invasions and foreign domination, the 18th century was a time of great suffering for Indians. People became much poorer, and there were terrible famines, especially in British-ruled Bengal. Intriguingly, the Marathas, Rohillas,

Sikhs and Afghans – none ever formally replaced the Mughal emperor. Even the British were reluctant to change this until the Uprising of 1857, such was the lustre of the Mughal dynasty.

Political History

Shah Jahan had started a bad habit – each new Mughal emperor was crowned after bloody warring within the family. After Aurangzeb's death, powerful nobles became kingmakers – raising and toppling princes on and off the throne, while grabbing the real power themselves. Mughal emperors quickly became weak puppets, even as different court factions like the Turanis, Iranis and Afghans became stronger.

The Turanis were highly favoured as they were from the Central Asian Mongol homeland. The Iranis were Shias from Persia and, although few in number, reached high positions in court. Opposed to these was the home-grown Hindustani party, which included nobles whose ancestors had come to India many generations ago, as well as Hindu rulers like the Rajputs.

The Mughal court was in a shambles – nobles carved out their own quasi-states, refused to pay revenue to the treasury, and did not maintain the troops they were meant to. So the Mughal army was large on paper, but irregularly paid and hardly battle-ready.

Later Mughals

Aurangzeb had outlived six of his children and left behind three ageing sons. His son Muhammad Muazzam won the accession war over his brothers, and became emperor Bahadur Shah I when he was sixty-three! He was an able and mostly benevolent emperor, but died after just five years in 1712.

During his rule, Banda Bahadur led the Sikhs into open rebellion against the Mughal Empire. Bahadur Shah I also tried to confiscate some Rajput princedoms, causing the kings of Amber and Jodhpur to join the Rana of Mewar's fight against the Mughals.

Bahadur Shah's favourite son Azim-ush-Shan was heir apparent, but when the time came, a noble called Zulfikar Khan ganged up with Prince Azim's three brothers and defeated and drowned him! Zulfikar (predictably) killed off the younger princes, and made the oldest one emperor. Pleasure-loving Emperor Jahandar Shah was happy to let Zulfikar Khan run the empire, as long as he could frolic with a musician called Lal Kunwar (a descendant of Tansen!). Historians would dub him the 'Lord of Misrule'. Lal Kunwar was given a flabbergasting annual allowance,

and her large musician family and friends were made high-ranking nobles and given *jagir*s.

When her brother tried to become Governor of Multan, a fed-up Zulfikar Khan demanded a bizarre bribe of 1,000 sarangis, later telling Jahandar Shah that as only musicians seemed to be getting important political positions, he wanted to gift sarangis to all other nobles to try their luck!

Jahandar Shah, the eighth emperor of the Mughal Empire

Meanwhile, dead prince Azim's son Farrukhsiyar reached

Bengal to raise support and men. He fell in with the soon-to-be-notorious Sayyid brothers, Hasan Ali Khan and Hussain Ali Khan, who came from a very old aristocratic military family. Old enemies of Jahandar Shah, they rustled up other malcontents and raised money for an army by raiding royal caravans, forced loans and even theft!

Jahandar Shah eventually bestirred himself to meet the approaching army; but his soldiers had not been paid even once in the past year! Their salaries had been frittered on frivolities like a weekly Diwali-style 'illumination' of the royal fort.

So now, gold vessels from Akbar's time were melted down, then jewelled objects were taken, then fine clothes and wall hangings. Finally, even the gold-roofed rooms were broken down to pay the soldiers!

When Jahandar Shah was defeated anyway, his own wazir Zulfikar Khan took him prisoner, to use him to save his own skin. But other nobles treacherously had both Zulfikar and Jahandar Shah strangled, trampled and stabbed to death, starting an awful tradition of murdering Mughal emperors, not just heir apparents!

Farrukhsiyar was crowned in 1713. The Sayyid brothers grabbed all the high positions for themselves and their group. As they were part of the Hindustani group, the Iranis and Turanis got squeezed out at court, while the Rajputs and Jats were rewarded.

Farrukhsiyar was an insecure type and began a flurry of strangulations of nobles. It became so bad that whenever they were summoned to appear before the emperor, Mughal nobles said their final goodbyes to their families, just in case they did not make it back home!

The Emperor Farrukhsiyar on his balcony

Farrukhsiyar met all with false flattery and rich gifts, but was known for his fickleness, disregard for loyalty, and casual treachery. He was also easily persuaded, and some nobles soon convinced Farrukhsiyar that the Sayyid brothers were going to replace him. He had three young royals blinded (just in case!) and tried to treacherously capture the Sayyids at court. When they got wind of his plans and tried to resign their posts and return to Bihar, he would not let them.

Fickle Farrukhsiyar was the one who, in 1715, set in motion the events that would lead to total British domination of India – he granted the East India Company tax-free trading rights across Bengal when an English doctor treated an unmentionable disease!

The tense situation with the Sayyids continued. Farrukhsiyar eventually sent off one brother to 'retake the Deccan' from the rival Marathas, while secretly requesting them to kill him off! The Sayyids turned the tables and marched to Delhi alongside an army of Marathas. A terrified Farrukhsiyar kept alternately reconciling with and betraying the Sayyids, before finally hiding in the women's quarters, guarded by female Turki bodyguards! He was dragged to the Sayyids, bareheaded and barefooted, immediately blinded, jailed and strangled soon after. He had been emperor for six years.

The Sayyid brothers now considered starting a new dynasty of their own, but finally decided to install another imprisoned Mughal puppet prince. They asked for the reasonably competent Prince Bidar Dil to be fetched. When the guards could not find him, they randomly picked another prince, Rafi-ud-Darjat, from the harem! He was marched off in his plain clothes, parked on the magnificent Peacock Throne and declared emperor!

Rafi-ud-Darjat was kept under firm guard and even his meals were served on order of the Sayyids. The accidental young emperor was an opium addict and had a wasting disease. As he weakened and approached death, he pleaded for his elder brother to take his place. In a fine farce, Rafi-ud-Daulah was next, crowned Shah Jahan II. A sickly youth, equally addicted to opium, he too died of disease after just three months.

Dozens of later Mughal princes were kept imprisoned by ambitious kingmakers, to be crowned and killed at whim! **FUN FACT!**

A 17-year old Muhammad Shah was now installed on the throne in 1719. However, the Turanis and Iranis finally united and managed to get rid of the Sayyid brothers. The elder was assassinated, the younger killed in battle, and the age of the Sayyids ended abruptly.

In the 12 years since Aurangzeb's death, six Mughal emperors had come and gone, and the empire was in a proper mess.

Muhammad Shah would rule for 30 years, in a pleasure-seeking reign that earned him the moniker 'Rangeela' (colourful). Mornings were devoted to animal fights, evenings to amusements and circuses. Painters and poets, musicians and dancers were lavishly patronized.

Muhammad Shah did not lead a single military campaign and large chunks of the empire broke away under provincial governors. In 1739, Delhi would experience one of its worst sackings ever.

Nadir Shah of Iran

Meanwhile, over in the West, as the 200-year-old Persian Safavid Empire fell into disarray, Persia had been ravaged by Afghan tribals. Nadir Quli, an obscure Persian tribal who had risen through the royal army, quickly retook Persia and crowned himself Shah in 1736. A brilliant military general, he soon started eyeing the fantastic Mughal wealth. He captured Kandahar and Kabul in short order – where Mughal troops had not been paid for five years!

Kabul's governor sent a panicked plea to Delhi for reinforcements, but when the messenger requested an urgent audience, Muhammad Shah was so furious at being disturbed during a party, he drowned the message in wine and sent the messenger to be tortured!

As Nadir Shah made for Lahore and then Delhi, Muhammad Shah belatedly divided the military command among three quarrelsome generals, including the Nizam-ul-Mulk of the Deccan and Saadat Khan, the nawab of Awadh, who refused to agree on anything.

The Mughals finally faced the Persians at Karnal, only 100 km from Delhi. Though they outnumbered the Persians six to one, they were routed in just three hours. When the Nizam-ul-Mulk negotiated a large (though not utterly ruinous) war prize of 20 million *rupiya*s, his rival, the Persian-origin Saadat Khan, convinced Nadir Shah that he could extract far more from the Mughals!

Nadir Shah promptly forced Emperor Muhammad Shah to visit him in his camp. As Persian was also the Mughal court language, the two could talk comfortably. Nadir Shah gave Muhammad Shah a fine lecture on what a bad emperor he was, saying '... you are puffed up with childish conceits'. He then invited himself to Delhi, where the Mughal court went all out to entertain him with sumptuous banquets and lavish entertainment!

Nadir Shah initially threatened harsh punishment for those of his soldiers who misbehaved with the locals. But when one day, some Persian soldiers were killed in a quarrel with local shopkeepers while haggling over prices,

Nadir Shah on the Peacock Throne after his victory at the Battle of Karnal

excited Delhi citizens 'poured like a torrent towards the Castle', and tried to shoot Nadir Shah as he rode out to see the corpses of his men. An enraged Nadir Shah climbed to the roof of a mosque near the Red Fort and drew his sword, ordering his men on a *qatl-e-aam* (general killing spree) until he sheathed it. He stood with the sword outstretched for six hours. His soldiers butchered young and old, male and female, until 30,000 people lay dead. Shops were looted, women were enslaved and huge amounts of money violently taken.

The wealth of Delhi, accumulated over 340 years since the last sack by Timur in 1398, was transferred to Nadir Shah in one go. He and his soldiers carried off perhaps 800 million *rupiya*s worth of loot (about 400 billion rupees today), including the priceless Peacock Throne and Koh-i-noor diamond. He excused all taxes in Persia for three years! Nadir Shah soon grew erratic, violent and suspicious, and was assassinated by his own soldiers in 1747.

Muhammad Shah continued to rule over the broken Mughal Empire until his death ten years later. He was succeeded by his son Ahmad Shah, who was installed by Safdar Jung in 1748, who had followed his father-in-law Saadat Khan as Awadh's governor. Ahmad Shah's mother, the dancing girl – Qudsia Begum, carried on an as depraved a life as her husband. Despite the recent devastation, she spent obscene amounts of money, including 20 million *rupiya*s on her birthday celebrations! Court nobles rabidly hated her and her favourite, the handsome Irani eunuch, Javed Khan.

Ahmad Shah's reign was quite as turbulent as his father's, as tribal Rohilla Afghans rebelled across north

India, and the Afghan king Ahmad Shah Abdali began his many raids into India.

Ahmad Shah Abdali

Nadir Shah had hired many Afghan soldiers in his army, including Ahmad Shah Abdali, whom he made the commander of his 4,000-strong personal palace guard. After Nadir Shah's assassination, most Afghans returned home and made Abdali the very first king of Afghanistan, who took the title '*Dur-i-Durran*', meaning the Pearl of Pearls.

Abdali quickly united the Afghan tribes, and grabbed land from the Persians and Mughals on either side. Like his countryman Mahmud of Ghazni, Ahmad Shah 'Durrani' also raided India numerous times. He soon took Lahore, and forced the Mughals to sign over Sindh and Punjab. During his fourth invasion in 1756, Abdali sacked Agra, Mathura and Vrindavan on his march to Delhi, where he married off both his son and himself into the Mughal royal family. Abdali looted Punjab so thoroughly that a popular

Ahmad Shah Abdali, the 1st emperor of the Durrani Empire

Punjabi saying goes: '*Khanda peenda lahe da, baki Ahmad Shahe da*', or 'only what we've eaten and drunk is ours, the rest belongs to Ahmad Shah'!

In 1761, he (along with his Rohilla and Awadh allies) crushed the Marathas at the Third Battle of Panipat. After his death in 1772, Afghanistan soon crumbled back into warring factions.

Back to the Mughals

Meanwhile, the inept Mughal emperor Ahmad Shah Bahadur was toppled and blinded in 1754 by the ruler of Hyderabad, Imad-ul-Mulk, and spent the remaining 20 years of his life as a prisoner.

Imad-ul-Mulk went back to Farrukhsiyar's family line, installing his 55-year old son Alamgir II, who had been raised as a caged Mughal prince and had no stomach for intrigue, instead spending his time on religion and books. Imad-ul-Mulk made treaties with the now powerful Marathas for 'protection' from the Rohillas and Abdali. After some years, they decided to get rid of Alamgir II anyway and had him stabbed.

The next king, Shah Jahan III, lasted only a year.

Alamgir II's fugitive son proclaimed himself Emperor Shah Alam II in 1759, but could not enter his own capital of Delhi for 12 years for the very real fear of treacherous Mughal nobles! The British fought and resoundingly defeated him, Awadh and Bengal at the Battle of Buxar in 1764. Shah Alam II was forced

Afghan royal soldiers of the Durrani Empire. The peacock feathers on their helmets were a symbol of royalty

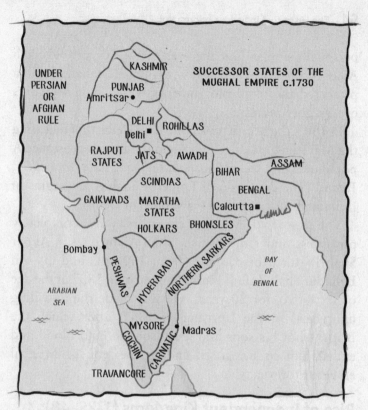

A map showing the autonomous states that formed as the Mughal Empire declined

to 'give' them the Diwani of Bengal, Bihar and Orissa in return for British 'protection'.

In 1772, Shah Alam II was 'rescued' from the British by the Marathas, and duly reinstalled at the Red Fort in Delhi, where he was 'persuaded' to appoint Mahadji Scindia as the regent of the Mughal 'Empire'.

In 1788, a Rohilla called Ghulam Qadir came and sacked Delhi – revenge for the unhappy childhood years that he spent as a prisoner at the Mughal court. Ghulam Qadir brutally mistreated the royal Mughal women and personally gouged out the eyes of the 60-year-old Shah Alam II before leaving. Many years later, Mahadji Scindia presented the blind old emperor with Ghulam Qadir's eyes in gory revenge.

In 1803, the British took control of Delhi after defeating the Marathas, making Shah Alam II a British pensioner. A popular saying went 'Badshahate Shah Alam, az Dilli ta Palam' (The dominion of Emperor Shah Alam begins in Delhi and ends at Palam – a suburb of Delhi).

The last two Mughal emperors were completely powerless under the British. Shah Alam II's son Akbar Shah II ruled for 31 years from 1806 CE, and his son Bahadur Shah Zafar became 'emperor' in 1837 at the age of sixty-two, for 20 years. He was made the unwilling figurehead of the Uprising of 1857, after which the British shot his sons and grandsons in cold blood and exiled him to Rangoon, ending the title of Mughal emperor forever.

Rise of Independent Kingdoms (1725–48)

We have been looking at what was happening in the imperial capital of Delhi. Let us take a quick glance at what was happening around the country in this same period.

As Mughal power declined after Aurangzeb's death, Mughal governors gradually carved out independent kingdoms, while still claiming to rule in the name of the emperor. These states, like Hyderabad, Awadh and Bengal, became very powerful.

The Central Asian Turki noble Chin Qilich Khan, who had been appointed the Nizam-ul-Mulk (literally meaning manager of the country!), broke away in 1724 to form the large and incredibly wealthy state of Hyderabad, which comprised parts of Maharashtra, Andhra Pradesh, Karnataka and Tamil Nadu.

Saadat Khan (who betrayed the Mughals to Nadir Shah) was governor of Awadh and started hereditary rule there.

The governor of greater Bengal, Murshid Quli Khan, declared himself the Nawab of Bengal back in 1717 CE. Siraj-ud-Daulah, the last independent nawab of Bengal, was betrayed by his own nobles and defeated by the British in the course-changing Battle of Plassey in 1757, which marked the beginning of British rule in India.

Other rulers were outright opponents of the Mughals, like the Sikhs, Marathas and Jats, and Rajput kingdoms like Mewar and Marwar. The disintegration was so widespread that, at the time of Indian independence in 1947, the 40 per cent of India's land still under princely rule had more than 550 different states!

The Sikhs

The Sikhs had been clashing with the Mughals since Jahangir's time, and relations deteriorated under Shah Jahan and Aurangzeb. Their tenth and last guru, Gobind Singh, organized the Sikhs into a battle-ready military force called the Khalsa (brotherhood). He told all Sikhs to build a bold identity. All Sikh men started calling themselves Singh ('lion') and women, Kaur ('princess'). Banda Bahadur took up the military baton, travelling

Banda Singh Bahadur, the leader of the Sikhs after Guru Gobind Singh

The Third Battle of Panipat

The Third Battle of Panipat in 1761 CE was one of the largest battles of the 18th century. It saw 70,000 Maratha soldiers facing 100,000 troops of the Afghan king Ahmad Shah Abdali and his Indian allies, the Rohillas and Awadh. The Marathas, led by the peshwa's inept brother, Sadashivrao Bhau, had inexplicably brought along 200,000 women, children and other non-combatants, to visit northern pilgrimage sites like Kurukshetra!

Though the Marathas had asked other kings to join them against the Afghans, most refused because they did not want the Marathas to become the unchallenged supremos of India.

As Abdali camped across the river, waiting for the monsoon to end, regional rulers like Mahadji Scindia and Raja Surajmal Jat advised Sadashivrao to send back the non-combatants but were rebuffed. As the Maratha troops moved north, Abdali did a surprise river crossing, cutting off their food supply. The Marathas' food ran out due to the number of non-combatants, because of whom the starving Marathas could not perform their usual quick retreat either.

They finally attacked Abdali on 14 January 1761, claiming it was better to die in war than of hunger. The battle raged for several hours and an entire generation of Maratha soldiers was wiped out in a single day. Eyewitnesses report that Abdali ordered 40,000 Maratha prisoners killed in cold blood, and many non-combatants. More than 100,000 Marathas were killed. Countless women and children were taken as slaves to Afghanistan.

Jankoji Scindia was gruesomely buried alive by the Rohillas, starting a terrible blood feud between their leader Najib Khan and the Scindias, ending only when his brother Mahadji Scindia killed Najib's grandson Ghulam Qadir after blinding and torturing him. It took the Maratha states a decade to recover from this disaster.

Detail from a painting of the Third Battle of Panipat

around Punjab with 30,000–40,000 people and harrying Mughal forces. He set up a capital in Lohgarh and even captured some parts of Mughal territory and became a real headache for the Mughals. Banda Bahadur was finally captured in 1716, brought to Delhi in chains along with 800 men, tortured and executed with his young son in his lap. Even hostile Mughal historians have remarked on the serenity of the Sikhs as each calmly refused to change his faith, and was killed in turn.

Emperor Farrukhsiyar continued a strict policy of persecution, and the Sikhs, who carried on guerilla warfare, were hunted and arrested on sight, and given a choice of death or conversion. Eventually, as part of a peace treaty, the Sikhs were given land and safe residence in Amritsar. They moved to Amritsar, where they were organized into two groups, the Budha Dal (old group) and the Taruna Dal (young group). However, peace lasted just two years and the Sikhs were soon on the run again.

Gradually, the Sikhs formed different armed groups called *misl*s which had about a 100 people each. To join a *misl*, a man only needed a horse and a gun. Booty from raids was equally divided.

In 1746, a Mughal official slaughtered all the Sikhs in Lahore to avenge his brother's death. This day is known as the *Chhota Ghallughara*, the Small Holocaust.

The Sikhs built up a bitter enmity with the Afghan marauder Ahmad Shah Abdali as he ravaged Punjab. He desecrated the Golden Temple in Amritsar, and in 1762, blew it up with gunpowder and had 30,000 Sikhs (one-third of the Sikh population) massacred. The Sikhs call this the *Vadda Ghallughara* (the Great Holocaust).

After Ahmad Shah Abdali, the Sikh *misl*s had a free run and no grave enemy to fight. They began to levy tribute called 'rakhi' from smaller kings and made their way up to the Ganga–Yamuna Doab. They captured Delhi in 1783 and left with a lot of loot and an agreement from Shah Alam II to maintain soldiers in Delhi and freely build gurdwaras there.

Rohillas

Over hundreds of years, many Afghan tribal highlanders had migrated to India to make their fortunes as soldiers. They became known as the Rohillas, from the Pashtun word for 'mountain'.

Aurangzeb had built up Rohilla loyalty by increasing their *mansab* ranks and giving them powerful positions. He even settled them in Uttar Pradesh to counter rebellious Rajputs. The area came to be called Rohilkhand, with its main city at Bareilly.

After Nadir Shah's disastrous invasion decimated the Mughals, Rohilla sardars carved their own small fiefdoms in Rohilkhand, ruling over the almost 100,000 Rohillas settled there. The Rohillas were caught between their acquisitive neighbour, Awadh, and the ambitious Marathas. In the Third Battle of Panipat in 1761, they sided with Ahmad Shah Abdali against the Marathas, creating a long, bitter enmity. After the battle, the chieftain Najib-ud-Daula was made 'regent' of the Mughal 'Empire'!

The Marathas recouped within ten years and retaliated brutally, ravaging Rohilla country. The Rohillas agreed to pay their neighbour, the nawab of Awadh, four million *rupiya*s to help defend them whenever the Marathas returned. After a quarrel, the nawab and the British East

India Company attacked them in the First Rohilla War in 1773. The British won, Rohilkhand fell to Awadh and most of the surviving Rohillas fled.

The Mighty Marathas

All said and done, 18th-century India was really the age of the mighty Marathas. Shivaji had carved an empire from under a furious Aurangzeb's nose, extracting large taxes called *chauth* and *sardeshmukhi* from Mughal-ruled Deccan.

As mentioned earlier, after Shivaji died in 1680, his son Sambhaji became king, but was captured, tortured and killed by Aurangzeb in 1689. His young half-brother Rajaram was made king. As the Mughals were battering away at his Raigad fort, Rajaram escaped to Jinjee fort in the deep south to continue Maratha resistance. Other Maratha chieftains kept harassing Mughal forces through their distinct guerilla moves, and recaptured many forts.

When Rajaram died of illness in 1700 at only thirty, his widow Tarabai took over as regent for her young son and very remarkably held off the Mughals!

A few years later, after Aurangzeb's death, the Mughals decided to release Sambhaji's son, Shahu, who had been brought up by the Mughals. Shahu and Tarabai went to war, and two different Maratha areas formed, with capitals at Satara and Kolhapur. As the Mughals had hoped, Shahu made peace with them and was given a high-ranking 7,000-*mansab*.

Shahu was aided by his prime minister, the peshwa (a Persian title used in the Deccan Sultanates!), an astute brahmin called Balaji Vishwanath. He was a clever political intriguer and got Tarabai deposed in 1713 and

Shahu recognized as Shivaji's real heir by the Mughal emperor, Farrukhsiyar!

After Balaji's death in 1720, his son Baji Rao I was appointed peshwa at the young age of twenty. The peshwaship became a hereditary role, and peshwas gradually became more important than the Maratha kings, like in the Japanese shogunate!

BAJI RAO I

As the Mughal Empire weakened, the Marathas went from strength to strength as Peshwa Baji Rao I (r. 1720–41 CE) grabbed long-held areas from them.

A great warrior and general, Baji Rao did not lose a single one of his 41 battles and once told his brother, 'Night has nothing to do with sleep. It was created by God to raid territory held by your enemy. The night is your shield, your screen against the cannons and swords of vastly superior enemy forces.'

The peerless peshwa, Baji Rao I

Baji Rao II, the last peshwa of the Maratha Empire

Baji Rao fought many battles against the Nizam-ul-Mulk over the Deccan, and in 1739, won Malwa. In 1741, the Marathas got the right to the *chauth* of Bengal, in exchange for giving military help to the Mughals.

Tarabai: The Spirited Maratha Queen

Tarabai was one of the most remarkable yet reviled women in Indian history. She headed the Marathas at their most vulnerable moment, and they survived and grew in strength under her brave leadership.

Married to Shivaji's younger son Rajaram at the age of eight, much of her youth passed in great danger, fleeing and hiding with her husband as he was hunted by the Mughals. When Rajaram died, 25-year-old Tarabai became regent for her young son Shivaji II.

One Mughal officer noted that Tarabai 'regulated things so well that not a single Maratha ruler acted without her orders'. Between 1700 and 1707, Tarabai single-handedly directed the Maratha defence against the mighty Mughals. Moving from fort to fort, she coordinated attacks while playing Aurangzeb's own game of bribing commanders on both sides.

Shahu was eventually released by the Mughals to counter Tarabai, and started ruling from Satara, and Tarabai was confined to Kolhapur in the south.

In 1714, Rajaram's other wife and son engineered a coup and imprisoned Tarabai and her son. She was rescued by her old enemy Shahu after 16 years, who reconciled with her and invited her to stay in Satara,

Tarabai, a portrait

where she was confined to the house until 1749. When Shahu died, the 75-year-old Tarabai produced an obscure 22-year-old grandson (she said she had hidden him in a village, and she later admitted that he was a fake) and had him crowned king as Rajaram II. When he did not toe the line, she had him jailed and ruled as his spokesperson!

She came into conflict with Peshwa Nana Sahib, who shifted his capital to Poona. She whipped up an anti-brahmin campaign, and asked Maratha enemies like the Nizam to attack the peshwa, but was not able to gather support. She finally had to spend her remaining days as a dowager, issuing edicts and building temples.

She died at the age of eighty-six, some months after the debacle at Panipat.

A painting depicting a Maratha Light Horseman

When the long-standing enemies finally met to sign a treaty, they flattered each other. The Nizam said, '*Ek baji, aur sab paji*' – 'Other than Baji, everybody is foolish' – to which Baji Rao replied '*Ek nizam, aur sab hajjam*' – 'Other than the Nizam, everyone is a barber.'

Baji Rao had a special relationship with the Bundela Rajput King Chhatrasal, who had fought the Mughals his whole life. In 1729, when attacked by the Rohillas, he urgently pleaded for Baji Rao's help. When the Marathas came and saved the day, a grateful Chhatrasal adopted Baji Rao, gave him one-third of his lands and his daughter Mastani, from his Persian wife, in marriage. Baji Rao and Mastani's

FUN FACT! Begum Samru, who started out as an Indian dancing girl in Delhi, rose to become the head of a very successful mercenary army with 100 European men reporting to her!

marriage caused an absolute scandal in Maratha circles, but they were devoted to each other – Mastani followed Baji Rao on all his military expeditions, riding alongside him, and fighting like any Maratha warrior. Baji Rao I died young at 41 in 1741, possibly of a heat stroke, and Mastani soon after. Their son, Shamsher Bahadur, was brought up as a Muslim and became the Nawab of Banda!

Baji Rao had made the Marathas the major power of India. From the Deccan, their lands now extended across north India – Rajasthan, the Ganga–Yamuna Doab and Punjab.

His son, Balaji Baji Rao (Baji Rao II) became the next peshwa and ruled for 20 years until 1761 over ever-increasing Maratha territories. He also persuaded the ailing Shahu to sign a deed that handed over Maratha power to the peshwa and accepted his bitter rival Tarabai's grandson as the next king! Maratha power now clearly lay with the peshwa and individual chieftains.

When Ahmad Shah Abdali started his raids, the Mughal emperor signed a treaty with Balaji – soon becoming a weak figurehead under Maratha protection.

Abdali and the Marathas kept skirmishing through the 1750s, and finally met on 14 January 1761 for the Third Battle of Panipat. By this time, the Marathas controlled most of northern and central India. The other large independent states were Awadh, Hyderabad, Mysore, and British-ruled Bengal. Abdali's artillery was superior and Maratha coordination weak. The Marathas lost disastrously and were slaughtered.

The massive rout, and the death of his brother and son broke Balaji Baji Rao, who died soon after.

Begum Samru: The Unlikely Ruler

Farzana, a beautiful Kashmiri girl, began life as a nautch girl. At the age of fourteen, she married a wandering soldier of fortune, the much older European, Walter Reinhardt Sombre. She took the name Begum Samru from 'Sombre'.

With his mercenary army, Reinhardt was given the small principality of Sardhana near Meerut. When Reinhardt died, Begum Samru was just twenty-seven, but she remarkably began to rule Sardhana and head the mercenary army herself, which had both European and Indian soldiers. Her wealthy *jagir* yielded 90,000 pounds per year, and she maintained a successful relationship with the British. She converted to Catholicism and built the largest Roman Catholic cathedral in north India.

A petite four-and-a-half feet tall, the Begum led her men into war, sporting a manly turban. As she developed a fearsome reputation, rumours spread that she was actually a witch who destroyed her enemies with black magic! She was a powerful force, and helped Indian rulers in many battles, including the Second Anglo-

Begum Samru, a portrait

Maratha War. The Mughal emperor Shah Alam II called her his 'most beloved daughter'. She built a magnificent palace in Chandni Chowk in a garden gifted to her by Shah Alam's successor, which still stands as Bhagirath Palace in Delhi, but in sad disrepair.

The flamboyant Begum maintained a formal Mughal-style court. She patronized Urdu poetry, and three of her European soldiers became recognized Urdu poets!

She died childless in 1836 at 85 years, leaving her immense fortune to David Ochterlony Dyce Sombre, her late husband's disreputable great-grandson. The East India Company seized Sardhana. Dyce Sombre married an aristocrat's daughter in England, but his wife got him certified as a 'lunatic'. He made a melodramatic escape to France, and continued a lifelong legal battle for his wealth, which the British government took over. The inheritance is worth about a billion dollars today and 'heirs' all over the world are still claiming it.

Maratha Confederacy

As the Marathas expanded, the peshwa handed over new territories to the chieftains who had conquered them. They ruled under the peshwa and did 'joint operations' under a unified Maratha force when needed. But after the debacle at Panipat, regional Maratha rulers refused to blindly accept orders from the peshwa.

Mahadji Scindia, founder of the princely state of Gwalior in central India

All the different Maratha kingdoms together formed the Maratha Confederacy. Malhar Rao Holkar started ruling southern Malwa from Indore. The Gaekwads ruled parts of Gujarat from Baroda. The Scindias ruled over northern Malwa from their capital, Gwalior. After Panipat, Mahadji Scindia (r. 1768–94), became the most important Maratha ruler, and rebuilt Maratha power to a new peak. He made Gwalior one of the richest and most powerful states in India. He was the 'protector' of the hapless Mughal emperor Shah Alam II and also defeated the British, the Rajputs and the Rohillas.

The Marathas remained India's premier power until the British finally defeated them in the beginning of the 19th century. Many Maratha kingdoms lasted (under British protection) until 1947, and even today, many former Indian royals are of Maratha heritage.

Ahilyabai Holkar
The Saintly Philosopher Queen

Ahilyabai, the Holkar queen of the Malwa kingdom

Ahilyabai Holkar (1725–95) was one of the greatest rulers of 18th century India. Her father-in-law, Malhar Rao Holkar, the Maratha king of Malwa, saw her in 1733 at a temple when she was only eight. Impressed by her bearing, he immediately married her to his son Khanderao Holkar. She was taught to read and write, trained in the art of governance and military skills, and given state responsibilities.

Her husband died when she was 29, but really astonishingly for her time, she did not commit sati. When her father-in-law followed in 1766, and her only son a year later, she applied to the peshwa for permission to rule directly, and was surprisingly granted the crown.

She did not observe purdah, and held daily public audiences. She had surprisingly modern views about individual rights. She loved to see bankers, merchants and farmers prosper, and very unusually proclaimed that she, their ruler, had no claim to their wealth!

Ahilyabai was a great builder. Not only did she build beautiful buildings across Indore and Maheshwar, and forts across Malwa, she constructed and repaired hundreds of temples and dharamshalas across the country at major pilgrimage spots like Dwarka, Benares and Somnath, using Holkar personal wealth.

Her capital of Maheshwar was culturally vibrant, with her patronage of Marathi and Sanskrit literature, music, art and sculpture, and industry and crafts.

Devoted to the welfare of her people, Ahilyabai Holkar is still considered a model ruler, and worshipped as a saint.

When she died at the age of seventy, all of Indore mourned their queen deeply.

What in the World Was Happening!
(1707–1820 CE)

Americas
- The United States of America becomes independent of the British and forms the world's first modern democracy.

Europe
- Advances in science and technology, like the invention of the Watt steam engine, give rise to the Industrial Revolution in Britain, which becomes a major power worldwide, with the defeat of France in the Americas.
- The Industrial Revolution spreads to other European countries.
- The French Revolution takes place, resulting in the first modern European democracy.
- Russia starts modernizing and increasing its territories, especially under Peter the Great and Catherine the Great.

Asia
- Colonization of India by the British and French.
- Japan remains closed to foreigners.
- European missions and trade with China begin.

Australia
- The British claim and colonize Australia.

Explore More

* FIND OUT about the warfare methods of the Marathas, especially against the Mughals. Some of these have become legends, such as the stories of Shivaji and Peshwa Baji Rao I.

* VISIT Indore and Maheshwar close by to see the many buildings built by Ahilyabai Holkar, including many temples.

A painting of a Mughal infantryman

* MAKE a scrapbook of sites in Maharashtra associated with the Marathas. Highlight their special features.

Shivneri Fort, the birthplace of Chhatrapati Shivaji

History in a Bowl of Paneer Makhani
The world in an Indian dish.

What we think is so typically Indian contains ingredients that have come to India from so many different countries, at various points in our history, through trade and invasions. A break-up of the ingredients of what we consider a classic Indian dish, paneer makhani, demonstrates how the current Indian culture is composed of so many influences.

Native to India:

• **Cardamom (*elaichi*):** A native Indian spice, it grew wild in Kerala.

• **Ginger (*adrak*):** This is native to India.

• **Black pepper (*kali mirch*):** A native Indian spice, black pepper was exported so long ago that it has been found stuffed up the nostrils of the mummy of Ramses II in Egypt, who died in 1213 BCE!

• **Bay leaf (*tejpatta*):** A native Indian spice, it was exported from India as *malabathrum* since olden times.

• **Garlic (*lehsun*):** This strongly flavoured condiment is native to India and the Mediterranean region. It was actually forbidden in Hinduism, Buddhism and Jainism.

• **Butter:** Butter and ghee were the major fats used by the Aryans. The Harappan civilization also had cattle.

From the Mediterranean, with traders and Greek invaders:

• **Coriander (*dhania*):** The oldest seeds have been found in Israel dating 7000 BCE. Coriander was used by ancient Egyptians and Greeks, and is mentioned in Panini's Sanskrit grammar from the fourth century BCE.

• **Cumin** (*zeera*): This spice is supposed to have originated in Egypt, and spread to the Mediterranean and India. Seeds have been found in Syria, dated 2000 BCE.

• **Fenugreek** (*methi*): This plant is native to the Middle East, and has, in fact, been found in Tutankhamen's tomb!

From Asia since antiquity:

• **Cinnamon** (*dalchini*): Dalchini (Cassia) originally came from China (*dal* – stem, Chini – Chinese!). Another variety is grown only in Sri Lanka.

• **Cloves** (*laung*): This fragrant spice came from Indonesia.

• **Nutmeg** and **mace** (*jaiphal and javitri*): Both spices came to India from Indonesia.

With the Portuguese from the Americas in the 16th century:

• **Green** and **red chillies** (*hari + lal mirch*): Chillies came from Mexico.

• **Tomato:** Tomatoes came from Mexico too.

• **Cashew nuts** (*kaju*): These nuts came from Brazil.

• **Peanut Oil:** Peanuts came from the Americas.

With the British

• **Cream:** Cream is something we learnt from the British (different from the Indian malai!).

Post-Independence:

• **Paneer:** *Panir* is the Iranian word for cheese, and it was not part of mainstream Indian cuisine until after Partition, when it was popularized by the Punjabi refugees. It was of course used for sweets in Bengal before that – they probably learnt *chhena* or *chhana* (cheese) making from the Portuguese.

5

Lifestyle in Mughal India

[1526–1857 CE]

'These Pathans (Mughals) built like giants and finished
their work like jewellers.'
– Bishop Heber, Bishop of Calcutta (1823–26) and man
of letters

5
Tales of Opulence and Decadence

The Mughals took the art of luxury to never-before levels and the aura of the Mughal emperor became semi-divine. From buildings to clothes to paintings to jewellery, everything Mughal was exquisite and extravagant in design, material and craftsmanship. European traders carried back fantastic tales of the 'Great Moguls', with their thousands of attendants, gold vessels, gem-studded shoes and perfumed baths. However, Mughal luxury came at a great human cost through ever higher taxation of poor peasants.

Social Organization
Only a few thousand Chagatai Turks came over with Babur, and had to quickly integrate into Indian culture. A steady stream of Muslims migrated from Central Asia and Persia, but the elite remained small and a combined Hindu–Muslim ruling class developed gradually.

Muslim society was also divided by rank, class and race, but the divisions were less strict than among Hindus.

The Persian immigrant Iranis ranked highest at the court, often sneering at other courtiers' looks and Persian accents. Next came the Turanis, Central Asian migrants, followed by the warlike Afghans. The native Hindustani Muslims were looked down upon by all immigrants. Hindus gained prominence as the Rajputs became the pillars of the Mughal army and the Marathas important in the Deccan. Still, the interaction between the Muslim elite and the masses was coloured by discrimination. Travellers noted that the nobility lived well due to their 'money, servants and whips'. Government servants were usually Muslims, and traders mostly Hindu.

RURAL SOCIETY

The rural upper class was made up of zamindars (Persian for 'landholder'), often chieftains with military forces, who gave the Mughal treasury a fixed sum after collecting taxes. Zamindari rights were hereditary, but could be bought and sold. Smaller zamindars were just a notch above farmers, while wealthier ones lived like minor nobles. The *Ain-i-Akbari* mentions their combined forces were about 400,000 *sawar*s and 4,300,000 foot soldiers.

The rural middle class was 10 per cent of the population and included *riyayati*s (privileged farmers who owned their land), brahmins, Rajputs and merchants. They paid reasonable taxes of around 25 per cent.

The *raiyati*s ('general public') often worked as tenant farmers and paid taxes as high as 50 per cent. Around a third were landless labourers, working for pitiful daily wages or food. Over time, the zamindars increasingly exploited the poor, who became indebted to moneylenders at cripplingly high interest rates.

THE MIDDLE CLASS

Cities had a thriving middle class of traders, shopkeepers, intellectuals and professionals including doctors, musicians, calligraphers, artists and writers. Those with court connections became wealthy.

The *kayasthas*, a community of imperial scribes, were known for their intellect and polish. They adopted courtly manners and had fewer food taboos than other Hindus.

The head of traders in each city was called the '*nagar seth*'. Gujarati merchants included Hindus, Jains and Muslim Bohras. Rajasthani merchants, called Marwaris, began migrating to Maharashtra and Bengal in the 18th century. Central Asian trade was controlled by Multanis, Afghans and Khatris. Chettiars on the Coromandel Coast, and Muslim merchants in Kerala dominated in the south.

Some merchants were very rich (merchants in Surat often owned up to 50 ships!), but the nobility could usurp their wealth through forced loans, and so most lived simply, hiding their wealth! Merchant groups employed 'lobbyists', nobles who spoke for them at the court.

THE CONDITION OF WOMEN

Both Hindu and Muslim societies were very patriarchal. A daughter's birth was received by silence. Akbar was rare in lavishly celebrating the births of his granddaughters. He also tried (unsuccessfully) to ban underage marriage and sati.

Mughal noblewomen observed purdah and lived in a heavily-guarded harem called the zenana, filled with official wives, semi-official concubines, female relatives and children. Eunuchs were in charge, and unrelated men who entered could be executed! The emperor rested and ate in the harem. This segregation spread to Hindu nobles, especially among Rajputs, where sati was also rampant.

Royal Mughal princesses often remained unmarried, and could be very powerful, like Jahanara, even issuing farmans (edicts). Some ladies were poets, like Salima Sultana, Jahanara, and Aurangzeb's daughter Zebunissa. Akbar started the yearly Meena Bazaar, in which royal and noble ladies sold luxuries, and the only male customer was the emperor!

Mughal princesses practising calligraphy (detail from a painting)

Common women worked alongside men, in construction, agriculture or domestic service, but got lower wages (so what's new?).

SLAVES

The Mughals did not put slaves in government and military positions, and slavery declined. People became slaves as prisoners of war or were sold by parents during famines. Akbar reduced this practice. The French and British dabbled in the slave trade, but the Dutch were very active in south India, where locals stopped going to markets because they were 'stolen upon the highways'! When the British abolished slavery in 1833, they carved out a special exclusion for Indian slaves! Portuguese and Arakanese slave traders terrorized Bengal and Odisha with their raids.

Trade and Economy

Agriculture remained the main source of Mughal income, and the tiny, ultra-privileged nobility controlled most of it. Just as an example, under Shah Jahan, 62 per cent of the revenue went to just 655 people!

As many as 155 cities thrived across the Mughal Empire and a huge 15 per cent of people lived in them. Some, like Delhi, Agra or Poona were political capitals. Patna, Ahmedabad and Surat became manufacturing and trading hubs. In the 17th century, the largest city was Agra, with a population of 500,000. In later decades, Lahore overtook it.

A unified rule helped law, order and trading, but wages stayed low. Corruption at the court kept worsening and English traders said that 'officers will do nothing without bribes, which is enforced as a duty'.

Manufacturing

Indian manufacturing was highly developed and, unlike Europe, not confined to large cities. Entire villages and tribes specialized in different crafts and the whole family worked, including children.

Textiles of dazzling variety dominated. People wanted shawls from Kashmir and Lahore, carpets woven in Agra and Fatehpur Sikri, and fine cotton cloth from Patan, Burhanpur and Dhaka. Woodwork, leather and metalwork were other major crafts.

Mughal royalty and nobility provided a lot of employment (though not well paid). Akbar employed thousands of tailors for the royal household! Royal *karkhana*s (workshops) produced the finest goods for royal use. Some regional master craftsmen set up private *karkhanas* – in Kashmir, shawl makers had up to 300 looms. There was resistance to labour-saving devices. When the Dutch introduced a technique in the Coromandel Coast to greatly increase the production of iron nails, the local authorities, worried about unemployment, banned it.

Even today in India, special crafts are made in *karkhana*-style workshops, artisans are paid per piece and technology is often resisted as it may cause unemployment!

Beauty and richness were the hallmarks of every little item in Mughal times

BANKING

Manufacturing and trading was helped by the *hundi* system of money transfer, based on a letter of promise. *Saraf*s or money changers in the *hundi* business grew so rich and powerful that even Mughal nobility had to negotiate with them. The incredibly powerful Jagat Seth family in the mid-18th century reportedly transferred 10 million *rupiya*s, Bengal's annual revenue, by a single *hundi* from Bengal to Delhi every year!

INTERNATIONAL TRADE

European traders – Portuguese, Dutch, English, French – were allowed to set up trading bases across India. The main ports were Surat in the west and Satgaon (Saptagram) in the east.

Slowly, the Europeans used their naval might to establish monopolies, and Indian rulers largely failed to counter them. The Portuguese controlled the Indian Ocean, and forced all ships to buy passes (*cartaz*) to cross!

Trade also thrived with Safavid Persia, Ottoman Turkey and Ming China, with Indian merchants settling in many countries – Gujaratis in Yemen, Jeddah and Africa, Odisha *klings* (from Kalinga) in South-East Asia and 10,000 Indian merchants in Persia!

India mainly exported textiles, sugar, cotton, pepper, indigo and, a new addition, tobacco. Indians, of course, imported horses and more horses! Luxuries like ivory, rose water, fruit, wine, almonds, Chinese porcelain and Venetian glass were favourites. Europe's thirst for Indian textiles became a cash cow for the later Mughals.

Science, Technology and Infrastructure

Emperors and nobles spent lavishly on great buildings, but not much on canals, bridges or irrigation systems. Cities were small urbanized pockets among forests. Akbar and Jahangir repaired and maintained royal highways, but, generally, roads were unpaved. Sher Shah Suri was the first medieval ruler to build four great roads, with 1,700 serais (inns) staffed by the government along the way, and trees for shade and rest. The poor walked everywhere, resting under large banyan trees at night.

Larger cities like Delhi and Agra had 'bridges of boats' or ferries to cross waterbodies. Very poor people crossed rivers using floating devices like dead sheep, whose carcasses had been greased and inflated into gruesome-looking balloons!

Goods were transported by pack animals from villages to *mandi*s (markets) in towns by nomadic tribes like *banjara*s with oxen, and even camels, in caravans of up to 10,000 oxen. Some *banjara* tribes stuck wheat grains in different patterns on their faces to advertise their trade! Goods were also carried on boats across the Yamuna and Ganga rivers. Travel insurance was as low as 1 per cent from Surat to Masulipatnam in Andhra Pradesh.

TECHNOLOGY AND SCIENCE

European science advanced greatly in the 16th and 17th centuries, laying the basis for the scientific revolution. However, by mid-18th century, India had stagnated badly. Europe and China were far ahead in wind and water technology, metallurgy, printing and nautical instruments. Military items like European guns, cannons and ships were copied, but new metallurgy techniques were overlooked. Glass manufacturing and printing were ignored.

There was enough time for India to adopt any Western technology before the Europeans became a serious threat, but they did not. Why? Was it due to so much cheap skilled labour? An arrogance and preference for fine, handmade quality over mechanical efficiency? Was science unable to break the shackles of religion? The debates continue.

A notable exception was Raja Sawai Jai Singh of Jaipur, whom Aurangzeb claimed was (*sawa*) 1.25 times more intelligent than others! He keenly followed advances in astronomy, sent scholars to Europe and Central Asia, employed Portuguese men, translated European astronomical texts, and imported instruments. He built five outstanding astronomical observatories, at Delhi (Jantar Mantar), Mathura, Benares, Ujjain and Jaipur.

Culture

Mughal emperors were patrons of all art forms. Jahangir and Shah Jahan created some of the most beautiful objects in history. Sadly, most of these treasures were carried away by Nadir Shah of Iran a century later, and destroyed in tribal looting. Luckily, Nadir Shah sent gifts from his Delhi loot to his neighbours, and some pieces survive in the Topkapi Palace in Istanbul and St Petersburg, Russia.

ART, SCULPTURE AND ARCHITECTURE

The Mughals left a glorious architectural legacy of fine Indo-Islamic fusion. Their buildings have a sense of airiness and symmetry, coupling grace with exquisite finishing. Running water is a distinctive Mughal feature.

Akbar built Humayun's tomb in Samarkand's Timurid style, but replaced Central Asian brick and tiles with sumptuous Indian stone. Akbar intermingled Islamic and Indian styles and his Agra Fort used local red stone, Rajasthani features like carved brackets and balconies, and animal motifs. Its Jahangiri Mahal has intricately carved stone pillars. His new capital of Fatehpur Sikri used red sandstone and each building was a unique experiment.

Nur Jahan was the first to use marble with pietra dura (inlaid gemstones) for her father's tomb. Displaying many features that later showed up in the Taj Mahal, Itmad-ud-Daulah's tomb is known as the Baby Taj!

However, Shah Jahan is the undisputed giant of Mughal architecture. Built by the heartbroken emperor as an eternal memorial to his beloved wife, the celebrated Taj Mahal, with its octagonal building, bulbous dome and tapering minarets, forms a visual treat. The designers had a deep understanding of perspective! The minarets are slightly inclined to fall outward in case of an earthquake and the foundation's centre is minutely higher than its sides, to avoid it looking like it is tumbling down!

The inlay work in marble at the Taj Mahal is peerless

Gorgeous white Makrana marble from Rajasthan was chosen – glowing softly at dawn, dazzling under the bright sun and luminous in moonlight. The massive blocks (up to 6 tonnes each!) were transported across 300 km by oxen or elephants, and pulleys used to lift the stone. The Taj is, in fact, built with millions of bricks, overlaid with marble. Many gems were imported for this multinational project – jade from China, lapis lazuli from Afghanistan, turquoise from Tibet and amber from Burma, as were stonecutters from Baluchistan, calligraphers from Syria and Persia, and inlayers from south India.

In 1655, the Taj was completed after 22 years, employing 20,000 workmen, and was instantly recognized as a masterpiece. French traveller Bernier says: 'The Tage Mehale deserves to be numbered among the wonders of the world much more than the pyramids of Egypt, those unshapen masses…'

Shah Jahan's other ambitious building project was his new capital Shahjahanabad, with stately avenues and pleasing gardens, built by 1648, in just nine years. It is most known for the magnificent palace fortress – the Red Fort – and the Jama Masjid, then India's largest mosque.

The Mughals loved gardens and built them all over the empire, including the famous Shalimar Gardens in Kashmir and Pinjore in Himachal Pradesh. The concrete jungles of Shalimar Bagh and Tees Hazari used to be real jungles with 30,000 trees! Mughal architectural styles influenced many future buildings, like the Golden Temple.

CITIES

Foreign travellers were in awe of Mughal cities. Agra and Lahore in the 17th century were grander than London.

An ideal Mughal noble's house had 'courtyards, gardens, trees, basins, small jets of water in the hall, and handsome subterraneous apartments furnished with large fans'. In stark contrast, the common people lived in cramped clay-and-thatch, limestone-washed huts. Each community had its own mohalla (neighbourhood). There was little city planning and frequent fires burnt down thousands of houses and shops.

In later times, the road to Delhi was dotted with ruins of tombs, the haunt of dacoits. A traveller mentions a Parsee bandit living in the basement of a Lodi Garden tomb!

PAINTING

Mughal miniatures were intricate paintings mostly used to illustrate manuscripts. They were initially heavily influenced by the Persian court. Calligraphy was prized and *nastalik* a favourite script. Akbar set up a royal workshop for artists of all kinds, including one Dashwant, a palanquin-bearer's son, found sketching on walls! Basawan and Manohar were other famous artists at his court. He commissioned an illustrated manuscript of the *Hamzanama*. A hundred painters from Gwalior, Gujarat, Malwa and elsewhere took 15 years for the book's 1,400 paintings! A focus on realism and portraiture developed, influencing later styles. Local Indian influences crept in, especially in the boldness of the colours used. Of the 17 most prestigious artists mentioned during Akbar's reign, thirteen were Hindus.

Jahangir, who boasted he could recognize the work of individual painters, dismissed many he thought unfit for the royal workshop, and gave favoured ones pompous titles like 'Nadir-az-Zaman' ('Wonder of the Epoch').

Artists replicated European paintings and picked up techniques like perspective and foreshortening, but European-style large canvases did not catch on. Under Shah Jahan, portraits became very formal, showing the emperor as an idealized, divine being. Aurangzeb thought painting un-Islamic. As royal patronage dried up, local styles like Rajasthani and Kangra came up, with Hindu religious themes. Today, the finest Mughal miniature paintings are lost to India – destroyed or in museums abroad. Beautifully painted frescos on walls still survive in Mughal buildings such as in Fatehpur Sikri.

Music

Mughal-era music saw true harmonization between Hindu and Muslim cultures as Persian and Indian styles, tunes and instruments were combined.

Akbar was very fond of music and played the *naqqara* (large kettledrums). In his reign, Muslim and Hindu singers worked together to compose beautiful ragas, many in praise of Hindu gods.

Surprisingly, young Aurangzeb was a very good veena player (before he banned music!). Muhammad Shah 'Rangeela' composed many *bandish*es, and his musicians Sadarang and Adarang shaped the khayal form of Hindustani classical music. Bahadur Shah Zafar composed many ghazals and thumris. A visiting European

Rembrandt and Mughal Miniatures

The famous 17th-century Dutch artist Rembrandt evokes great European masterpieces, biblical themes and realistic portraits. He was well-known for his curiosity about foreign peoples and places, and collected, copied and interpreted foreign art.

It is little known that Rembrandt once chanced upon a set of Mughal miniatures, known in Holland as 'Suratse teeckeningen' or 'drawings from Surat'! After studying these miniatures over a long time, Rembrandt sketched about 25 'Indian drawings', using oriental Japanese paper. These uncoloured, brown and black sketches are remarkable because Rembrandt interacted with a style so different from his own. Keeping some aspects of his style, Rembrandt added life and animation to the precise and formal Mughal art style by giving the figures a sense of action and movement.

He kept the essential form and figure of the Mughal dress, but discarded the details of fabrics that were a hallmark of Mughal art. He kept the formal three-quarter profile style, but did away with the colourful backgrounds, instead adding shadows (never used in the Mughal, or any Indian, style of art).

comments on the royal band, which kept playing through the day '... twelve trumpets and as many cymbals which play together... a roaring sound issues...'

Cultural Contributions of the Deccan states

The Deccan Sultanates were cultural enthusiasts, and intermingled Hindu and Muslim culture. Ali Adil Shah of Bijapur patronized Sanskrit and Marathi. His successor Ibrahim Adil Shah built Nauraspur, a new capital where musicians were invited to settle, and also patronized Hindu temples like Pandharpur. Bijapur's Gol Gumbaz, built after the Taj, has the largest single dome in India.

The Qutb Shahis of Golconda appointed Hindus to high posts, and as peshwa. They loved literature and built beautiful buildings, like the Charminar in Hyderabad.

Dakkhani Urdu was adopted as a literary language and Deccani paintings combined Persian and local forms.

Literature and Language

The early Mughals spoke Turki. Persian became the court language during Akbar's time. Sanskrit works flourished at traditional hubs like Benares. Regional languages grew, and beautiful bhakti poetry was composed in Bengali, Odia, Gujarati and Marathi. In later times, Urdu emerged in the fading grandeur of the Delhi court.

PERSIAN: A curious Akbar had many Indian books translated into Persian, including the Ramayana. Many histories were penned, like Akbar's biographies – the flattering *Akbarnama* and *Ain-i-Akbari*, and the far more critical *Muntkhab-ul-Tawarikh* and *Tabaqat-i-Akbari*.

Jahangir's memoirs, the *Tuzuk-i-Jahangiri*, is known for its easy style. During Shah Jahan's reign, historical works like the *Padshahnama* by Abdul Hamid Lahori and the *Shahjahannama* by Inayat Khan were composed.

Persian poetry became the rage and thousands of poets visited from Central Asia and Persia. Poets were gifted vast riches and even *mansab*s! Akbar's favourite, Faizi, was one of the three great Persian poets of his century, along with Ghizali and Naziri. Shah Jahan and Mumtaz Mahal occasionally conversed in verse! Aurangzeb disapproved of poetry, abolished the position of court poet laureate, and stopped most stipends.

HINDI: Hindi was not yet standardized and popular regional dialects included Awadhi, Braj Bhasha and Khari Boli. Akbar set up a court position of a Hindi poet laureate, or

Kavi Rai – Birbal was the first. Abdur Rahim was a great poet in Braj. Jahangir had a great command over Hindi. Hindu kings, especially Rajputs, patronized bards who composed poems of bravery (usually about them).

The great poet Goswami Tulsidas (16th century) composed the *Ramcharitmanas* and *Hanuman Chalisa* in

Awadhi, and helped popularize the Ramlila, a folk-form of Ramayana performed across north India. Meera Bai (1498–1546), daughter-in-law of Rana Sanga of Chittor, adored Lord Krishna as her husband, mortifying her family. After her husband's death, she, unusually, did not commit sati. Her over 1,000 poems and bhajans are still sung.

Meera Bai

URDU: When Muhammad bin Tughlaq shifted his capital south, a language called Dakkhani Urdu developed. In the 18th century, the Sufi poet Wali Muhammad Wali from Aurangabad impressed the Delhi court with his Dakkhani Urdu compositions. Delhi became the seat of literature in Urdu (from Zabaan-e-Urdu, 'Tongue of the Camp'), also called 'Hindustani' and 'Rekhta'. Urdu poetry developed forms like ghazals (rhyming couplets), *qasida*s (odes to benefactors), and *masnavi*s (long poems). Poets adopted *takhallus*, special pen-names. Muhammad Shah 'Rangeela' declared Urdu a court language. The three 'pillars of Urdu poetry' were Mir, Sauda and Dard.

Mir Taqi Mir (1723–1810) was known for his *Dil aur Dilli ke Marsiye* ('Laments for the Heart and for Delhi').

Mirza Sauda (1713–81) was a nobleman famous for his *qasida*s and sharp satirical eye about crumbling Delhi society. Khwaja Mir Dard (1721–85) was a celebrated Sufi mystic, who composed soulful, religious verses.

Many Urdu poets left troubled Delhi for Hyderabad, Patna and Lucknow. Awadhi Lucknow, a new cultural centre, saw Urdu poems that reflected frivolous court life.

The very famous Ghalib (1797–1869) lived at the tail-end of the Mughal Empire. A liberal mystic, he often criticized religious conservatism in his melancholic poems.

MARATHI: Marathi poems peaked with bhakti poet-saints Eknath (1533–99) and Tukaram (1608–49). Worshippers of Vitthala (a Vishnu form), they wrote devotional songs called *abhanga*s, still sung today. They spoke against untouchability, and conflicted with orthodox brahmins.

Slice of Life

About society, French physician and traveller Bernier comments sharply: 'In Delhi there is no middle state. A man must either be of the highest rank, or live miserably.'

Courtiers never sat in front of the emperor and greeted him with *kornish* (bowing) and *sijda* (kneeling and touching the forehead to the ground) in lavish durbars that could last over two hours. Fake flattery was the rule. A Persian proverb advised, 'If the monarch says that day is night, reply: The moon and stars shine bright.'

Shah Jahan was a master at extravagance — at 10 million rupiyas, his gem-studded Peacock Throne cost twice as much as the Taj Mahal, making it the most expensive object in history.

FUN FACT!

Mughal Camps

Mughal emperors spent a great deal of time shuttling between Agra, Delhi and Lahore, besides cooling down in Kashmir and travelling for war! The entire court and government machinery moved in a massive camp with the emperor, including records, treasure, library and harem. With up to 200,000 people, the camp took days to cross a point. Everything an emperor needed was carried along... imagine one at a modern airport! Two sets of tents were carried, so that while one was being used, the other was sent ahead to the next stop. As a chronicler described it: 'The Royal Camp looks like a great city travelling from place to place.'

Bernier describes a royal march. It began amid incredible fanfare. The heavy artillery and boat went first, followed by baggage, laden on hundreds of pack animals. Then 200 camels, loaded with silver *rupiya*s; a hundred camels loaded with gold, fifty camels carrying water and so on. Water carriers sprinkled the sandy paths and servants walked ahead with masses of white sheets, to cover any unpleasant sights. Then came the nobles, horsemen and foot soldiers accompanying the emperor. This was followed by the band, drumming and trumpeting loudly to announce the emperor's arrival.

Nobles got huge salaries, up to 10 million *rupiya*s a year (five billion rupees today!). A reasonably high-ranking 5,000-*mansabdar* got 350,000 *rupiya*s a year.

Amirs spent money recklessly on jewellery and clothes, living in mansions with costly stables. They tried to outdo one another in patronizing artists, poets and holy men, and extravagant gifts. Many were in perpetual debt. A few prudent ones, including royal women, invested money wisely. Noble lifestyles were propped up on the taxes squeezed from the common people. Peasants lived in *jhopdi*s, single-room mud houses with thatched roofs. They used leaf *pattal*s (plates) and terracotta to cook and eat. All were particular about brushing and bathing daily. European travellers marvelled that many old people had all their teeth! According to accounts, people even then spent far more than they could afford on weddings and death rituals.

CLOTHES

Mughal men and women both wore trousers and a tunic topped with an elaborate coat or vest called *qaba*, tied at the chest. The Hindus tied it to the left, and Muslims and Europeans to the right. Muslims wore white and round turbans, while Hindus wore bright, angular, high ones in infinite ways across region and tribe. Hindu women wore saris and *angiya*, and in western India, ghaghra-cholis. They covered their heads with dupattas. Manucci notes: 'It is bad manners to speak with your shoes on and your head uncovered.'

Jahangir fancied himself as a fashion designer and invented new styles that only he could wear – one was the 'kurdi', now known as the ubiquitous kurta!

FUN FACT!

Holi in the Mughal World

Akbar started grand Holi celebrations at court. Jahangir played Holi with his beloved Nur Jahan and called it Eid-e-Gulabi. It was played with red powder (*gulaal*), rose petals (*gulab paashi*) and rose water (*aab paashi*) as *nagara* drums beat in the background. For a few days strict social rules were relaxed, and men and women could mingle. The last Mughal emperor, Bahadur Shah Zafar, composed poems about Holi that remain popular even today.

Royal clothes were of exquisite fabrics, including fine muslin cloth called *ab-i-rawan* (running water), *shabnam* (dew) and *daft hawa* (woven air).

The Mughals were very fond of perfumes and *ittar*s. Akbar even created the *khushbukhana*, a department of perfumery! It was noted that 'all persons in India… spend a great deal for essences, rose water and scented oils…' As for jewellery, Abul Fazl describes 37 types of ornaments worn by women. The emperor gifted favoured nobles robes called *khilat*. Out-of-favour ones were given a poisoned *khilat*, to kill off the wearer!

FOOD

Mughal food was sumptuous and elaborate. Even frugal Akbar spent five million *rupiya*s a year on household expenses! Mughal emperors drank water only from the Ganga river. Yamuna water was used for cooking, with some drops of Ganga water added for 'purity'.

For the rich, a daily ice boat came from the mountains. Others chilled water by spinning flasks in water and saltpetre. Men started gathering in *qahwakhana*s across

Delhi to drink newly popular coffee, smoke hookah, and discuss poetry and life. Travellers say that the 'tender-hearted' Indian people did not sell young animals. Niccolao Manucci hilariously describes paan, '... everybody was spitting something red as blood.'

GAMES AND PASTIMES

Nobles loved hunting and kept pets like pigeons, parrots, falcons and dogs. Aurangzeb kept Uzbek hounds dressed in red velvet. Jahangir had 15 tame lions that went 'frisking between men's legs'!

Daily quail and partridge fights saw noblemen strutting around with their prized birds. Common people enjoyed goat, ram and cockfights, as well as *ishqbaazi*, where trained pigeons flew in formation, somersaulted and spun in the air. Large-scale *patangbazi* (kite-flying) matches were held on the Yamuna's banks. Wrestling and boxing were popular, and Akbar kept Persian and Turani boxers. He also forced noblemen to play polo, day and night!

In later times, a peculiar type of gallant called *banka* arose in Delhi society, known for his funny, loitering walk, expertise at sports and fighting, and idiosyncrasies, like keeping half a moustache!

Street entertainers became popular: jugglers, magicians, acrobats, jesters called *bhand*s, sword and fire swallowers, and *bahurupiya*s who changed their looks.

Chess was an obsession, both two- and four-people versions. Akbar played it with real people as chess pieces in Fatehpur Sikri! Fierce international matches were held. *Chaupad* remained popular and matches could last for months! *Ganjifa* playing cards were works of art.

A ganjifa card

Explore More

* VISIT Mughal architectural monuments such as the Taj Mahal, Humayun's Tomb and Red Fort.

* TRY Mughlai dishes such as biryani, Mughlai paratha, korma, kebabs and phirni.

* READ or listen to ghazals written by Mirza Ghalib, Mir Taqi Mir and Dagh Dehlavi. Make a list of clues you get about the social life of the time from them.

* VISIT the National Museum in New Delhi and look at Mughal exhibits such as the portrait of Mughal emperor Shah Jahan, painted circa 1660–70, the waistcoat armour of Aurangzeb, the inscribed battleaxe of Nadir Shah and the inscribed bow of Bahadur Shah II.

The Europeans Arrive

6

[1498–1803 CE]

'Consider the situation in which the victory at Plassey had placed me. A great Prince was dependent upon my pleasure; an opulent city lay at my mercy; its richest bankers bid against each other for my smiles; I walked through vaults which were thrown open to me alone, piled on either hand with gold and jewels! By God, Mr Chairman, at this moment I stand astonished at my own moderation.'
– Robert Clive, defending himself on corruption charges to the British Parliament

6

The Fortune Hunters

From the 15th century, European ships started sailing out to explore the globe, with a dramatic impact on world history. We still live in the 'Age of Europe' today – Europeans have settled North America, South America and Australia; much of the world speaks English or Spanish, and 30 per cent has become Christian. Europe profited wildly from its adventuring, and her countries are still some of the wealthiest in the world.

People often wonder – how could such small groups of people conquer far richer and more crowded nations like India and China? How could they utterly overwhelm the Americas and Australia?

Colonial Europeans patted their backs and came up with theories like the inbuilt racial superiority of the 'white man', or how people from cold climates simply worked harder... none of which explained most of history where Europe was not dominant!

So how did it happen? In the 1440s, Johannes Gutenberg invented a new sort of printing press that made faster and cheaper mass printing of books possible – which allowed the new knowledge bubbling up in the European Renaissance to be shared widely. Scientists like Galileo Galilei, Isaac Newton and Francis Bacon came up with new theories and the modern 'scientific method'. New academies of science led to huge technological developments.

So when they reached the Americas, Europeans had far more advanced items, like guns and steel, than native societies like the Mayas, Aztecs and Incas, which still mostly used stone weapons and tools. More tragically, the natives had almost no immunity to commonplace Old World diseases like influenza and the measles, which rapidly killed off millions of locals. Imagine, within 100 years after the Europeans reached the Americas in 1492, ninety per cent of the Native American population was wiped out, falling from about 55 million to five million!

But this still did not explain what happened in the East. Asian countries like India and China already had guns, steel and many, many more germs than Europe. They *were* part of the Old World! However, it was improvements in ship design, navigation, cartography, guns and cannons in the 18th century that gave the Europeans a clear edge there. Essentially, they could sail further, faster, longer, and fight harder!

Europeans could not immediately dominate India and China in the 17th and early 18th centuries, remaining at the fringes for hundreds of years as traders. As strong empires fragmented into regional kingdoms, they cunningly offered their cutting-edge military services to local rulers in return for large amounts of land and money.

Why did Indian and Chinese rulers not copy this European military technology? Rich Asian kingdoms had themselves become narrow-minded, and considered themselves far superior to European 'barbarians', sure that they had nothing to learn from them. This attitude would cost them dearly.

The Portuguese

In 1497, a young Portuguese called Vasco da Gama, left Lisbon with four ships and 170 men. He sailed around the tip of Africa and hired an Indian navigator to speedily guide him across the Indian Ocean using the monsoon winds. When the ship arrived in Calicut (now Kozhikode) in Kerala in May 1498, the Portuguese sailors met two Muslim Moors from Tunis, who exclaimed, 'The Devil take you! What brought you here?' The sailors replied, 'We came to seek Christians and spices'!

The Portuguese actually believed they had found an eastern land full of Christians! They visited a 'church' where worshippers chanted 'Maria' (probably Mariamma, the Hindu goddess of smallpox). Inside was an image of 'Our Lady' and 'other saints painted on the walls, with crowns, teeth protruding from the mouth and four or five arms'. The 'priest' gave them 'holy water' and ash, which they assumed was a deviant Eastern custom!

The Hindu Samudri or 'Zamorin', Manivikraman Raja, was excited to meet these new type of foreigners, but would soon regret it.

Vasco da Gama sold his pepper cargo for 60 times his expedition's cost. The Portuguese kept returning and dominated the Indian Ocean for the next 100 years, invariably winning all battles at sea. They built

FUN FACT!

One theory goes that the Bengalis learnt the art of cottage cheese making from the Portuguese, which led to the sandesh and rasgulla!

The Age of Discovery

During the 'Age of Discovery' in the 15th and 16th centuries, countless European ships sailed forth to explore the unknown world. It began in 1415 CE with a young Portuguese prince called Henry the Navigator, who dreamed of finding a direct sea route to India to buy spices, and bypass Muslim-ruled Middle-East and Turkey.

Prince Henry the Navigator

Henry got merchants to fund many official Portuguese sea voyages down the African coast, venturing further south with each trip – possible with more accurate charts and maps, and new ships like the caravel. The ships returned with extremely profitable slaves (one European horse fetched 100 slaves in Senegal, who were sold for 800 per cent profit back home). The Portuguese rounded the tip of Africa in 1488, naming it the Cape of Good Hope (in hopes of good trade with India!).

Italians also had a long history at sea. Many Genoese sailors became jobless after their rival Venetians struck exclusive trade deals with the Ottoman Turks and started leading expeditions for different countries. One such sailor, Christopher Columbus, tried long and hard to get Portuguese, Venetian or English funding to find a westward route to India. (Columbus was quite wrong – believing Japan was 4,000 rather than 20,000 km away!).

In 1492, Columbus finally convinced the Spanish king to fund three ships – they struck it lucky on their very first 'venture capital' project when Columbus discovered the Americas (still believing it was Asia!). The Spanish hastily got the Pope to divide all new lands – 'giving' Portugal Africa, Asia and Brazil, while Spain 'got' the rest of the Americas and Polynesia. The Spanish and the Portuguese dominated their respective seas even as other European countries began funding their own expeditions. In 1497, the British John Cabot (actually Giovanni Caboto of Venice) reached North America and in 1503, the French landed in Brazil. The Dutch reached the Indonesian Spice Islands (the Moluccas) in 1595. Slowly, the entire world was explored and mapped (and taken over!) by the Europeans.

their first fort in Cochin (present-day Kochi) in 1503, and set up naval bases all across the Indian Ocean – in Mozambique, Muscat, Bengal, Sri Lanka, the Malaccas, Macau and even Japan! They forced all passing ships to buy a Portuguese permit (*cartaz*). In the Battle of Diu in 1509, they got a huge boost when they beat the combined naval fleets of Egypt and Gujarat. The Portuguese also ran a profitable business selling Africans, Indians, Sri Lankans and Burmese into slavery.

Under Governor Afonso de Albuquerque, they won Goa from the Bijapur Sultanate in 1510, and the ports of Daman, Salsette, Bombay and Diu.

Portuguese savagery was a shock to Indians. When Vasco da Gama seized a ship carrying back Muslim pilgrims from Mecca, he looted it and burnt alive all 400 men, women and children aboard, despite being offered a large ransom. When the Zamorin sent a Hindu priest to negotiate, he was returned with his lips and ears chopped off and dog's ears sewn to his head.

An illustration showing Vasco da Gama landing at Calicut (Kozhikode)

NOBODY EXPECTS AN INDIAN INQUISITION

Few people know that there was an Indian edition of the medieval Christian Inquisitions! Launched in 1560 CE, the

Portugal in Our Dining Room

With their early colonization of Brazil, the Portuguese had a direct link to the New World, and introduced many fruits and vegetables considered 'typically' Indian today! The Portuguese also took the Indian *narangi* to Europe – in Portuguese called *naranja*, in Greek – *portokali*, and in English – *an orange*, which evolved from *a norange*.

Can you identify some?

1. This root quickly became a worldwide staple. The devastating Irish famine in the mid-19th century was caused by its crop failure.
2. This grain is typically eaten with *sarson ka saag* in Punjab.
3. This bean's name sounds like 'royal mother' in Hindi and is eaten with rice in Kashmir and Punjab.
4. A Spanish festival is celebrated by pelting this fruit, but most consider it a vegetable.
5. This nut's oil is used for cooking. A famous saying goes, 'If you pay _____, you get monkeys.'
6. The sap of this popular brown fruit is used to make chewing gum, and a famous brand is named after it.

7. This Brazilian nut is very popular in India and a Goan liquor is made from it.
8. This plant's scientific name means 'food of the gods'. Mixed with milk and sugar, this bitter bean is a favourite.
9. Allahabad is famous for this multi-seeded fruit. In Mumbai, it is named after a South American country.
10. The Carnatic music composer, Purandara Dasa praised this in the 16th century: 'I saw you green, then turning redder as you ripened... saviour of the poor, enhancer of good food, fiery when bitten.'

Answers: 1. Potato; 2. Maize; 3. Rajma; 4. Tomato; 5. Peanuts; 6. Chiku – the sap is chicle; 7. Cashew nut – the liquor is called *feni*; 8. Chocolate, Theobroma; 9. Guava, called Peru; 10. Red and green chillies

Goa Inquisition lasted a good 250 years, where more than 15,000 people were put on trial for 'anti-Church' activities. Wide prohibitions included banning Indian greetings and Hindu names after conversion, and suppression of the Konkani language. The Inquisition was also harsh on Syrian Christians and Sephardic Jews (who had historically fled to India to escape European persecution).

The Portuguese started losing out to the Dutch, and by the 18th century, were left only with Goa, Daman and Diu, which they clung on to stubbornly – until forcibly evicted by independent India's military in 1961.

Interestingly, one theory is that the Bengalis learnt the art of cottage cheese making from the Portuguese in Bandel, which led to the sandesh and rasgulla!

OTHER EUROPEAN POWERS

The Portuguese had a 100-year headstart, but other European powers gradually followed them east. In 1605, the Dutch East India Company started setting up bases in Tamil Nadu, Bengal, Gujarat and Ceylon (Sri Lanka) – to source Indian textiles in exchange for spices. (They earned far more through abducting and selling Indians as slaves to Jakarta, Malacca and Ceylon.) Dutch power gradually declined and they surrendered their last Indian bases to the British by 1825.

Even Denmark was in India! The Danes started setting up bases in 1620 in Tranquebar (Tamil Nadu), Serampur (Shrirampur, West Bengal), and the Nicobar Islands. They were forced to relinquish these to the British by 1845 CE.

The French reached India late, establishing their first factory in Surat only in 1668 CE.

Europe's ill-gotten silver from America poured into India at a great rate, to buy spices and textiles!

The British

THE BEGINNING (1600–1700 CE)

It was the small island nation of Britain that would come to utterly dominate vast and wealthy India for nearly 200 years. In fact, the British East India Company was called 'the Grandest Society of Merchants in the Universe'.

After Britain's spectacular victory in 1588 CE over the much more powerful Spanish Armada, emboldened English merchants got a monopoly from Queen Elizabeth on all trade east of Africa. The British East India Company was formed, and a massive 70,000 pounds raised from 218 'subscribers' (shareholders)... at a time when a skilled English carpenter earned seven pence a day!

The first expedition set sail in 1601 CE with four ships, and returned from Indonesia with substantial loot from Portuguese ships and enough black pepper to cause a glut on the market – English merchants complained of unsold pepper even seven years later! Over the next few years, English traders bought calico and muslin fabric from India to pay for Indonesian spices, which they sold back home for a handsome profit.

The Company took over the tiny nutmeg producing island of Pulo Run in Indonesia, which King James called 'as valuable to him as Scotland', but was soon driven out by the Dutch. To avoid paying scarce gold for the spices and Indian muslins, calico and chintzes that had also become wildly popular in England, they tried to sell English woollen broadcloth, but no one in Asia wanted to buy it... until eventually an Indian king bought some to cover his horses and elephants!

In 1608, Captain William Hawkins led the first British East India Company expedition to India. Jahangir took to him, impressed by his fluent Turki. He was given a high salary and made one of the emperor's 'drinking companions' – but not allowed to set up a trading post!

In 1613, the first British trading post, called a factory, was finally opened in Surat in Gujarat. King James sent over Sir Thomas Roe as his ambassador. The factory prospered and Jahangir wrote to King James I:

> Upon which assurance of your royal love I have given my command to all the kingdoms of my dominions to receive all the merchants of the English nation as the subjects of my friend; that in what place they choose to live, they may have free liberty without any restraint; and at what port they shall arrive, that neither Portugal nor any other shall dare to molest their quiet...
>
> For confirmation of our love and friendship, I desire your Majesty to command your merchants to bring in their ships of all sorts of rarities and rich goods fit for my palace; that our friendship may be interchanged and eternal...
>
> – Nuruddin Salim Jahangir

The Company happily set up 23 factories across India to buy fabrics, silk, indigo dye, saltpetre and sugar. However, for the first 50 years, most of the Company's trade and profits still came from pepper!

In 1639, the Company built its first fort at Madras (now Chennai), called Fort St George. In 1668, the British received Bombay as dowry when the Portuguese princess,

Catherine of Braganza, married Charles II. The British shifted there from Surat, which was being raided too often by Shivaji (whose men they called 'Seevages'!). King Charles II granted the Company powerful rights: to raise its own army, to rule territory in its own name and to mint its own money!

By 1688, the Company got cocky and blockaded Mughal ports on India's western coast. A furious Aurangzeb sent a fleet of Mughal ships to attack Bombay, confiscating all Company territory except Madras. Trade fell to a tiny fraction, the Company neared bankruptcy and desperately pleaded for Aurangzeb's pardon. Its envoys were made to lie in front of Aurangzeb to beg forgiveness and pay a large fine, before being allowed to re-establish themselves – Aurangzeb needed the large taxes the Company brought in!

THE QUIET YEARS (1700–40)

In 1717, the Company got an amazingly favourable trade agreement (farman) from the Mughal emperor Farrukhsiyar, partly by 'influencing' his advisers. The British wrote home, 'With a little patience and good bribery, our business may be now properly said to have received a good foundation; God grant a happy conclusion to the whole.' Happy for some, anyway!

The terms were frankly foolish and loss-making for the Mughals. For a small annual fee, the British East India Company could trade without paying any taxes in Bengal and Surat. The Company's Bengal trade (naturally) thrived.

THE RISE AND RISE OF BRITISH POWER (1740–65 CE)
BENGAL

The British soon became smug and started building illegal fortifications in Calcutta. When Siraj-ud-Daulah became the nawab of Bengal in 1756, he ordered the British to demolish these. When they refused, he seized Calcutta and imprisoned British captives in a small room overnight, where many died due to suffocation and heat in an infamous incident called the 'Black Hole of Calcutta'.

Robert Clive led British troops from Madras, reoccupied Calcutta and decided to 'change' the nawab. Clive went to war, having secretly hatched a conspiracy with the nawab's generals – Mir Jafar and Rai Durlabh, the ultra-rich banker Jagat Seth, and the British agent Aminchand.

A British troop of just 3,000 (with 1,000 Europeans) met Siraj-ud-Daulah's 50,000 soldiers at the Battle of Plassey (Palashi) in June 1757. What followed was more a farce than a battle. The 38,000 troops commanded by Mir Jafar and Rai Durlabh simply did not fight, and the few soldiers that did, were ordered to withdraw. In this 'epic' battle, just 500 of Siraj-ud-Daulah's men and 18 of Clive's died! One of the

most important battles in the world was just a pre-planned palace coup.

In India, the term 'Mir Jafar' is still used for a traitor, much like Benedict Arnold in the USA or Quisling in Europe.

A portrait of Robert Clive

Mir Jafar became nawab and executed Siraj-ud-Daulah. The Company was given the zamindari of the '24 Parganas' area of Bengal, that is, the right to collect taxes, while passing on a fixed amount to the nawab. Mir Jafar was unable to pay Clive the agreed sum of 234,000 pounds (a posh London mansion cost 10,000 pounds then!), and so made Clive the feudal ruler of '24 Parganas' instead. In a strange twist, the Company's employee became the Company's landlord!

Mir Jafar soon tried to get the Dutch to oust the British, but they were defeated in 1759 and the angry Company replaced Mir Jafar with his son-in-law Mir Qasim. When he too tried to get rid of them, the British crowned the deposed Mir Jafar again!

Mir Qasim now joined forces with the nawab of Awadh and the weak Mughal emperor, Shah Alam II, meeting the British at the Battle of Buxar near Patna in 1764.

Buxar was a true battle – but the 7,000 Company troops still defeated the 40,000-strong Indian alliance. Mir Qasim and the nawab of Awadh abandoned Shah Alam II to his fate and fled.

In a farcical scene, an armchair was perched atop a dining table in Clive's tent to make a 'throne'. Sitting upon it, the hapless Shah Alam II hastily conferred the Diwani of all of Bengal on the Company in return for 2.6 million *rupiya*s a year through the Treaty of Allahabad.

Astoundingly, the British East India Company now had the right to collect revenue from 30 million people across 400,000 sq. km, with an expected annual profit of two million pounds! The Company could pay for their imports from Bengal with the money collected from the people of Bengal. The Company's share prices (naturally) boomed. Canny Clive had bought

Chowringhee (in Calcutta) in 1798

lots of shares before announcing the treaty, and made a fortune! He was accused of 'enriching himself' in the British Parliament, and though eventually acquitted, shot himself in 1774.

To maximize the money they received, the Company auctioned tax collection rights of different areas of Bengal to the highest bidders, who forced money from the peasants through fair means and foul. Adventurers joined the Bengal Gold Rush to become 'nabobs'.

The Company started forcing far more tax from the same peasants – collections went from 800,000 pounds in 1764 to 2,700,000 pounds 30 years later. While earlier rulers had spent their money in Bengal itself, providing employment, the Company took it away to Britain, and it proved utterly disastrous for Bengal.

In 1769, a catastrophic famine struck after a poor monsoon. Usually, people would have bought grain from other areas, but now they had no money left and started dying of starvation. Other rulers would have reduced or excused taxes, but the Company decided to still collect every penny and even announced a further 10 per cent increase in taxes! Within four years, around ten million people, one-third of Bengal's population died. One-third of the land stopped being cultivated as entire villages were abandoned.

An official British report said: 'All through the stifling summer of 1770, the people went on dying. The husbandmen sold their cattle; sold their implements; devoured their seed-grain; sold their sons and daughters, till no buyer of children could be found; they ate the grass of the field; and the British Resident affirmed that the living were feeding on the dead.'

SOUTH INDIA

The French started setting up Indian bases in 1668, in Surat (Gujarat), Pondicherry (now Puducherry), Chandernagore (now Chandannagar in West Bengal) and Mahe (on the Kerala coast).

At this time, England and France often went to war. In 1744, when the two nations began fighting again, their armies began fighting in south India as well! In the First Carnatic War, the British captured French ships, and the French briefly captured the British city of Madras. In 1746, one small battle would have a mind-blowing impact on world history, as European military superiority became starkly clear for all to see.

Ten thousand of the nawab of Carnatic's (who was helping the British) horsemen faced just 400 French riflemen at the Battle of Adyar. The cavalry charged, confident about overrunning the French before they could fire a second time, as guns normally took three minutes to reload. However, using sequenced firing and better guns, the French fired 20 rounds a minute! The Indians suffered a great defeat.

The French commander Dupleix seized this new-found opportunity and started offering his military services to help Indian princes against their rivals (like mercenaries!). And so, with French aid, Chanda Sahib became the nawab of Arcot, and Muzaffar Jung became the Nizam of Hyderabad, giving the French a lot of land on India's east coast.

In less than a year, the French became the most powerful force in south India. The important British port of Madras was totally surrounded by hostiles and the British were about to write off south India.

However, Robert Clive besieged Arcot and won against overwhelming odds, which led to an aura of British military invincibility. The British and the French kept fighting across India (and the world). Eventually the French were forced to capitulate to the British in 1761. They lost most of their Indian land, and the French commander was recalled home and executed! This marked the end of French imperial ambition in India, though they held on to some scattered outposts like Pondicherry until after Indian independence.

MYSORE

The British faced their stiffest opposition from father and son Hyder Ali and Tipu Sultan of Mysore state, and were twice defeated by them.

Hyder Ali had been the chief minister of the Wodeyar king of Mysore (Karnataka), before styling himself as sultan. From humble beginnings, he was an illiterate child prodigy with a superb memory, who spoke Kannada, Telugu, Tamil, Hindi, Marathi and Persian fluently. He was good at ruling, diplomacy and battle – one of the few Indian rulers to get French guns and gunners, and train his troops in modern European military techniques.

His great expansion of Mysore's territories worried the British, who allied with the Marathas, Hyderabad and the Carnatic to attack Mysore in the First Anglo-Mysore War (1767–69).

Hyder Ali chased the British almost until Madras. The panicked East India Company signed a treaty in 1769 – the first time it was defeated in the 18th century by an Indian.

In 1778, the British and French went to war again. Hyder Ali allied with the French, and along with the Marathas and Hyderabad (who had changed sides!), attacked the British with an army of 80,000 soldiers in the Second Anglo-Mysore War (1780–84).

The first British governor general in India, Warren Hastings, remarked grimly that the British seemed to be fighting most world powers at the same time – France, Spain, Holland, the Americans, Hyderabad, the Marathas and Mysore! Backup ships were sent from Britain and France to India.

Hyder Ali died in 1782 of illness, but his son Tipu Sultan kept up the fight, and captured many British locations, getting the extremely favourable Treaty of Mangalore. This humiliation made the British determined to defeat Mysore and this would be the very last time any Indian ruler would sign a treaty on equal terms with the British.

Tiger Tipu

Born in 1750, Tipu Sultan was a remarkable ruler, a rare 18th-century Indian who recognized the importance of the outside world. He tried to create anti-British alliances with many foreign powers like the Ottomans, Afghanistan and France! He loved his image as the Tiger of Mysore, and used the symbol everywhere.

He sent a grand mission to Louis XVI at Versailles, France, in 1788 and got back skilled munition experts, gunsmiths, porcelain and glass makers, watchmakers, doctors, engineers and gardeners. Like Europeans,

Tipu Sultan put up a stiff resistance to the British

Tipu set up a network of state factories around the Arabian Sea. He produced guns, paper and knives and imported Persian silkworms – introducing silk manufacturing in India!

In 1789, the British started the Third Anglo-Mysore War, allying with the Nizam and the Marathas (who had switched sides yet again). After Tipu's capital Seringapatam (Srirangapatnam) was besieged, he was forced to sign the humiliating 'Treaty of Seringapatam' in 1792, where he had to surrender half his land, hand over two of his sons as hostages and pay a huge war indemnity of 33 million *rupiya*s.

Napoleon invaded Egypt in 1798, planning to send '15,000 men from Suez to India, to join the forces of Tipu Sahib and drive away the English.' He was defeated in the Battle of Nile by Horatio Nelson, but a few French troops from Mauritius came to help Tipu.

Under the new Governor General Lord Wellesley, the British started the Fourth Anglo-Mysore War (1798–99) along with Hyderabad and the Marathas. Tipu Sultan died on the battlefield while defending a breach in the walls of Seringapatam, which was brutally sacked. The British parcelled out some of Mysore to their allies, while keeping most of it.

Tipu Sultan, who used the tiger as his emblem, had this mechanical tiger built by French engineers

The British admired Tipu's bravery. When Napoleon surrendered in 1814, Scottish novelist and historian Sir Walter Scott wrote, '... I did think he [Napoleon] might have shown the same resolve and dogged spirit, which induced Tipu Sahib to die manfully upon the breach of his capital city, with his sabre clenched in his hand.'

MARATHAS

By 1771, the Maratha Confederacy had recovered from the disastrous Third Battle of Panipat and regained their power. Mahadji Scindia of Gwalior became the most powerful regional Maratha king, and 'the nominal slave, but the rigid master of the unfortunate Shah Alam, Emperor of Delhi'.

However, constant Maratha infighting gave the British a chance. In 1773, the young Peshwa Narayanrao's uncle murdered him, but Maratha ministers like Nana Phadnavis supported his infant son, Madhav Rao II, as the next peshwa. The uncle, Raghunathrao (Raghoba), was unwilling to surrender his ill-gotten peshwaship and appealed to the British, sparking the First Anglo-Maratha War (1775–82). The British eventually defeated the Marathas, but in the Treaty of Salbai, Madhav Rao II was recognized as peshwa after all, Raghoba was pensioned off and the British got some land (Salsette).

The British and the Marathas kept peace for the next 20 years as Nana Phadnavis became powerful – with an iron grip on the young Peshwa Madhav Rao and shrewdly holding together the fractious Maratha kings. The Europeans started calling him the Maratha Machiavelli! Mahadji Scindia died in 1794 when his heir was young, and soon after, the powerless young Peshwa Madhav Rao fell off (or jumped off, we don't know) a building.

Once Nana Phadnavis died in 1800, Maratha unity rapidly crumbled as the new Peshwa Baji Rao II began quarrelling with regional Maratha rulers. When toppled by Jaswant Rao Holkar of Malwa, he too went to the British for help. In return for being restored as peshwa, he signed a Subsidiary Alliance (which signed over a king's military and political power over to the British) on behalf of the Marathas! This gave the British great influence over the mightiest power in India.

Regional Maratha chiefs were aghast, and united to fight the British in the Second Anglo-Maratha War (1803–05). The war took place all across India, with 300,000

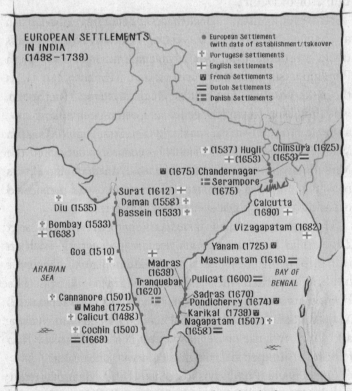

EUROPEAN SETTLEMENTS IN INDIA (1498–1739)

● European Settlement (with date of establishment/takeover)
✛ Portugese Settlements
+ English Settlements
▦ French Settlements
═ Dutch Settlements
⁝═ Danish Settlements

✛ (1537) Hugli
+ (1653)
Chinsura (1625)
(1653) ═
▦ (1675) Chandernagar
⁝═ Serampore (1675)
Surat (1612) +
Daman (1558) ✛
Bassein (1533) ✛
Calcutta (1690) +
Diu (1535)
✛ Bombay (1533)
+ (1638)
Vizagapatam (1682)
Yanam (1725) ▦
Goa (1510)
Madras (1639)
Masulipatam (1616) ═
ARABIAN SEA
Tranquebar (1620)
Pulicat (1600) +
BAY OF BENGAL
✛ Cannanore (1501)
▦ Mahe (1725)
✛ Calicut (1498)
Sadras (1670)
Pondicherry (1674) ▦
Karikal (1739) ▦
✛ Cochin (1500)
═ (1669)
Nagapatam (1507) ✛ (1658) ═

A look at how European settlements dotted India by 1739

A painting of the Battle of Assaye, fought between the British and the Marathas

Marathas facing off 55,000 British troops. The British won the Battle of Assaye (now a village in the Jalna district of Maharashtra) in 1803, led by the Governor General's younger brother, Arthur Wellesley. He ranked this as the greatest victory of his life – which is saying something, as he would become the Duke of Wellington and defeat Napoleon at the famous Battle of Waterloo! The British continued to beat the Marathas, including at the Battle of Patparganj in Delhi. The Mughal emperor passed from Scindia's protection to British protection. The Bhonsles and Scindias were forced to hand over large territories. Lord Wellesley was recalled by the Company for conquering too much territory for the British! Ironically, the new Governor General, Lord Hastings, came in 1813 with an even greater expansionist agenda!

The Marathas rose once last time to fight the Third Anglo-Maratha War (1817–18), where they lost most battles. The British abolished the peshwaship forever, and Baji Rao II was exiled to Kanpur, but Indore and Nagpur were allowed to keep small territories.

THE REST

During this time, the British were also conquering other parts of India, forcing one ruler after another to sign their infamous Subsidiary Alliances, (which signed over a king's military and political power over to the British), including many Rajput kingdoms. When the Commander-in-Chief of British India and Governor of the Bengal Presidency, General Cornwallis, forced the Nizam of Hyderabad to cede his coastal dominions in 1788, the British got a coastal corridor straight from Madras to Bengal.

For many years, the Company also acted like mercenaries in battles between regional powers, like the Rohillas and Awadh in 1774. The British and Awadh almost exterminated the Rohillas. Warren Hastings defended himself from harsh criticism in British Parliament by replying that it was to improve 'Company finances'!

The British method of gaining power was like a *Panchatantra* tale

'The Political Banditti assailing the Saviour of India' (1786), political cartoon on the Hastings trial

The Richest Pirate Loot in History

In 1695, the English pirate Captain Avery attacked Aurangzeb's heavily armed royal ship, the *Ganj-i-Sawai*, as it returned from Mecca. The pirates abused royal Mughal women and brutally tortured the men – one later testified on his deathbed that the 'inhuman treatment and merciless tortures inflicted on the poor Indians still affected his soul'. A few survivors were allowed to return to Surat on the empty ship. The pirates took around 600,000 pounds in gold, silver and gemstones, worth 250 million dollars today... probably the largest pirate loot ever taken!

An enraged Aurangzeb closed the East India Company's factories. Its officers were almost lynched by mobs of angry Indians. Every Englishman in Surat was rounded up and clapped in irons.

Near ruin, the Company penitently agreed to reimburse the entire treasure, and to capture the pirate. They placed a 1,000-pound prize on Avery's head, leading to the first worldwide manhunt on record! One Captain William Kidd, given a contract to hunt him, in a twist, himself became a famous pirate who attacked Mughal ships!

Avery vanished from the public eye and started living in disguise in the Bahamas. Speculation was rife in England that he was still in hiding there. The tale caught the imagination of writers like Daniel Defoe, who wrote a novel, *The King of Pirates: Being an Account of the Famous Enterprises of Captain Avery, the Mock King of Madagascar with His Rambles and Piraci*, based on it.

about a monkey who offers to impartially divide a roti that two cats are fighting over. While pretending to make the two pieces exactly equal, he keeps taking bites and finishes the whole thing off, while the cats are still squabbling!

Explore More

- Have a holiday in Goa. Visit Portuguese churches such as Se Cathedral, Church of Our Lady of the Immaculate Conception and the Bom Jesus Basilica. Enjoy Portuguese food like canja de galinha, chorizo, camarao tigre and fusion dishes like chamucas.

* Visit the French quarters in Puducherry to see the French influence in India. Visit Dansborg Fort and the Ziegenbalg House and Chapel in Tamil Nadu to see the Danish influence.

Consulate of France at Goubert Avenue, Puducherry

St Mary's Church, Chennai

* Watch The Birth of Empire: The East India Company, a BBC documentary on the establishment of the East India Company and its subsequent fall. https://www.youtube.com/watch?v=x+jbHm64cpY

* Visit St. Mary's Church in Chennai. It is the oldest Anglican Church in South Asia and the oldest extant British monument in India.

7

The Uprising of 1857 [1820–1858 CE]

'Every day a dozen... are hanged. Their corpses hung by twos
and threes all over town... For three months did eight
dead-carts go around from sunrise to sunset, to take down
corpses hung at the crossroads and market places, poisoning the
air, and throw their loathsome burdens into the Ganges.'
— Lieutenant Pearson on the punishment of rebels in
Allahabad, in a letter to his mother

7

Tales of Horror and Courage

The British were masters of strategy and excelled at playing off one Indian kingdom against another. With their superior guns, navy and military organization, they were valuable allies for any feuding king's army, and began to demand land in exchange.

By 1818, the British East India Company directly or indirectly controlled the vast majority of the Indian subcontinent. Few pockets of resistance remained, in Assam, Sindh and Punjab. This began the 'Pax Britannica' (British Peace), where Indian states stopped fighting each other under the 'protection' of the British. However, to most Indians, this was the 'Tax Britannica', because whenever the British acquired a territory, they increased the tax rates hugely!

Sher-e-Punjab Maharaja Ranjit Singh
The East India Company's march across India was temporarily halted by Maharaja Ranjit Singh, the Lion of Punjab, who formed the magnificent, if short-lived, Sikh Empire.

The Sikhs had been a growing force for a few centuries, having first armed themselves into the Khalsa under Guru Gobind Singh, the tenth guru, in the 17th century, against Aurangzeb. In the 18th century, twelve Sikh clans arose, called *misl*s (meaning 'similar'). They varied in size and strength, and often fought each other, but always united under a common banner when faced with an outside attack. These included the unrelenting invasions by the brutal Afghan Ahmad Shah Abdali. *Misl* leaders gathered in Amritsar twice a year for Sarbat Khalsas, to pass collective laws binding on all *misl*s and Sikhs.

Ranjit Singh was born in 1780 to the leader of the powerful Sukerchakia *misl*. As a child, he lost an eye due to smallpox. He became chief at a young age. At nineteen, he captured Lahore from the Bhangi *misl* in his first major conquest, and made this formerly great Mughal city his capital. He was soon crowned 'Maharaja', and had coins struck in the name of the Sikh gurus. Over the next few years, he defeated the other *misl*s and brought all of Punjab under his

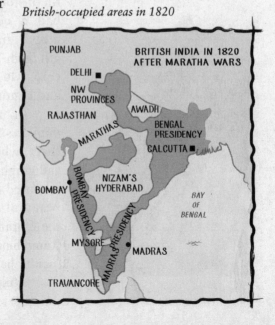

British-occupied areas in 1820

flag. In 1819, he annexed Kashmir, and later, Ladakh and even parts of Tibet.

A strategic thinker, Ranjit Singh recognized British military superiority, and in 1820, began to modernize his army. He hired European officers, many of them French and Italian generals who had fought for Napoleon until his recent defeat! He created the Fauj-i-khas ('special army') brigade, led by Generals Jean-Baptiste Ventura, Jean-Francois Allard, Auguste Court and Paolo Avitabile. Punjabi troops traditionally relied heavily on cavalry, but this model brigade focused on a well-trained artillery and infantry. Sikh engineers skilfully copied British cannons. The generals settled in Lahore and adapted to Indian culture, marrying Indians and employing court artists.

Ranjit Singh created the only independent kingdom in the history of Punjab. He had a culturally diverse army and court and, although Sikhs formed its core, Muslims, Christians and Hindus were included as commanders and ministers. A legend goes that when a Muslim calligrapher, who had laboured to make a beautiful illustration of the Quran, presented it to Ranjit Singh, the Maharaja paid a handsome sum for it, saying, 'God meant for me to look upon all

The British never dared to wrangle with Maharaja Ranjit Singh

The Legend of the Koh-i-noor

Until the 18th century discovery of Brazilian mines, diamonds came solely from India, and the fiery stones from Golconda were highly prized. The Koh-i-noor, the most famous diamond in the world, has never been sold, and has only changed hands as a spoil of war, through treachery, or in exchange of favours!

Legend has it that when the Persian Nadir Shah sacked Delhi, he heard that the Mughal Emperor had a priceless diamond hidden in his turban. When leaving, he suggested exchanging turbans and the hapless Muhammad Shah had to agree. When Nadir Shah saw the gem, he apparently exclaimed – 'Koh-i-noor!' – meaning 'mountain of light' in Persian. From Persia, the Koh-i-noor eventually found its way to the Afghan royal family, and when the deposed Shah Shuja (Ahmad Shah Abdali's descendant) sought refuge with the Sikhs, it was passed on to Ranjit Singh, who wore it mounted on an armlet.

It was ceded to the British when they defeated the Sikhs in 1849. The British resident's brother, John Lawrence, took it, but mislaid it! It was rediscovered by his valet and entrusted to Lord Dalhousie, who carried it in a belt sewn around his waist. Queen Victoria received it in 1850. Prince Albert had it recut to increase its brilliance, thereby reducing it in size by 40 per cent, from a whopping 186 carats to 105 carats! It is now set in the Crown Jewels of England, and on display at the Tower of London.

religions with one eye; that is why he took away the light from the other.'

In his long-running battle with the Afghans, Ranjit Singh pushed them out of Punjab and the North-West Frontier Provinces (NWFP, currently Khyber Pakhtunkhwa) occupying Attock in 1813 and Peshawar by 1834. At its peak, the Sikh empire consisted of Punjab (across India and Pakistan), Himachal Pradesh, Jammu and Kashmir, and the NWFP.

Interestingly, the covetous British never fought Ranjit Singh, whom they regarded as a military genius, even comparing him to Napoleon! In 1809, the British and Sikhs signed the Treaty of Amritsar, with the Sutlej river as their border. The English diplomat Francis D'Arcy Osborne describes Ranjit Singh sitting cross-legged on a golden throne, robed simply in white, with a belt of large pearls and the Koh-i-noor diamond displayed on his arm!

Ranjit Singh could see the writing on the wall, and when shown a map of India with the still-modest British

The 'Black Prince' of Perthshire

In 1849, the British defeated the last Sikh Maharaja, Ranjit Singh's youngest son, Duleep Singh. He became Christian following his British guardian's preaching and was exiled to England at fifteen, where Queen Victoria took a great shine to him! She showered affection on him and apparently exclaimed, 'Those eyes and those teeth are too beautiful'.

He lived like a British aristocrat, but was not allowed to marry an Englishwoman, eventually wedding the daughter of a German banker and an African slave. They lived in Elvedon Hall, and transformed the run-down estate into an efficient game preserve. Queen Victoria was godmother to many of his children.

As he grew older, he longed to meet his estranged mother, who  was struggling in Nepal. He was allowed to bring her to England in 1861. He started mourning the loss of his throne, reconverted to Sikhism and went to St Petersburg to (unsuccessfully) persuade the Tsar to invade India via Afghanistan!

He lived in exile and poverty on the European continent, dying early at the age of fifty-six. He was forgiven by the queen in his last days, and his remains brought back to England. His eight children died without heirs, ending this Sikh dynasty.

holdings coloured in red, remarked prophetically, '*Sab laal ho jayega*' (It will all turn red).

As soon as Ranjit Singh died of illness in 1839, the British started snapping at the heels of the Sikh Empire – helped by their infighting. The inevitable collision took place in late 1845. In the hard-fought First Sikh War, the British finally won by 1846 at the Battles of Aliwal and Sobraon. They demanded their usual war indemnity, reduction of the Sikh army and the placement of a British Resident, Henry Lawrence (who later founded the Lawrence School at Sanawar). The Jalandhar Doab and Kashmir were handed over. The British then sold Kashmir back to the Dogra ruler of Jammu for 750,000 pounds!

A mutiny in the Sikh troops in 1848 was used as an excuse to invade Punjab by the aggressive new Governor General Lord Dalhousie. In the Battle of Chillianwallah in 1849, the British lost 3,000 men, their worst defeat in India. However, they soon defeated the Sikhs at the Battle of Gujrat (in Pakistani Punjab now). They said of the Sikhs: 'No troops could have fought better, no army was worse led.' The 10-year-old Maharaja Duleep Singh was forced to sign over Punjab and become a British pensioner, exiled to London.

The First Afghan War

Now for Afghanistan and Russia. The Russian Empire was formed by Tsar Peter the Great in the late 17th century, who scientifically and culturally modernized his empire. By Catherine the Great's reign, Russia had become a major European power, encompassing modern Russia, Mongolia, Kazakhstan and many Central European countries.

After defeated rival European powers united and defeated Napoleon at the Battle of Waterloo in 1815,

Russia started conquering more and more land from the Persian and Ottoman Empires. By the late 19th century, Russian borders touched Afghanistan, having absorbed Kazakhstan, Tajikistan, Uzbekistan and Kyrgyzstan. It was now only a hop, skip and jump to India – only Afghanistan stood in the way.

In came Captain Alexander Burnes of the East India Company's army, who, in 1831, undertook an adventure-filled journey (in disguise!) from India, through Afghanistan and Uzbekistan, to Persia. He wrote a wildly successful book about it and became known as 'Bokhara Burnes'. Britain and Russia both became paranoid about each other, and Afghanistan became a playground of shadowy spy games – called 'The Great Game' or the 'Tournament of Shadows'.

Ahmad Shah Abdali's descendant Shah Shuja (not to be confused with Shah Jahan's second son) had been overthrown by Dost Muhammad in 1826, who in 1838, entered into a Perso-Russian alliance. The worried British decided to replace him with their puppet, Shah Shuja. They occupied Kabul in 1839, but Shah Shuja proved very unpopular, and Afghan mobs started killing important British officials (like Alexander Burnes). The British were forced to surrender Afghanistan to Dost Muhammad in exchange for safe exit from Kabul! In 1842, some 16,500 people started out – 4,500 troops (690 of them Europeans) and 12,000 camp followers. They were attacked by Afghan tribes all along, through a freezing winter. Only one survivor, Dr William Brydon, reached the British camp in Jalalabad.

The remaining British troops retreated to India from Kandahar and Jalalabad, but detoured hundreds of kilometres, to sack Kabul, Ghazni and other cities. They carried back the 'Gates of the Somnath temple' taken to Ghazni 800 years ago, which the new Governor General Lord Ellenborough (in office: 1842–1844) publicized as 'revenge by India' to restore British prestige (the gates proved to be fakes!).

The First Afghan War was a bitter lesson for the British. It cost them 20,000 lives and 15 million pounds. It also destroyed the myth of British military invincibility. Indians were amazed that the British could be so battered by tribal warriors and started thinking that they too could beat them.

Stirrings of Discontent

By the early 19th century, the British had alienated many sections of Indian society, from princes to landowners to peasants, and Hindus and Muslims alike.

THE DOCTRINE OF LAPSE AND SINDH

After the disastrous First Afghan War, the British deliberately began to overthrow native Indian princes to bring their lands under direct British rule – princes who had already signed treaties and were living by British terms. They spared not even their faithful allies, starting by capturing Sindh most unjustly in 1843. The commander, Major General Sir Charles Napier, confessed that 'we have no right to seize Scinde'. The famous *Punch* magazine printed a cartoon showing Napier saying 'Peccavi: I've Scinde' (Peccavi means 'I have sinned' in Latin).

LORD DALHOUSIE ARRIVES

The Scottish Earl, Lord Dalhousie (in office: 1848–1856), was made India's youngest-ever Governor General at

Dalhousie used the Doctrine of Lapse to snatch away kingdoms

thirty-six. An energetic, efficient administrator, he was firmly convinced that Western rule, laws and customs were superior in all ways to Eastern ones.

He began to modernize Company-ruled territories at breakneck speed, setting up railways, telegraph, post offices, irrigation canals and universities. Dalhousie believed that Britain's interest was best served by expanding directly ruled Company territories, and aggressively applied the 'Doctrine of Lapse' introduced by the Company back in 1834. This rule said that if Indian princes were either 'unfit to rule' or did not have 'biological sons', their kingdoms would 'lapse' back to the Paramount Power – the British. Adopted sons could not be heirs unless permitted by the Company. (One wonders why, despite many wives, so many kings did not have any natural-born heirs!)

Dalhousie often disallowed adopted heirs, and used loose definitions of 'incompetence', claiming that British rule was for the 'good of the governed', and native rule 'fraught with suffering'. In seven years, Dalhousie took over seven states, including Satara, ruled by Shivaji's descendants; Nagpur ruled by the Maratha Bhonsles; and Jhansi, a minor Maratha state, which the British needed for their new railway lines from Bombay to the United Provinces!

Dalhousie even used the Doctrine to discontinue pensions of deposed kings. He refused to acknowledge as heir the adopted son of Baji Rao II and discontinued

Delhi's Last Flame

After Delhi's Pax Britannica in 1803, it got a welcome respite from its regular looting and saw a brief renaissance, before its flame was drowned by the bloody 1857 Uprising. The population had shrunk dramatically to a few lakhs, but life within the walled city flourished. British bungalows dotted the Ridge, and European interaction sparked cultural mingling. The latest fabrics and accessories were sold in the shops of Chandni Chowk, and Delhi had the most fashionable

women, sophisticated people, and the best etiquette and language. Lucknow and Delhi competed for the best dancers and cooks.

Bahadur Shah Zafar, the last Mughal emperor, was a good poet, and had great Urdu poets like Mirza Ghalib, Zauq and Momin at his court. A verse by him:

Kitnaa hai badnaseeb 'Zafar' dafn key liye,
Do gaz zamin bhi na mili kuu-e-yaar mein.
(How unfortunate is Zafar in his burial,
He could not even get two yards of space in his beloved land.)
– Bahadur Shah Zafar, during his last days in exile in Burma

his large yearly pension of 80,000 pounds. The adopted son, Nana Sahib, and his general Tantia Tope would play important roles in the rebellion.

In February 1856, with one month left of his governership, Dalhousie applied the Doctrine of Lapse to Awadh, a loyal ally of the British for 100 years, claiming 'intolerable misgovernment'. This truly shook the good faith of the Indian princes in the British. Nawab Wajid Ali Shah of Awadh was a cultural enthusiast only interested in dance, music and theatre, and used to immediately agree to any and all British demands.

British troops marched in and the nawab was speedily pensioned off to Calcutta, where he settled in Matia Burz, creating a centre for culture. The famous thumri '*Babul Mora*' (probably composed by him) expresses a bride's anguish at leaving her father's home, and represents the nawab's parting from his homeland. As many as 40,000 disbanded Awadhi soldiers, fuming at their ruler's shoddy treatment, were absorbed into the East India Company's army.

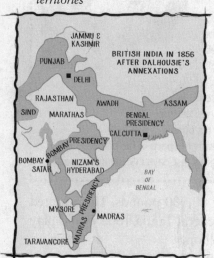

Dalhousie was able to annex large territories

Lord Dalhousie returned to England expecting a hero's welcome. He had reported, 'By the territorial acquisitions... the Revenue of India has increased from £26,000,000 in 1847 to £30,000,000 in 1854...' British leaders were initially full of praise, but after the Uprising, he was roundly accused of having incited it. His health suffered and he died young at the age of forty-eight. Ironically, he died without any natural heir, and the earldom passed on to a distant cousin (Doctrine of Lapse!).

Interfering with Local Religions

The British East India Company had historically disallowed Christian missionaries into India, claiming this created social unrest. Over time, as the power of the Company shifted to the British government, this policy changed. One of the British Parliament's conditions for the Company's 1813 Charter renewal was to actively promote missionary activity in India.

At that time, British people genuinely believed that Hinduism was a barbaric religion and many considered it British duty to enlighten Indian natives. Missionary societies for India came up in England. In reality, the missionaries made few converts – in 1851, there were probably fewer than 100,000 Protestant Christian converts (as per the Church of England). However, missionaries began setting up English-language Christian schools for Indian children on a large scale, actively funded and supported by the Company.

With the Governor Generalship of Evangelical sympathizer Lord William Bentinck (in office: 1828–35), many social laws were passed – outlawing sati for widows, and allowing Hindu widows to remarry and converted ex-Hindus to retain inheritance rights. The British also tried to remove ancient social constraints like foreign travel. Railway carriages were not segregated, and Indian sepoys were sent to Burma (Myanmar).

As modern Indians, we may recognize that some of these reforms were needed, but so many changes in such a short time proved one too many. People started believing in a grand conspiracy to force the entire country to convert to Christianity. Indeed, an American evangelist who visited after the Uprising said, '… these dreadful developments… contradict our pleasing anticipations that this great and idolatrous land should soon be transferred to the Christian faith…'

THE ROTI RUMOURS

In the tense atmosphere of early 1857, a new, disturbing movement came to British attention. A minor British magistrate in Mathura found four 'dirty little cakes of the coarsest flour' on his desk. He was told that a 'man had come out of the jungle, given them to the watchman with instructions to make four more and to take these to the watchman in the next village, who was to do the same'.

And so began the 'chupatty' movement. Thousands of Indian rotis, with no distinguishing marks or messages, were mysteriously passed from village to village across north India.

The British grew spooked that the chapattis could travel at a rapid rate of 100 to 200 miles per night, much faster than the swiftest British mails. With barely 100,000 British ruling over a population of 250 million, they knew they did not stand a chance if the natives turned on them. Indians believed unholy items had been mixed into the rotis, to corrupt both the Hindu and Muslim religions.

FUN FACT! The British were convinced that the Uprising was planned using chapattis to convey secret messages across north India!

Tension was simmering and the temperature was soaring as summer approached. Everyone was on edge.

THE LAST STRAW

Even a fleeting spark was bound to create a bonfire.

There was talk of a new rifle for the Company army's use. In the Enfield rifle, the soldier had to tear open the cartridge with his teeth (because his hands were full), to pour the gunpowder down the barrel before the bullet was rammed down. For smoothness, the cartridge was greased. When the rifle was first developed in Britain, the grease used was standard animal tallow (fat). In India, it took on a new meaning, as the fat was of the cow and the pig. For Hindus, the cow is sacred, and for Muslims, the pig unclean. So there was absolutely no question of Indian soldiers putting this foul cartridge in their mouths.

The British recognized the potentially explosive nature of this problem early on, and replaced the grease with vegetable fat, but conspiracy theories spread like wildfire in the army ranks, including rumours that this was intentional, so that the sepoys would be excommunicated and forced to convert to Christianity.

The Uprising

There were small-scale protests against Enfield rifles across north Indian army bases, including a one-man rebellion in Barrackpore by a brahmin sepoy, Mangal Pandey, who was hanged. Attitudes grew sullen and minor acts of arson began. Some sepoy units were dishonourably disbanded.

In this tense atmosphere, a British commander at the large garrison at Meerut decided to 'encourage' sepoys to get over their phobia by holding a military parade! The soldiers made a group pact to defy him, and 85 soldiers were court-martialled, stripped of their uniforms, put in chains and handed long prison sentences. The next day, on 10 May 1857, their angry colleagues killed their European officers and set off for Delhi.

In Delhi, the sepoys 'persuaded' the unenthusiastic 82-year-old Bahadur Shah Zafar, living quietly as a

A sketch showing Tantia Tope's soldiers marching on

British pensioner, to sign a proclamation that he was now the emperor of India! As more people joined in, the sepoy insurrection became a full-blown attempt to expel the British. Uprisings broke out across the United Provinces and Bihar. In many places, British men, women and children were slaughtered.

In Kanpur, the former peshwa, Nana Sahib, accepted British surrender and promised safe conduct to Allahabad. However, when the British began boarding the boats, the men were butchered at Satichaura Ghat (still known as Musker Ghat – from 'massacre') and the women and children were imprisoned. A few months later, they too were massacred in the infamous Bibighar. Only four men escaped. These killings horrified the British, and 'Remember Cawnpore' became a war cry.

In Lucknow, the rebels were led by Begum Hazrat Mahal, wife of the deposed nawab of Awadh. More than 20,000 rebels besieged the fortified British Residency, which held out for four months (with 1,800 British and 2,000 Indians) before being evacuated.

The British were initially slow to respond, stunned by the speed and ferocity of the uprising. They had believed Indians were 'used' to British rule. However, British troops began winning by July. Delhi was retaken after a two-month siege, followed by looting and massacre. A letter claims: 'all the people found within the walls of Delhi were bayoneted on the spot...' Bahadur Shah Zafar's sons and grandsons were shot, and their bodies hung at the Khooni Darwaza ('Bloody Gate'). Bahadur Shah was exiled to Rangoon, where he died soon after. Delhi's grand buildings and stately homes were looted and smashed – it is almost impossible to find a house in Delhi from before 1857. Jhansi was taken in April 1858. The Rani of Jhansi and Tantia Tope briefly captured Gwalior, but the British retook it in two weeks.

The British carried out horrific massacres. One officer recalled their frequent breaks, as their arms tired of the incessant killing. British volunteer hanging parties went out in search of natives, grotesquely hanging victims in figures of eight. For actual 'mutineers', the British inventively

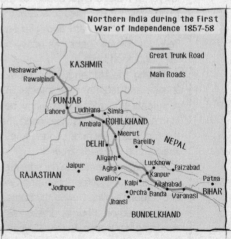

The cry for independence swept across northern India

Northern India during the First War of Independence 1857-58

Great Trunk Road
Main Roads

KASHMIR
Peshawar
Rawalpindi
PUNJAB
Lahore Ludhiana Simla
Ambala ROHILKHAND
Meerut
DELHI Bareilly NEPAL
Aligarh
Jaipur Agra Lucknow Faizabad
RAJASTHAN Gwalior Kanpur
Jodhpur Kalpi Allahabad Patna
Orcha Banda Varanasi BIHAR
Jhansi
BUNDELKHAND

'blew them from the guns'. Sepoys were escorted to the parade ground with an English band playing a lively tune, tied with their backs to the muzzle of small cannons, which

Rani of Jhansi

Rani Lakshmibai was a heroic face of the Uprising of 1857. Born in 1827 to a poor brahmin at the exiled court of Peshwa Baji Rao II, she hung about Nana Sahib and other students. Unlike most girls, she was raised as a scholar and warrior. She spoke Marathi, Hindi, Sanskrit and Persian, was fond of wrestling and sword fighting, and was a skilled horse rider.

She was married at 15 to the much older ruler of Jhansi, a small, infertile land in Bundelkhand, and led a confined, traditional life until her husband died, soon after adopting an infant son, Damodar Rao. The British refused to accept his claim and annexed Jhansi under the Doctrine of Lapse. Lakshmibai hired a successful English lawyer to make a legal appeal to the Court of Directors in London, to no avail. When urged to accept the British pension, she famously said 'Meri Jhansi nahi doongi' ('I will not surrender my Jhansi'). Tensions rose in Jhansi, as heavy-handed British treatment turned the population hostile.

During the Uprising, local sepoy mutineers killed the British in Jhansi, and left Rani Lakshmibai in charge. She created women's regiments and militarized many people in anticipation of war. In March 1858, the British besieged Jhansi. Despite a valiant defence, the fort was breached. Looting and massacre orders were given for Jhansi, and it was destroyed.

The Rani escaped with her son, meeting Tantia Tope at Kalpi, where they lost again, before capturing Gwalior. The British soon besieged and retook Gwalior. During the battle, a British officer shot her as she sat mounted on a horse, dressed as a cavalry officer, hair shorn off, exhorting her troops. Barely 30 years old, she died soon after.

were then fired. The British took a year to fully douse the pockets of resistance offered by uncaptured rebels.

Was the revolt of 1857 a Sepoy Mutiny or the First War of Indian Independence? And why did it fail?

Only about one-third of Indian soldiers mutinied, mostly from the Bengal division. Though people of all types joined in the fight, if the British had been defeated, India would have probably reverted to a group of squabbling kingdoms. The rebellion was confined to the northern and eastern Hindi-speaking plains of India. Madras, Bombay, Bengal and western Punjab were undisturbed. Many Indian rulers, like those of Nepal, Gwalior, Hyderabad and Bhopal, provided troops to the British. As Governor General Canning said, they 'acted as breakwaters to the storm which would have swept us in one great wave'. The 1857 Uprising failed due to a lack of central authority, unity and leadership on the Indian side, and their lack of modern weaponry.

The Aftermath

The Uprising was suppressed with great ferocity. North India lay dotted with countless burned villages, devastated fields and destroyed cities. More than 100,000 Indian

Retribution from the British came in the form of countless public hangings and execution by tying people to the mouth of a cannon and firing it

sepoys were killed. British labour records show that manpower dropped between 20 and 30 per cent!

With the Queen's proclamation in 1858, the Crown assumed control of India, formally ending East India Company rule. The Governor General now became the Viceroy. In reality, the British Government had already been in charge for a long time.

Steps were taken in British colonies across the world to avoid 'copycat rebellions.' Further annexation of princely states was stopped, and Indian princes persuaded that their interests lay with British rule. The British ceased interfering with religion. The army was reorganized, and

A Crocodile's Point of View

In 'The Undertakers', a story by Rudyard Kipling, a crocodile reminisces about the Mutiny as the good old days, when he feasted on dead bodies:

'... the river was low, smooth, and even, and, as the Gavial had warned me, the dead English came down. I got my girth in that season...

'One lay still in the slack-water and let twenty go by to pick one... The news was that the English were being hunted into the rivers, and by the Right and Left of Gunga!

'When I had reached Arrah and the back-waters behind it, there were no more dead English. The river was empty for a while. Then came one or two dead, in red coats, not English, but of one kind all – Hindus and Purbeeahs – then five and six abreast, and at last, from Arrah to the North beyond Agra, it was as though whole villages had walked into the water.... and every ripple brought more dead.'

Heroes of the Uprising

Begum Hazrat Mahal

• **Begum Hazrat Mahal:** Wife of the deposed nawab of Awadh, Begum Hazrat Mahal declared her young son, Birjis Qadar, the ruler of Lucknow, and fought alongside Nana Sahib and the Maulvi of Faizabad. She fled to Nepal and died in obscurity in 1879.

• **Nana Sahib Peshwa:** Kanpur's revolt was led by Peshwa Nana Sahib, the adopted son of Baji Rao II. He became infamous for two massacres during the Uprising, then vanished and was never heard of again.

• **Tantia Tope:** Nana Sahib's general was defeated when the British captured Cawnpore. He and Rani Lakshmibai briefly captured Gwalior. He escaped when the British retook Gwalior and kept up an active resistance for over a year, before he was betrayed in 1859 and executed.

Tantia Tope

• **Maulvi Ahmadullah Shah:** He travelled across north India, trying to exhort Indians into rebellion. Jailed for distributing incendiary pamphlets, he escaped during the Uprising and led troops with Begum Hazrat Mahal. He was murdered in 1858 for the prize money of 50,000 rupees on his head.

• **Veer Kunwar Singh:** He was the Rajput ruler of Jagdishpur in Bihar, and took up arms (again!) at the age of eighty! He won victories through guerrilla warfare. When struck by a bullet, he cut off his left hand near the elbow (!) and continued fighting. He died, without surrendering, after a year.

the Company's army disbanded and replaced by Royal British troops. The Bengal infantry regiments, the largest and strongest, were scaled down from 74 to 15. The ratio of British to Indian soldiers was increased to 1:3, from 1:9. Only British soldiers could now handle artillery.

The British developed a theory of the 'Martial Races', which claimed that some sorts of Indians were 'naturally' more suited to battle. They massively increased recruitment

FUN FACT! The ancient Indian 'wootz' steel technology, much prized throughout the world, was lost forever after the British banned local weapons manufacturing post—1857.

from 'martial' races, conveniently those groups who had stayed loyal, and almost stopped recruiting from 'non-martial races', meaning those who had revolted! This appalling policy, formally documented in British Army manuals, affected relations between Indians. Thus began the crafty policy of 'divide and rule' in the British Indian Army, later used in political arenas.

The year 1857 was a defining one for Britain. The British Empire was by now the largest and richest in the world, and the British widely believed that they were the 'chosen race', to rule and bring Western civilization to backward countries. The rebellion shocked the British into realizing that perhaps not all 'natives' wanted to be 'civilized'! The British public widely approved the viciousness of British revenge, against sepoys and ordinary Indians.

Charles Dickens said, 'I wish I were commander-in-chief in India... I should do my utmost to exterminate the Race.' When Governor General Canning asked moderation from his troops, the British press scorned him as 'Clemency Canning'.

A scene from 1857

What in the World Was Happening! (1820–58 CE)

Europe

- GREAT BRITAIN: The Industrial Revolution gathers force; the steam engine and railways are invented.

  Queen Victoria accedes to the throne in 1837, starting the 'Age of Imperialism'.

- FRANCE: Napoleon conquers most of Europe, but is defeated by Britain and its allies in 1815, at the Battle of Waterloo.

- Russia and Great Britain go to war in Crimea in 1854.

Americas

- UNITED STATES OF AMERICA: The newly independent United States expands and industrializes; pioneers settle the west coast, displacing Native Americans.

- SOUTH AMERICA: South American countries win freedom from Spain.

Asia

- CHINA: Opium Wars are fought in China involving disputes between Britain and China over British trade in China and Chinese sovereignty.

- INDONESIA: The British return to the Dutch, their empire in Indonesia in 1816.

- VIETNAM: The French occupy Vietnam.

Africa

- France occupies Algeria.

Australia

- Gold Rush in Australia.

Explore More

* WATCH the movie *Junoon* directed by Shyam Benegal. Starring Nafisa Ali and Naseeruddin Shah, it is based on Ruskin Bond's *A Flight of Pigeons* and revolves around the 1857 Uprising.

* READ 'Aankho Dekha Gadar' by Amritlal Nagar, containing an eyewitness account of the Uprising of 1857.

* WATCH THE FILM *Shatranj Ke Khiladi* directed by Satyajit Ray. Based on Munshi Premchand's short story of the same title, the movie is set around the annexation of Awadh in 1856.

* WATCH the TV series 'Mirza Ghalib' produced and written by Gulzar, with Naseeruddin Shah in the lead role.

* VISIT Jhansi Fort, which was once the residence of Rani Lakshmibai of Jhansi, who died fighting for independence in 1858.

Jhansi fort (c. 1882)

8

Reform and Renaissance

[1780–1913 CE]

'What Bengal thinks today, India thinks tomorrow, and the rest of the world the day after.'
— Gopal Krishna Gokhale, founding figure of the Indian independence struggle

8

A Nation Awakens

Through the 19th century, after the Enlightenment and Industrial Revolution, European society slowly started moving towards equality, democracy and women's rights. In British-ruled India, Western and Indian ideas mingled, and Indians began to critically examine their past, which led to the 19th-century Bengal Renaissance. New generations wanted reason and equality rather than blind belief in tradition. Many people started societies for education, and for religious and social reform.

Why Bengal? Bengal was the first area ruled by the British, and Calcutta was the seat of the British Empire in India. Calcutta, the City of Palaces, became a centre of buzzing business and intellectual activity, where people flocked from all over the world.

Indians also had to deal with changing attitudes in the smug Victorian era, when the British considered 'the Gentoo (Hindu) deficient in intellect and depraved in morals', and somehow find a sense of pride in their own heritage.

The Backdrop

From their memoirs, we realize what a culture shock many of the British got in India. From lush stone sculptures to tangle-locked, naked yogis, to sati and human sacrifice, they gaped disapprovingly at this 'heathen' culture.

The Hinduism of the day was bound up in a thousand restrictions, with rigid rules about ritual 'purity' and 'pollution'. Those who disobeyed were shunned and disinherited. Eating with non-caste Hindus was taboo as was travel abroad, especially by sea. Child marriage was common. Female infanticide was rampant due to large dowries. If widows somehow escaped sati, remarriage was unthinkable. Women were kept illiterate, as there was a genuine fear that an educated woman would cause her husband's death! Lower-caste people led terrible lives.

Any attempt at changing these practices inflamed passions, and earlier rulers had learned to leave them alone. Even Akbar had to agree when a brahmin teacher refused to enter his 'polluted' palace. Akbar heard his lessons from a balcony, while the pandit sat on a cot hung outside!

Among Bengali upper classes, as the Dayabhaga school of Hindu law allowed widows to inherit wealth, sati was often forced upon young childless widows to keep property within the family.

The Orientalists

Once they gained Bengal, the East India Company transformed from 'petty traders quarrelling over their seats in church into imperialist swashbucklers and large-scale extortionists'. The old India hand and first Governor General of India, Warren Hastings, believed that if the

British were going to rule millions of Indians, they needed to absorb Indian culture, customs, and all the languages in use, like Persian, Arabic, Sanskrit and Bengali. The Fort William College was started in 1800, during Lord Wellesley's Governor Generalship (in office: 1798–1805), to create a university 'comparable to Oxford or Cambridge' to train British officials in Indian languages. Hastings also nurtured an intriguing group of Company employees, who became passionate students of everything to do with India!

The most famous was a Supreme Court judge, the scholarly Sir William Jones, who spoke 28 languages. As the Company had decided to use Hindu and Muslim laws (dispensed by British judges), Sir William began learning Sanskrit to understand ancient Hindu laws. He found Sanskrit had startling similarities to Greek and Latin, and his sensational theory that all European and Indian languages came from one source caused a furore!

He started the famous Asiatic Society of Bengal, whose members studied all aspects of India – its history, languages, culture, arts, medicine, geography and people. Indeed, there was a lot to be discovered – the world had forgotten about the Harappans, Ajanta, Ellora, Ashoka and Chanakya's *Arthashastra*, to name just a few!

The society became a haven for passionate Indologists. who painstakingly pieced together the jigsaw puzzle of India's past. James Prinsep deciphered the long-forgotten Brahmi script in his spare time and gave the world a new hero in Emperor Ashoka. H.T. Colebrooke translated many ancient scientific Sanskrit works into English. Company soldiers wrote regional histories, like James Tod's *Annals and Antiquities of Rajasthan*. Jonathan Duncan, the Governor of Bombay, stamped out female infanticide in Benares by using arguments from the Hindu scriptures! These lovers of India became known as the Orientalists. All these discoveries sparked India's pride in her own past.

The Anglicists Rise

Meanwhile, evangelical Christians considered Indians 'as depraved as they are blind, and as wretched as they are depraved...' and convinced Parliament to actively promote missionary activity in India. Intellectuals called 'utilitarians', like Jeremy Bentham and James Mill, believed that government should act for the 'maximum good for the most people' and wanted to rid society's 'superstitious respect for antiquity'. The evangelicals and utilitarians became very unlikely allies, and together were called the Anglicists. As the East India Company was committed to saving profits not souls, relations were always tense between the Company and zealous Baptist missionaries.

The Anglicists Win

The Orientalists viewed the growing power of the evangelicals and utilitarians in Britain as a disaster in the making, sure that if they had their way, 'indignation will spread and fifty million people will drive us out'.

In came Lord Thomas Babington Macaulay, a committed Anglicist, as part of India's Supreme Council. The Orientalists wanted education for Indians in their native languages and subjects, while the Anglicists were

Lord Macaulay believed in the superiority of Western education

Governor General Bentinck replaced Persian with English

adamant that government funds should be spent purely on English-language, Western-style education. In his famous 1835 Minute (a formal written note), Macaulay denounced India, claiming that 'a single shelf of a good European library is worth the whole native literature of India and Arabia'.

He urged the government to spend their (measly) 100,000-rupee budget to, 'form a class as interpreters between us and the millions whom we govern, Indian in blood and colour, but English in tastes, opinions, morals and intellect.' Macaulay was in luck, as his boss, Governor General William Bentinck, was a fellow evangelical and utilitarian! The Orientalists received a death blow. Persian was replaced by English as the official language, the Orientalist Fort William College made obsolete and Western-style universities established in major cities!

Social and Religious Reform

With Western-style education came a new class of Indians, exposed at home to traditional Indian texts, and at school to modern, radical Western literature and thought. They started questioning age-old traditions and launched reform movements, leading to churn and change, which also led to an intense backlash from orthodox Hindus. Some reformists started eating with other castes (and even Europeans). Many fought against child marriage and sati. Most believed that British rule was good for India, and would drag her into the modern world, kicking and screaming in protest if necessary.

RAJA RAM MOHAN ROY

One of the earliest reformers was Ram Mohan Roy. Born in the 1770s into a wealthy Bengali Kulin brahmin zamindar family, he was married off thrice by the age of ten. A very sharp student, he studied Persian, Arabic, Sanskrit, and Hindu classical texts. Though he only learned English at twenty-two, he started printing an English journal, and an Englishman later said, '... I should have ascribed it to the pen of a superiorly educated Englishman.' He worked for the East India Company but retired at forty-two, gathering Indian and European intellectuals around him in Calcutta and starting social work. He published journals and newspapers in English, Urdu and Bengali. Incidentally, he was the first Indian ever to use the word 'Hinduism'!

In 1828, he founded the Brahmo Samaj, which renounced idol worship, speaking of the one, all-knowing God, hailing the Vedas and Upanishads for proof. The Brahmo Samaj was against child marriage and polygamy, and encouraged widow remarriage, inter-caste marriage and foreign travel. It became very popular with Bengali intellectuals. As someone who had himself seen screaming widows being led to the funeral pyre, Ram Mohan Roy vigorously opposed sati (though he was unable to prevent sati in his own family). He faced great opposition, but in 1829, sati was outlawed by the British. Startlingly for those times, Roy believed that women equalled men in intellect, writing: 'When did you ever afford them a fair opportunity of exhibiting their natural capacity? ... you keep women void of education...'

Although loyal to the British, he did not hesitate to oppose them – often and very publicly! When press

Ram Mohan Roy led the Indian Renaissance

freedom was restricted, he challenged it in the Supreme Court of Calcutta and even wrote to the British king! This idea was truly revolutionary – that an Indian could go to a British court, the British Parliament and even the British king for justice against the British themselves. In 1830, the powerless Mughal emperor Akbar Shah II persuaded Roy to plead his pension case to the Company in London, and bestowed the title of 'Raja' on him.

Among the first high-caste Hindus to sail from India, Roy took along a brahmin cook, just so that his angry family could not have him legally disinherited (they had been piling lawsuits on him)! In England, he met with the king, addressed Parliament, and mingled closely with British intellectuals and nobles. An admirer wrote, 'No one ever came clothed in such wisdom, grace and humanity...' However, he soon contracted fatal meningitis. He was buried in Bristol as England had no concept of cremation. A memorial *chhatri* erected by his English friends still stands here.

THE TAGORES
The Tagore (Thakur) family became very influential and threw up many notable figures. The Tagores had worked with the British from very early on. Dwarakanath Tagore (1794–1846) raised the family fortune to new heights – with investments in steam engines, tea estates, banks, silk,

sugar and his own fleet of ships! 'Prince' Dwarakanath lived flamboyantly. His mingling with Europeans horrified his conservative family, who kept rushing

off to purify themselves! His parties in Calcutta were comparable only to the British Governor General's, and entertainment included jugglers and fireworks!

He was a philanthropist and was deeply influenced by Ram Mohan Roy and the Brahmo Samaj. He supported modern scientific education, and even donated cash prizes to encourage upper-class Hindu medical students to overcome fear of 'pollution' and dissect corpses!

In 1842, he set off to visit Britain in his private steamer. He meandered across Europe, dining with governors, nobles and merchants, and called on the Pope in Rome. Queen Victoria wrote, 'The Brahmin speaks English remarkably well, and is a very intelligent, interesting man...' He threw a lavish boat party on the Thames, attended by authors like Charles Dickens and William Makepeace Thackeray. 'Dwarky', as an English lady called him, returned a celebrity.

Abanindranath Tagore's depiction of Bharat Mata became an enduring nationalist concept

DAVID HARE

David Hare (1775–1842) was a Scottish watchmaker, who moved to Calcutta for the watch business but stumbled into education. Along with Ram Mohan Roy, he set up the prestigious English-medium Hindu College (now Presidency University) to give Hindu boys a liberal Western-style education; it gave rise to remarkably freethinking youth. Hare started the School Book Society to prepare textbooks, and the Calcutta School Society to launch English and Bengali schools.

His own schools became famous for their high standard and non-religious approach. He also fought tirelessly for the freedom of the press and against indentured labour. Members of Young Bengal wrote: '... a man who has breathed new life into Hindu Society... the friend of a friendless people, set an example to his countrymen and ours...' When David Hare died in 1842, thousands of Indians attended his funeral.

ISHWAR CHANDRA VIDYASAGAR

Ishwar Chandra Bandyopadhyay (1820–91) was born in an impoverished brahmin family. His student years passed in a flurry of academic prizes and scholarships and earned him the title Vidyasagar ('Ocean of Knowledge'). He became the principal of Sanskrit College, Calcutta, at just 30 years of age. He wanted education for all, and along with the government's Education Department, set up 20 Bengali-medium 'model schools' across rural Bengal. He wrote the still-used Bengali textbook titled *Adarshalipi O Saral Barnaparichay* ('Ideal Script and Easy Introduction to the Alphabet').

Vidyasagar had an untiring commitment towards women. He hated polygamy and child marriage, rampant in Bengal, wanted widows to remarry, and all girls to study. His survey of Kulin brahmins in the Hooghly district showed that 130 men had more than four wives each, of which the top ones had more than 80 wives each! When he tried to get the British to ban polygamy, they refused to act for fear of hurting religious sentiments.

Vidyasagar worked committedly to have the remarriage of widows legalized

He was threatened on the streets of Calcutta, but managed to get the Widow Remarriage Act finally passed in 1856. The first widow remarriage created a huge furore throughout Bengal.

HENRY LOUIS VIVIAN DEROZIO

Born to a mixed Portuguese-Indian family, Derozio (1809–31) started teaching English literature and history in the new Hindu College. A firebrand teacher, he encouraged his students to question everything. He often met them in the evenings outside college, where along with poetry, touchy subjects like religion and patriotism were discussed.

His followers known as 'Derozians' and 'Young Bengal' wanted radical change, mingled for meals and drank wine. Their excessive free thought antagonized both conservative Hindus and Christians. Derozio was forced out of the college and died shortly after, but his radical ideas kept shaping the attitudes of countless young Bengalis.

Raja Radhakanta Deb

The story of the Bengal Renaissance would be incomplete without mentioning the fierce opponent of many liberal reformers, who opposed all the 'dangerous' and 'radical' new ideas. An accomplished scholar from an elite Calcutta family, Radhakanta Deb (1784–1867) vigorously defended ancient Hindu traditions, and believed that the British government, to whom he was loyal, had no business interfering with religious customs.

Intriguingly, he was a great supporter of English-language education, and worked with Baptist Christian missionaries to set up girls' schools across Calcutta. He also funded students to go to England for higher studies, and was a driving force behind Hindu College.

Prarthana Samaj

'The Prayer Society' was formed in Maharashtra in 1867, springing out of a previous secret society called the Paramhamsa Sabha, where people met to sing devotional hymns and eat a meal prepared by a low-caste cook. Prarthana Samaj founders, like Justice Govind Ranade and Sir Ramakrishna Bhandarkar, were inspired by historical Maharashtrian reformers like Tukaram.

Its members considered themselves Hindus and did not formally renounce idol worship. The Samaj worked on issues like women's education, widow remarriage, banning female infanticide and child marriage, and caste-related issues like inter-dining and inter-caste marriage.

Dayanand Saraswati and the Arya Samaj

A great Sanskrit scholar and monk from Gujarat, Dayanand Saraswati (1824–83) became disenchanted with idol worship. Harking back to the Vedas, he spoke of a monotheistic faith. In 1875, he began the Vedic Arya Samaj in Bombay, and published its main text, *Satyartha Prakash* ('Light of Truth'). The movement spread like wildfire, and idols were publicly smashed or thrown into rivers.

He denied foreign travel was 'polluting', and wrote, 'Those who go abroad augment their political power and prosperity by combining the good qualities of foreigners and rejecting their faults.' He believed that women and men were equal in the Vedic age, and favoured widow remarriage and women's education. An arch-nationalist, he first used the words 'swadeshi' and 'swaraj', which later became bywords in India's independence struggle.

After he died, the Arya Samaj continued to grow and began a *shuddhi* or 'purification' movement to reconvert Indian Christians and Muslims to Hinduism. It also set up Dayanand Anglo-Vedic (DAV) Colleges.

RAMAKRISHNA PARAMAHANSA

Born into a poor brahmin family in rural Bengal, Ramakrishna Paramahansa (1836–86) became the priest at a Kali temple at Dakshineshwar

A Paramahansa Parable: The Blind Men and the Elephant

Four blind men met an elephant. One touched its leg and said, 'The elephant is like a pillar.' The second touched its trunk and said, 'It is like a thick stick.' The third touched its belly and said, 'It is like a big jar.' The fourth touched its ears and said, 'It is like a basket.' A passer-by approached the arguing group and said, 'None of you has seen the elephant... its legs are like pillars, its belly is like a vessel, its ears like baskets... the elephant is a combination of all of these.' In the same way, those who quarrel have seen only one aspect of the Deity.

near Calcutta. He adopted the old bhakti tradition of detachment, simplicity and devotion. He believed that all religions led to the same god. He was sparsely educated and his parables were in simple Bengali, but left a deep impression. His following grew rapidly, and he became known as the living Saint of Dakshineshwar.

SWAMI VIVEKANANDA

Narendranath Dutta (1863–1902) was born to a liberal, cultured, affluent lawyer. With a modern, Western-style education, as a student he corresponded with European scientists about the theory of evolution, and dabbled with the Brahmo Samaj and the Freemason Society. He was introduced to Ramakrishna Paramahansa on a whim when his English teacher suggested he visit the ascetic to understand what the word 'trance' meant!

Gradually, he became deeply influenced by Ramakrishna's ideas, and studied the Vedas, Upanishads and the Bhagavadgita. He took a vow of celibacy, the name Vivekananda ('the joy of wisdom') and walked across India.

In 1893, Swami Vivekananda represented Hinduism at Chicago's novel World Parliament of Religions. He electrified his audience and became an overnight celebrity, showing the world a new face of Hinduism when he proudly claimed, 'We believe not only in universal toleration, we accept all religions as true... the West can learn tolerance from India.' The *New York Herald* noted: 'After hearing him we feel how foolish it is to send missionaries to this learned nation.' He was invited to become a professor at Harvard University!

In 1897, Vivekananda started the Ramakrishna Mission to spread Hinduism worldwide, and over the

The World Parliament of Religions

In 1893, Chicago, USA, hosted a novel World Parliament of Religions as part of a World Fair with tens of millions of visitors. Four thousand people watched the religious representatives enter hand in hand. A bell tolled ten times, in honour of the ten great world religions: Confucianism, Taoism, Shintoism, Hinduism, Buddhism, Jainism, Zoroastrianism, Judaism, Christianity and Islam. Forty-one religious traditions were represented through 400 delegates. Swami Vivekananda began his address with 'Sisters and Brothers of America', and immediately got a thunderous standing ovation from the massive crowd. He was catapulted to instant fame, and an American newspaper described him as 'an orator by divine right and undoubtedly the greatest figure at the Parliament...'

Vivekananda (fourth from right) at the World Parliament of Religions

next century, as many as 200 branches were opened from America to Japan to Brazil. Swami Vivekananda urged his countrymen to awaken from age-old slumber: 'What makes the difference between the Englishman and you? The Englishman believes in himself and you do not...' He passed away at the young age of 39 due to diabetes, leaving behind a towering legacy.

SIR SYED AHMAD KHAN

Born into Delhi Mughal nobility, Sir Syed Ahmed Khan (1817–98) worked for the British East India Company. Though he stayed loyal to the British during the 1857 Uprising, his criticism influenced British policy.

After visiting England, he started dreaming of setting up a 'Muslim Cambridge' and spent his time after retirement towards realizing his dream. The Mohammedan Anglo-Oriental College was started in 1875 in Aligarh, eventually becoming the famed Aligarh Muslim University. It taught science and religion, and Western and Indian subjects. Sir Syed was elected to the Imperial Legislative Council where he had a say in the laws being passed for Indians. He was liberal-minded for his times, but was against democratic elections, preferring British rule to 'Hindu' rule.

Literature

Regional Indian literature flowered. Over time, grammars of various languages were formalized and prose, poetry and novels, all began to express social problems, the plight of women and the exploitation of the poor.

MICHAEL MADHUSUDAN DUTTA

Madhusudan Dutta (1824–73), born in Jessore (Bangladesh), was raised in Calcutta in a traditional

Michael Madhusudan Dutta became a literary luminary

Hindu family. At Hindu College, he became fascinated with English language, literature, people and culture and whimsically converted to Christianity. He was kicked out of his home, moved to Madras Presidency, married an Englishwoman, switched to European dress and took on the name Michael.

He began writing and publishing English works, but suddenly, living in abject poverty, abandoned his family and returned to Calcutta. When commissioned to translate Bengali plays into English, he wrote his own Bengali play to prove he could do better! His *Sharmishtha* was a story from the Mahabharata, styled on Western lines. He invented a form of Bengali blank verse and composed his masterpiece, *Meghanadabadh Kavya*. The confirmed anglophile became an unlikely giant of Bengali literature!

He continued to flit between England, France and Calcutta, married another Englishwoman and fancifully named his children Sharmishtha, Milton and Napoleon!

BANKIMCHANDRA CHATTOPADHYAY

One of the two earliest graduates of the newly established University of Calcutta, Bankimchandra (1838–94) worked for the British as a civil servant, but was one of the first to voice an anti-British nationalist spirit. Surprisingly, he was awarded the Order of the Indian Empire in 1894.

He was also one of the earliest novelists in India and his first work, *Rajmohan's Wife*, was in English. He introduced historical fiction with his first Bengali novel, the runaway bestseller *Durgeshnandini* (set in Akbar's time). His Bengali novels created a stir as he exhorted Indians to waken from their long apathy, which had led to centuries of colonial oppression. *Anandamath* was a historical novel about a band of Hindu ascetics who took up arms against Warren Hastings, to fight for 'Mother India', all crying 'Vande Mataram' (Hail, Mother) as they charged. The chant 'Vande Mataram' would become the rallying anthem for the Indian freedom movement.

MODERN HINDI IS BORN

When the British started ruling, there were a range of Hindi-like dialects, from Rajasthani to Bihari to Persianhybrid Hindustani. When the Company realized there were no textbooks or formal rules for any of these, Hindi in the Devanagari script emerged for the first time.

The father of Hindi literature, Bharatendu Harishchandra, came from a wealthy, intellectual trading family of Benares and contributed immensely to Hindi literature in his short 35 years. He translated and wrote around 175 Hindi histories, poetry (humorous too!), prose and plays on nationalism, love and religious devotion. He rejected Sanskritized Hindi, preferring a more colloquial language. The title of a still-popular political satire sparked off a popular saying, '*Andher nagari, chaupat raja*', which signifies a ruler who is foolish beyond belief.

Science

In India, colonial education did not emphasize sciences like physics, chemistry and mathematics. However, some Indian scientists still contributed greatly.

Jagadish Chandra Bose was a scientist way ahead of his times

Jagadish Chandra Bose

He studied at Cambridge and became a physics professor at Presidency College in Calcutta, at a time when only Englishmen taught 'sciencey' subjects. In 1895, Bose (1858–1937) was the first to prove that electrical signals could be transmitted without wires, beating American and Italian scientists to it. (Unsurprisingly, it was Italian Dr Guglielmo Marconi who received the 1909 Nobel Prize in Physics for 'wireless telegraphy.') He set up the Basu Bigyan Mandir ('Basu Temple of Science') or Bose Institute in Calcutta. Bose kept his discoveries patent-free, giving up millions of dollars. He also wrote one of the first Indian science-fiction stories, the Bengali *Niruddesher Kahini*, a fictional tale about controlling a cyclone using hair oil!

PRAFULLA CHANDRA RAY

After studied chemistry in Britain, Prafulla Chandra Ray (1861–1944) was able to overcome racial discrimination with Bose's help and get a post with Presidency College. He published over 200 original research papers on chemistry and set up Bengal Chemical and Pharmaceutical Works, India's first pharmaceutical company that prepared 'indigenous drugs' with 'up-to-date scientific methods'.

Art

After William Hodges became the first professional European artist to visit India in 1780, a steady trickle of European artists travelled across India, painting landscapes, portraits and miniatures, showing the country to the British public in all her colourful glory, from the Benares ghats to her exotic monuments, dancing girls and clothes. The most famous were Thomas Daniell and his nephew, William Daniell, whose paintings are valuable documents of late-18th-century life in India.

Raja Ravi Varma (1848–1906), from the royal family of Travancore, painted Indian mythological scenes in Western-style oil paintings that were a runaway success. His style of depicting deities continues into the present! His works were presented at international conventions in Vienna and Chicago, but he refused to go abroad for fear

Ladies in the Moonlight
by Raja Ravi Varma

of excommunication. Through his paintings, he also popularized the style in which the sari is draped today (called Nivi)!

The Kalighat style developed when Patua folk artists, who painted scrolls with vegetable and mineral dyes, settled around the famous Kalighat temple in Calcutta, and sold paintings of Hindu deities as inexpensive souvenirs. The handmade paper slowly morphed into standardized sheets, and the natural dyes into imported British paints. The Kalighat style took on social commentary and satire, and influenced artists like Jamini Roy.

India's earliest modern artists were Abanindranath and Gaganendranath Tagore. Abanindranath's experimental mixed Mughal–Western painting won the top prize at the Delhi Durbar of 1903. Modern themes were influenced by Mughal miniatures and the recently discovered Ajanta frescoes. Some artists worked with Japanese artists to develop Pan-Asian styles. M.A.R. Chughtai and Nandalal Bose were major artists of the Bengal school.

Women in Public Life

Even in conservative Victorian England, women were meant for hearth and home. In India, people were fighting for very basic rights for women: primary education, widow remarriage and abolition of sati. However, a few women slowly started coming into public life as writers, doctors and lawyers.

ROKEYA SAKHAWAT HOSSAIN

Begum Rokeya Sakhawat Hossain (1880–1932) was an early feminist and author in Bengali and English. She was unique in her time as the only one to demand *equality* for women, rather than just education. Her scathing writing, (particularly *Sultana's Dream*) laced with wit, humour and logic, spared nobody, not men, not religion, nor women themselves. She set up schools for girls where they were taught sciences and physical education. She is particularly revered in Bangladesh today. A quote: 'May I ask, Astronomer sir, why do we not find your wife with you? When you are engaged in measuring the distance between the earth and the sun or the stars, where is your wife occupied in the measurement of pillow covers?'

RASASUNDARI DEVI

Rasasundari Devi (1810–90) published the first ever Bengali autobiography. Her *Aamaar Jiban* (My Life) describes what life was like for Indian women back then. Married off at twelve, she compares herself to a sacrificial goat, 'the same hopeless situation, the same agonized screams...' Doing chores from dawn until midnight, at 26 years, she secretly taught herself to read Hindu texts, by stealing pages from the *Chaitanya Bhagavat*, and comparing its letters to a paper on which her son had practised his alphabet. She read every book in her household and learned to write in her mid-fifties, and then published her memoirs in 1876 at 66 years of age!

Toru Dutt

Coming from a privileged, intellectual Calcutta family, Toru Dutt (1856–77) learnt Bengali, English, French and Sanskrit. Ostracized after her father's conversion to Christianity, her family moved to Europe for a spell, living in England (London and Cambridge) and France (Nice), which sparked her deep love for French literature. Upon their return to Calcutta, Toru wrote for newspapers, translated French poems into English, wrote a French novel and a book of English poems called *Ancient Ballads and Legends of Hindustan*. She died of tuberculosis at only 21 years of age.

Our Casuarina Tree (An excerpt)

When first my casement is wide open thrown
At dawn, my eyes delighted on it rest;
Sometimes, and most in winter,—on its crest
A gray baboon sits statue-like alone
Watching the sunrise; while on lower boughs
His puny offspring leap about and play;
And far and near *kokila*s hail the day...

Toru Dutt, the poet

Haimabati Sen

Widowed at 10 years, Haimabati Sen (1866–1933) was cheated out of her inheritance and ended up in Benares with no money or refuge. She eventually went to Calcutta and remarried a religious yet progressive Brahmo, Kunjabehari Sen, who supported her decision to become a doctor. She came first in her course, among both men and women, but had to settle for the silver medal after enraged male students went on strike! She practised medicine for many years.

CORNELIA SORABJI

A brilliant student with a pukka British upbringing, she was the first woman graduate of Bombay

Cornelia Sorabji was the first ever woman lawyer in the British Empire!

FUN FACT!

University in 1892. She went to Oxford to study law, though she was denied a scholarship just because she was a woman (sympathetic British ladies raised the money). She became the first female lawyer in the British Empire. She worked to help the *purdahnashin*, secluded Hindu and Muslim women often cheated by male business agents. A British loyalist, she travelled across America, speaking in favour of British rule.

The Russian Adventurer Who Pioneered Modern Indian Theatre

Born impoverished in Catherine the Great's Russia, Gerasim Lebedev travelled across Europe as a musician with the Russian Embassy, before absconding to India. In Calcutta, he became fascinated with Indian culture and mythology, and began writing music that blended Indian tunes with Western musical instruments. In his spare time, the Russian translated English comic plays into Bengali, transplanting the locale to India and giving the characters Indian names!

European-style theatre was unknown in India. Lebedev built a 400-seat European theatre and hired local Bengali male and female actors (women in theatre was a shocker!). His plays were a runaway success, especially as Lebedev showed Indians and Hinduism in a kindly light. Calcutta's British residents, however, unhappy with a Russian adventurer's thundering success, forced the theatre's closure and hounded him out of India in 1797. Eventually, he went back to Russia, where he set up the first printing house in Europe using Bengali and Devanagari scripts, financed by the Russian Tsar!

Explore More

Left: Dhruva by Asit Kumar Haldar; right: Pratima Visarjan by Gaganendranath Tagore

• VISIT the National Gallery of Modern Art in Delhi to see Bengal School painters. Look out for these names: Nandalal Bose, M.A.R Chughtai, Sunayani Devi (sister of Abanindranath Tagore), Manishi Dey, Mukul Dey, Kalipada Ghoshal, Asit Kumar Haldar, Sudhir Khastgir, Kshitindranath Majumdar, Sughra Rababi, Debi Prasad Roychoudhury, Bireswar Sen, Beohar Rammanohar Sinha, Kiron Sinha, Gaganendranath Tagore (Rabindranath Tagore's brother) and Sarada Ukil.

* READ 'Those Days (Sei Samay in Bengali) by Sunil Gangopadhyay, an award-winning novel set against the backdrop of 1857 and the Bengal Renaissance.

* READ the memoirs of Haimabati Sen. You might find the book in a library.

* VISIT the Bose Institute in Kolkata to see Bose's 60 GHz microwave apparatus (right),

Calendars, Indian Style
Indian calendars are similar, but differ on the zero dates.

Most calendars followed in the world are either purely solar, like the Gregorian calendar followed the world over, of 365 days to the year, or purely lunar, like the Muslim Hijri calendar, which has 12 lunar months as a year of 354 days. However, twelve lunar months are only 354 days, which is 11 days shorter than a solar year. For spring or summer to come at the same time every year, this needs to be reconciled to the solar year.

The Hindu calendar is a solar–lunar calendar: the months move according to the moon and the year is 354 days long. However, every third year, the leftover 33 days (11x 3) are adjusted by creating an extra lunar month of 29 days. Four days are adjusted off here and there. An example of a date would be – Ekadashi, Shukla Paksh, Kartik Maas, Vikram Samvat 2057 – 11th day of the fortnight of the waxing moon, the month of Kartik, year 2057 of the Vikram Era.

The method of calculation of the dates is quite standard across the various calendars used in India, and other Indian-influenced calendars like those in South-East Asia. However, the zero dates vary!

An interesting habit of Indian kings was to found a new era starting from the beginning of their dynasty. This new zero date would be followed in their kingdom and by their feudatories, until they were replaced by a new dynasty and a new calendar was inaugurated with a new zero date. Hundreds of such calendars were created over the centuries, including the Gupta Era beginning in 319 CE, and the Harsha era beginning with 606 CE.

The really odd thing is that there is much confusion about the origins of the two calendars in common use today, the Vikram Samvat with a zero point of 57 BCE and the Shaka Samvat with a zero point of 78 CE. The Vikram era is variously supposed to have been founded by the Shaka king Azes, or the legendary King Vikramaditya, but we have no historical records of any Vikramaditya in that period. The Shaka era is

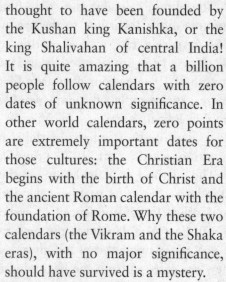

thought to have been founded by the Kushan king Kanishka, or the king Shalivahan of central India! It is quite amazing that a billion people follow calendars with zero dates of unknown significance. In other world calendars, zero points are extremely important dates for those cultures: the Christian Era begins with the birth of Christ and the ancient Roman calendar with the foundation of Rome. Why these two calendars (the Vikram and the Shaka eras), with no major significance, should have survived is a mystery.

A page from the Hindu calendar 1871–72

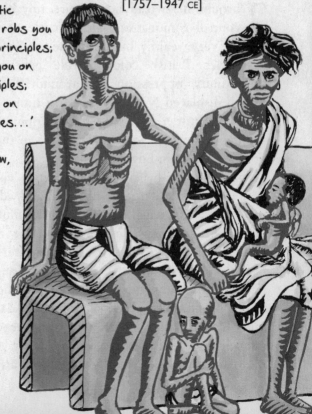

'When an Englishman wants a thing... he waits patiently until a burning conviction comes into his mind that it is his moral and religious duty to conquer those who have got the thing he wants... He does everything on principle. He fights you on patriotic principles; he robs you on business principles; he enslaves you on imperial principles; he bullies you on manly principles...'
– George Bernard Shaw, Victorian playwright

9

Impact of the British Raj

[1757–1947 CE]

9

Plucking the Golden Bird

Through her worldwide empire, tiny Britain came to control a monstrous global cycle of profit, which made it very wealthy, but devastated entire continents.

In fact, British colonial rule believed in equal-opportunity oppression all around the world. The British displaced Native Americans; transported African slaves like cattle; addicted China to opium; starved and subjugated Indians – all to drink tea in their new posh drawing rooms in England.

Many Indians believe that the British 'civilized India', with railways and roads, industry and education, and the English language. They forget the motives and the numbers. The British established peace in India, but bled her dry. They set up the judiciary, but applied laws unfairly. They believed they were morally superior, but let millions of Indians starve to death under their noses.

The profit motive ruled supreme. As Adam Smith had said, Britain was a 'Nation of Shopkeepers', and the moment they had to spend on any public good in India, they usually found themselves 'unable to afford it'.

India Beggared

India had long had many thriving industries – its craftsmen created valuable products from raw material, like fine muslin cloth from cotton fibre. Britain's 200-year rule reduced India's rich economy to tatters. Trade, wealth, industry and people, all suffered deeply compared to other countries. India became poorer and poorer – going from earning 25 per cent of the world's income in 1750 to a measly 4 per cent, 200 years later! Imagine, in 1600, Indian and British workers earned the same amount of money, but by 1875, the average Indian earned Rs 30 per year, while the average Briton earned Rs 450!

A Colossal Drain of Wealth

India's wealth was methodically drained back to Britain. An intellectual and trader, Sir Dadabhai Naoroji (1825–1917) was one of the first to estimate that, in just 37 years (between 1835 and 1872), around 500 million pounds were transferred out of India through land taxes, British salaries, profits of British companies exporting goods to India and so on!

This staggering sum could have been used to build roads, schools, hospitals and factories in India. It could have prevented millions from starving to death. But it enriched Britain instead. Indeed, many of today's wealthy families in Britain made their initial fortunes in India.

A second reason for India's fall was how Indian industry was almost completely destroyed by the

Dadabhai Naoroji first brought attention to India's wealth being drained to Britain

British, especially its glorious tradition of textile exports. The British initially forced Indian weavers to sell them fabrics at really low prices, using 'persuasion' tactics like flogging, and then sold them for a fat profit in Europe.

Once Britain's Industrial Revolution was sparked with the invention of the steam-engine, there was a dizzyingly rapid switch to machines using steam power. British companies began making cheap cloth in large quantities, and selling it in India. The government helped them by putting huge taxes on Indian cloth imported into England!

Millions of skilled Indian artisans were forced to return to basic agriculture. Governor General William Bentinck wrote in 1834, 'The misery hardly finds parallel in the history of commerce... the bones of the cotton weavers are bleaching the plains of India.'

Dadabhai Naoroji pleaded in British Parliament against these unfair British policies. He said, 'The Indian starves in peace and perishes in peace, with law and order... If, as in England, the revenue raised from the people is returned to the (Indian) people – there be no need for famines... or poisoning with opium, millions of the human race.'

Show Me the Money

After the Company conquered Bengal, its profits began to come from taxes and monopolies rather than trade. They bumped up taxes and changed how they were collected, with truly horrendous results.

In Bengal, the British declared a Permanent Settlement of the land, making zamindars the outright, permanent 'owners' of the land, who had to pay a fixed annual amount. The Company auctioned zamindari rights to the highest bidder and threw off old zamindar families

How to Start an Industrial Revolution

It began with the agricultural revolution, where in the 17th century, scientific farming methods like rotating crops, animal breeding and new types of ploughs greatly increased food crops in Britain. The following population explosion provided the first thing needed for an Industrial Revolution, the *workforce*.

New *technology* allowed steam power to be used to run machines to quickly make textiles. Next, *capital*, the money to start expensive new cotton mills, came from the fortunes made previously through trade in India and elsewhere.

Lastly, the *market* for the finished goods was India itself, becoming the largest market for British cloth and goods, buying 40 per cent of British exports. The Indian handloom textile industry collapsed.

from their lands for late payments. Many new zamindars lived far away and appointed agents, who were often oppressive. After protests, the British changed the law – making it tough and dangerous for peasants to complain! The Permanent Settlement caused great misery and impoverishment across Bengal.

The British tried different methods to collect revenue in other areas. In the Ryotwari system, each small farmer paid a fixed revenue directly to the Company. This system was introduced in the south, and expanded across Maratha lands, Uttar Pradesh and Punjab. In the Mahalwari system, the zamindar and the village were jointly responsible for paying the taxes, and it was common in parts of Uttar Pradesh, Delhi and

Khwaja Salimullah was a rich zamindar in Bengal with large landholdings

Punjab. Peasants began to stay in debt, in near-slavery, for their whole lives, and even put their children in the clutches of moneylenders, who charged exorbitant interest.

Tea

When the British Parliament removed the Company's monopoly over the extremely profitable China tea trade, they decided to start growing tea in India instead! The first tea plantation in Assam was set up in the 1830s. For the intensive labour, planters liked 'hardy' tribals from Jharkhand (then Bihar), who would endure the awful working conditions. They are still called the tea tribes of Assam.

Opium

The East India Company started trading with China in 1672, importing silk, porcelain china and a brand-new drink called tea, which became enormously popular in Europe and America. Like with India, Britain worried about the outflow of gold and silver to China, and soon started to fund their goods by selling the drug, opium, to the Chinese, which they forced Indian farmers in Bengal and Bihar to grow!

Only the Company could decide who could grow opium in India, how much and for what price. Opium cakes were packed at Company factories and auctioned to European merchants who would smuggle it into China (after opium imports were banned by the Chinese emperor). Eventually, Britain fought the 'Opium Wars' to force the Chinese to allow

FUN FACT! The British funded their tea-drinking habits by forcibly selling Indian-grown opium to China, until one in four Chinese men became drug addicts.

Workers at a typical indigo farm with British watchers; synthetic indigo is still used to dye blue denim

Indigo Blues

Indigo plants had been used to make gorgeous blue dye since antiquity ('indigo' comes from the Greek word for India). As colonial demand for indigo boomed, European plantation owners were given permission to 'persuade' farmers and workers in Bengal and Bihar to grow and make indigo for them. The farmers were reluctant as they got very low prices, and the indigo crop often failed. The planters resorted to brutal thuggery by seizing lands illegally, sharply increasing rent, and beating farmers. Bonded labourers, brought over under false promises, stayed in near-slavery for generations after their initial 'contracts' were over.

The peasant indigo revolt, *nilbidroha*, broke out in Bengal in 1859 against the brutal oppression of farmers. The Bengali play *Nil Darpan*, written by Dinabandhu Mitra, was published under a pseudonym in 1860. It was translated into English by Reverend J. Long for which he was sentenced to prison and charged with sedition!

them to sell opium. China's addiction became the largest and longest drug epidemic ever seen in the world!

Greater Bengal became a beehive of this very profitable (and seedy) trade. By 1858, India exported almost 5,000 tonnes of opium every year! By 1900, opium made up 15 per cent of all Indian revenue!

Salt Tax

The British taxed and put monopolies (only the Company was allowed to sell that product) on many common goods – like household salt! Between 1780 and 1788, the long-existing salt tax was sharply increased to 3.25 rupees per maund (about 38 kg). This made salt totally unaffordable – an average Indian peasant had to pay one month's wages just to buy salt for his family! Salt taxes made up a huge part of British revenue, but many (already malnourished) Indians fell severely ill due to lack of iodine and sodium. The salt tax was severely criticized, even by British officials and doctors.

Famines

During the 19th century, world population nearly doubled to 1.7 billion, as much more food was grown, and fewer people died, thanks to better hygiene and medicine. However, in this same time, India's population increased by just 10 per cent, from 250 million to 280 million.

So what happened in 19th-century India? Mainly, famines on an unimaginable scale, with widespread starvation invariably followed by deadly epidemics of cholera, plague, smallpox and malaria. Some estimate that 60 million Indians died due to famine under British rule – almost a quarter of the population.

Some Major Famines during the British Raj

- Great Bengal Famine (1769–70): 10 million deaths
- Madras and Chalisa Famines (1782–84): 11 million deaths
- Skull Famine (1791–92): 11 million deaths
- Orissa Famine (1865–67): 1 million deaths
- Rajputana Famine (1868–70): 1.5 million deaths
- Great Famine (1876–78): 6–10 million deaths
- Indian Famine (1896–97): 5 million deaths
- Indian Famine (1899–1900): 1 million deaths
- Bengal Famine (1943–44): 2–5 million deaths

While in the 700 years before British rule, there had been (on average) a major famine every 50 years, during Company rule this jumped to one every six years. Once the British Crown officially took over in 1858, there was a big famine every two years!

So what happened during British rule? Firstly, there was forced diversion of land from food crops to cash crops like indigo and opium. Then, India was always (and is still) dependent on moody monsoon rains, and regularly experienced droughts and food shortages. When this happened, Indian rulers usually reduced or excused taxes and even distributed extra stored grain.

In contrast, the Company even increased taxes, and always 'proudly' reported it had collected every penny, despite the raging famine! This caused 10 million people to die in the 1769–73 Bengal Famine in just two years, amounting to one-third of Bengal's population!

The Company followed a chaotic policy towards famine relief. It sometimes banned grain export and sometimes fixed maximum prices, but taxes always stayed sky-high.

By 1858, British officials were obsessed by new economic theories of Free Trade, which claimed that people needing, and people selling, grain would match themselves naturally. Officials claimed to be shocked when this did not happen, and panicked people hoarded their grain instead of selling it! Once, when rice was imported and fewer than 50 people died, the Governor, Sir Richard Temple, was heavily criticized... for spending too much on importing grain!

During the Great Famine of 1876–78, the government was determined to save... money. A senior official claimed, 'The task of saving life is beyond our power.' The same Sir Richard Temple now hastily removed 500,000 people from the scant government relief scheme (where some food was offered in exchange for hard labour) and slashed the food given to just 450 g of rice. This infamous Temple Ration was less than what was given to prisoners in Nazi concentration camps in the Second World War.

There was a public outcry in Britain over the high death rates in India, but it was also the general British view that India was overpopulated, backward, and famine was inevitable, as Indian peasants were 'extravagant' and did not save money for bad times! Ironically, India produced enough grain, but most was exported to Europe, even during the worst famines.

Who remembers these lost 60 million dead Indians?

How the British Ruled India

In Britain, its Parliament voted in laws, while its subgroup, the government, made the daily decisions. Independent judges ensured laws were applied fairly and to everyone. These groups provided checks against one another.

In India, this was not the case. The British Parliament granted powers to the Company to run India on its behalf. The main British official was the Governor General, who lived in India for his term and had a small council of four to six British people as advisers. This group, 'the Governor General in Council' was the all-in-one team. Helped by civil servants, they made laws, oversaw judges and law and order, decided tax rates and generally made the decisions. It was gradually expanded, but had no Indians for a long, long time.

So, just a tiny handful of British people controlled the destiny of millions of Indians, their smallest decisions – good, bad, absurd – becoming firmly etched into law.

After 1757, Calcutta became the capital city and home to the Governor General, and presidencies like Bombay and Madras became like states, with their own Governors.

The British government (called the 'Home Government') set up the India Office in London, headed by a Secretary of State for India, which controlled the 'Indian Government'. The Home and Indian governments often clashed!

COLOUR-BLIND JUSTICE?

Until the Uprising of 1857, the laws governing personal life depended on one's religion. Criminal law was Mughal and civil law was British. The British had set up Supreme Courts in Calcutta, Madras and Bombay, and lower courts in the districts. The Army kept its own military courts.

After the Uprising, there was a flurry of activity, and all laws were ordered and organized (called codification), like the Indian Penal Code (framed in 1860), still the main criminal code for India (though heavily amended). Indeed, the familiar Hindi term 'chaar-sau-bees' (420) is from Section 420 for fraudsters, from the original Indian Penal Code!

The Indian Penal Code was hailed as proof that British justice was fair and impartial, as the same law applied to both the British and Indians. Well, almost. Europeans in India could choose to be tried by a 'white' judge.

Most of the deadly violence presented to courts was committed by European planters and British soldiers on powerless Indian peasants. The accused were routinely let go – sometimes the judges would simply refuse to believe eyewitnesses, or often, murders became smaller crimes of 'causing hurt' or 'accidental death'.

The British even came up with a theory that Indians were 'pathologically weak' with 'fragile spleens' (that easily burst and killed by internal bleeding). This clear bias was a big factor in rising Indian nationalism. The Bengali daily *Amrita Bazar Patrika* sarcastically wrote, 'Judicial officers should be aware that for Europeans to commit murders is an impossibility.'

THE HEAVEN-BORN SONS

People often celebrate the British Raj for starting the Imperial Civil Service (or informally, Indian Civil Service). Why was it a big deal? They were the very engine of the British government in India, the ones who kept the country going, even as viceroys came and went. This small, (very) well-paid group of around 1,000 people, handled everything from collecting taxes, suppressing revolts and drafting laws, to building hospitals and dams. They were called the 'heaven-born sons', due to their incredible power and privilege!

In 1806, an 'East India College' was established at Haileybury in England, to train British people to run India as 'civil servants' (that is, non-military). Its recruits were chosen by the Company's Court of Directors.

Eventually, this system became heavily tilted towards favours and bribes. In 1851, the British Parliament introduced 'merit-based' competitive entrance exams. Any British subject (English or Indian) who met the requirements, could appear for these annual tests in England. Subjects mostly had nothing to do with India – English, history, ancient Greece and Rome, mathematics, sciences, and just a smattering of Sanskrit and Arabic!

Indians who tried to take these tests, faced serious obstacles. They had to travel to very expensive and far-off England at a young age (the age limit was 21 years), after overcoming the stigma

Satyendranath Tagore, Rabindranath Tagore's elder brother, was the first Indian to qualify for the Indian Civil Service

associated with foreign travel. This made for few Indian applicants and even fewer successful ones.

Satyendranath Tagore was the first Indian to qualify for the Imperial Civil Service in 1863. Even by 1900, Indians were just 5 per cent of the force. The Indian employees of less powerful branches like the Provincial Service and Subordinate Service were hardly ever promoted to the Imperial Civil Service. Other services like the Indian Forest Service, Indian Medical Service and Indian Police Service were also set up.

Modernization

Britain ruled over India during a time when Europe was bubbling with scientific discoveries, utterly transforming Western society at a speed never seen before. New technologies usually came to India within years of their introduction in Europe.

Knowledge Reaches the Masses

India's first newspapers were produced by Englishmen. *Hicky's Bengal Gazette* was launched in 1780, a 'weekly political and commercial paper open to all parties but influenced by none'. It had a tiny circulation (about 200 copies) and covered matters of the small British populace. Many English newspapers were soon launched, including

the *Bombay Courier*, *Madras Herald*, *Madras Courier*, *Madras Gazette* and *The Oriental Star*.

Mumbai Samachar *is the oldest running newspaper in Asia*

The Great Hedge of India

Imagine a long, long hedge, 12 feet tall and 4 feet thick, made up of dead, thorny plants or living shrubs like *babool*, *karonda* and Indian plum – which stretched the same distance as from London to Istanbul! This really existed. It was the Great Hedge of India, the Inland Customs Line, running 4,000 km from Punjab, across to Odisha! It was built to stop the frequent salt smuggling from the princely states into British-controlled India, due to the crazy salt tax, which was much higher in British India! Once the salt taxes were equalized across all of India in the 1870s, the hedge became redundant and was abandoned. Today, not even a trace of it remains.

The first Indian-language newspaper, the Bengali *Samachar Darpan*, came in 1818. The Gujarati *Bombay* (now *Mumbai*) *Samachar* followed in 1822, and remains the oldest running newspaper in Asia! Indian press was subject to strict British control, but restrictions were removed in 1835, and the British squarely blamed the 1857 Uprising on the 'sedition' spread by Indian papers!

However, only a tiny fraction of Indians could read even by the end of the 19th century.

RAILWAYS

British industry wanted to use railways to quickly ferry Indian raw materials to ports. In 1853, the Great Indian Peninsular Railway began the first train line for passengers between Bombay and Thane. Tempted by financial guarantees, many private British companies flocked to

Passenger train crossing the Dapoorie Viaduct to Thane in 1858

gradually build 55,000 route km of railway lines across India. The railways truly connected India, as roads were patchy and water transportation limited.

Unexpectedly, there turned out to be huge demand from ordinary Indians, and the railways began earning most of their income from passengers rather than goods. The first and second classes were used by government officials and wealthy Indians, the intermediate class by middle-class Indians and working Europeans. The third class came to define Indian rail travel, as large Indian masses stacked up like sardines on their journeys.

IRRIGATION

The British dug many irrigation canals, from many rivers (irrigating 20 million acres), to boost farming production (and increase taxes collected!). Punjab and Sindh developed one of the largest canal networks, which transformed dry Punjab into a prosperous farming state.

SHIPS

Britain's mighty navy patrolled the world's oceans and its merchant ships made the world a global marketplace. But ship journeys were long and uncomfortable – Europe to India took four months around Africa. With steamships and the opening of the Suez Canal in 1869, sailing times shrank dramatically and the journey time from England to India went from four months to three weeks!

COMMUNICATIONS

Electric telegraphs made the world a tiny place, with almost instant communication. The first telegram was sent from Mumbai to Pune in 1854. By 1856, miles of telegraph lines connected Calcutta, Agra, Bombay, Peshawar and Madras. This played a big role in allowing the British to quell the 1857 Uprising, as British outposts were quickly warned. The Oriental Telephone Company set up the first telephone exchanges in 1881 in Calcutta, Bombay, Madras and Ahmedabad.

INSTITUTIONS

The British set up many formal institutions. Banks became an alternative to informal credit from moneylenders, and friends and family. The Bank of Hindustan was started in 1770 in Calcutta. The Bank of Bengal followed in 1806, eventually becoming the State Bank of India, still the largest bank in the country today. The British also standardized Indian currency. When they first seized power, nearly 1,000 different coins were in circulation. In 1835, the Company issued a uniform coin across India, a silver rupee of 1 *tola* or 11.66 g. Each rupee was divided into 16 annas, and each anna into 4 paise.

Modern companies and factories were launched. The first life insurance company was set up in 1818. The first Indian stock exchange was launched in 1875 in Bombay.

The Surprising Origin of Standardized Written Exams

The Chinese Imperial Civil Service had had an open, objective, examination-based system to select their government officials for thousands of years. The British 'borrowed' this idea to find the most talented recruits for the East India Company's civil service. As more young people started going to school across Europe and America, standardized written examinations were considered a good way to test large numbers of students quickly and fairly.

So the next time you want to complain about a school test, you can blame the British East India Company (or the Chinese emperors)!

Explore More

HPS2 Class 4-6-0 no. 24467 locomotive at the Rail Museum in Delhi

* VISIT the National Rail Museum in New Delhi and take a look at the collection of rail engines and coaches from the colonial period, which are on display. Some popular attractions are the 'Fairy Queen' built in 1855, the 'Mysore Maharaja Saloon' from 1899, the 'Prince of Wales Saloon' of 1875 and the 'John Morris Fire Engine' built in 1914.

* WATCH the film Lagaan, directed by Ashutosh Gowariker and featuring Aamir Khan, which revolves around the issue of high tax — and during a rainless period — that was levied on Indians during British rule.

* FIND OUT more about the taxes imposed by the British in India. Compare it to the number of taxes levied on the people now. Study the differences between the kind of commodities that were taxed and those that were not.

* VISIT the Reserve Bank of India's Monetary Museum in Mumbai, which houses a vast collection of currency from ancient India to modern times. All the coins and currency notes introduced during the British rule, such as the anna, paisa and the rupee are displayed.

10

The Raj in India

'The gentlemen had a great feast last night. There was a little hog on the table, even the women ate of it...Having stuffed themselves with the unclean food; and many other sorts of flesh, taking plenty of wine, they made for some time a great noise, doubtless from drunkenness. They all stood up, crying, "Hip! Hip!" and roared before they drank more wine. After dinner, they danced in their licentious manner...'
– Excerpt from a local Persian newspaper in Delhi in 1837, describing a British dinner

10
Memsahibs and Box-wallahs

The British developed their own cocooned way of life in India. Whatever their background back in Britain, they immediately jumped to the top of the social hierarchy here. Indian princes also led hectic, lavish social lives under the Pax Britannica, disconnected from the masses.

Life became worse for the vast majority of Indian peasants, who still eked out an uncertain existence from the land. As the world modernized rapidly, changes came to India as well, but mainly benefited tiny, elite sections of Indian society.

Education
When the Company first took over, it only set up colleges to study religious texts to administer law. Evangelical missionaries gradually started schools across India. Macaulay famously ensured that money was spent 'on English education alone'. Gradually, English-language universities, and medical, engineering and law colleges came up. In general, even as Europe and America were passing laws to make primary education compulsory

for all children, the British decided that in India, they could not afford to start primary schools, which should be run privately! By 1900, more than 95 per cent of Indians remained illiterate.

The Hindu College in Calcutta, started by Raja Ram Mohan Roy and David Hare, is one of the oldest educational institutions to survive till today, now known as Presidency University

Medicine

Western medicine's rapid advance in the 19th century, with discoveries of germs and vaccinations, helped to drastically reduce early deaths and epidemics in Europe and America. In India, most public works like building sewerage and drainage systems did not take off, as the British found them 'too expensive'. Smallpox vaccination drives slowly became compulsory in big cities, but rural Indians were very wary of modern medicine.

The Princely States

After 1857, the psychologically scarred British wanted to avoid another uprising at any cost. The map of India was frozen as it was. About 60 per cent of India came under direct British rule and the rest stayed with the princely states, which had just 25 per cent of India's population.

There were about 565 princely states. Most were little more than glorified zamindaris, and only a handful were large and wealthy – like Hyderabad, Kashmir, Jaipur, Baroda, Gwalior, Kolhapur, Mysore and Travancore.

Each princely state had signed a Subsidiary Alliance – officially acknowledging Britain as the Paramount Power that decided all foreign and military policy. They had to pay for British troops and a 'British Resident' to live lavishly on-site. Only 21 states even had their own governments; most 'contracted' with the British (for a fee, naturally) to govern for them! Residencies were managed by the Indian Political Service, the government's diplomatic (and spy!) arm.

As the British wanted to protect India and their sea routes to her at all costs, they developed 'British protected states' all around India to keep away their rival French, Italians and Russians, across Bhutan, Nepal, Afghanistan and even Arabia and Somalia.

LIFESTYLE OF THE PRINCES

With not much else to do, the Indian princes led wildly indulgent lifestyles. The British made up titles and coats of arms and very intricate social rituals for Indian princes. Indian royals entered these social competitions with gusto – comparing which British royals had deigned to visit them, how elaborately they were entertained and so on. Princes and British officials socialized lavishly, for galas and house parties and polo.

The British also decided how many guns saluted a ruler as he arrived for official functions. The highest was a 21-gun salute, enjoyed by the Nizam of Hyderabad, the maharaja of Mysore and a handful of others. The viceroy got a 31-gun salute, while there were 101 for Queen Victoria!

Shikar (hunting) was very popular. Huge parties would perch on planks on trees with their rifles, waiting to shoot from safety tigers who were lured by goats or oxen to a chosen spot and sometimes even drugged! The poor beasts had no chance. From Indian royals to minor British

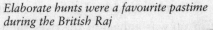

Elaborate hunts were a favourite pastime during the British Raj

officials to tourists – everyone wanted to boast about their kills. Tiger populations plummeted, while lions were hunted to near extinction.

Pig-sticking was also supposed to be 'good, clean fun' – where a wild boar was chased on horseback and speared to death. Other favourite hunting targets were elephants, birds, deer – basically anything that moved.

THE DURBARS
To show off their imperial might, the British also began organizing Mughal-style 'Durbars', where Indian nobles would come pay homage to them. The biggest spectacles were the three 'Imperial Durbars' held in 1877, 1903 and 1911, which the British held in the old Mughal capital of Delhi rather than their grand capital of Calcutta.

Viceroy Lord Lytton (in office: 1876–80) held a two-week-long extravaganza in 1877, where English-style coats of arms were designed (out of thin air!) for the 63 princes and hundreds of chiefs who attended. Queen Victoria was proclaimed the '*Kaiser-i-Hind*', the empress of India, amidst cheering crowds. Or at least, her portrait was, as Victoria was still in London!

Commissioned by Lytton, the British painter Valentine Princep was aghast at the over-the-top decor, exclaiming, 'Oh Horror! What have I to paint? ... never was more atrocious taste... like a gigantic circus...'

Of course, while the government was busy throwing an expensive party, India was in the throes of the devastating Great Famine, which claimed 10 million lives in two years.

The durbar of 1903 celebrated the newly crowned Edward VII (who did not attend either). Viceroy Lord Curzon planned the festivities meticulously. An elaborate tented city was built, as was a temporary railway service to ferry spectators! There were souvenir guidebooks, special stamps, exhibitions and firework displays.

However, all the dazzle and pomp could not disguise the increasing resistance to the British Raj, and these durbars were severely criticized by the Indian press, who saw them as a hypocritical waste of money.

Immigration and the Indian Diaspora

The tiny island nation of Britain controlled one-fourth of the earth and the destiny of billions. Proud Englishmen proclaimed that 'the sun never sets on the British Empire'. There were immense mass migrations across this vast global network – mainly forced, like the transportation of British convicts to Australia.

INDENTURED LABOUR

When Britain abolished its slave trade in 1834 after rising public protests, it caused acute labour shortages in plantations around its empire (free men refused to work in such awful conditions). Innovatively, the British decided to 'hire' Indian workers for pitiful wages to work in sugar,

The Nizam of Hyderabad at the 1911 Durbar in Delhi

Imperial Spectacle

The final, glittering Delhi Durbar of 1911 marked the coronation of George V, who astonishingly, decided to attend! Practically every prince and important personage in India came to bow before the emperor and empress. As the royals left the specially built amphitheatre, people rushed to kiss their thrones and carried out a mass puja. The king and queen also gave a 'darshan' (sighting) to their Indian subjects from the balcony of the Red Fort, like Mughal emperors used to.

tea and rubber plantations in Ceylon, Burma (Myanmar), Malaya, Fiji, Mauritius, Africa and the Caribbean. They were promised land or passage back to India after some years.

Indian indentured labourers in Trinidad in 1855

Agents called *kangani*s would go around the country, lying to starving, illiterate peasants, and get them to sign '*girmit*s' (from 'agreement') with the government. The '*girmitiyas*' were in for a rude shock. Force-marched to Indian ports, they were held in filthy, overcrowded emigration depots like animals, and packed tightly into waiting ships. On the long journeys, they were poorly fed and harshly treated – large numbers died.

Plantation owners treated these 'coolies' no better than actual slaves, and literally worked them to death, even young children. Up to 10 per cent died every year. As most *girmitiya*s arrived in debt, they never became free due to their pitiful pay. By the time the system was finally abolished, almost 100 years later, millions of Indians had been transported as indentured labour to various corners of the world, which are still enclaves of Indian culture and religion.

AND THE OTHERS

Enterprising Indian businessmen also went and settled in British colonies all over the world. East Africa got a sizeable Gujarati community, and traders from Kerala and Tamil Nadu started shops and moneylending in Burma, Ceylon and Malaysia.

Many would have moved to the USA and Canada too, if these countries had not passed specific laws to disallow Indian immigration! America's 1917 law banned 'undesirables' like Asians, and 'idiots, imbeciles, alcoholics, criminals, beggars, anarchists'! Canada allowed in only those landing after a continuous ship journey, which was not available between India and Canada!

Hardly any Indians moved from India to Britain, except for the few who went as the servants of returning British officials and the odd Indian Lascar (sailor) who jumped ship. Slowly, some Indians started studying in England, some of whom stayed on and even entered British politics! They learned how different the British were at home and in India and became Indian nationalists – Jawaharlal Nehru, Mahatma Gandhi and Sardar Patel all studied law in England.

Calcutta was the second city of the British Empire, and people from as far as China, Armenia and Baghdad migrated to make their fortunes and live the Indian dream!

FUN FACT!

SOME CAME TO INDIA TOO

Calcutta was the second city of the British Empire, ranking only below London, and attracted many foreigners. Europeans set up businesses, factories and plantations. The Chinese became carpenters, traders and leather workers. Chinese festivals are still celebrated in Kolkata's Chinatown, where the beloved Indo-Chinese fusion cuisine also originated!

Interesting Indian Migrants to Britain

Sake Dean Mahomed: He was a Company soldier from Bengal, who accompanied his Irish friend to Ireland. He married an Irish girl after converting to Christianity (because interfaith marriage was illegal!). They moved to England, where he opened the first Indian restaurant in England in 1810, called the 'Hindoostanee Coffee House'. He later started Britain's first 'shampooing' (*champi*) house in Brighton, advertising that this Indian head massage cured all sorts of ailments. It was a big hit and he became wildly popular as Dr Brighton, and was appointed the king's 'shampooing surgeon'!

Abdul Karim: Towards the end of Queen Victoria's long reign, a 24-year old Indian clerk from Agra came as a *khidmatgar* (attendant) to the royal household in 1887. The 68-year-old queen took a real shine to the tall and charming Abdul Karim who introduced Indian curries to the royal kitchen and gave the queen daily Urdu lessons. Karim improbably became  the queen's close companion and accompanied her everywhere, even advising her on Indian matters. Their closeness caused a right scandal in uptight Victorian England. After Victoria died, her son, King Edward VII, promptly dispatched Abdul Karim back to India, and had their letters burnt!

Arabic-speaking Jews (called Baghdadi Jews) came in large numbers from Iraq, Iran, Syria and Afghanistan, for both business opportunities and religious freedom. Most moved to Israel after its formation in 1948.

British Lifestyle in India

When the British first came to India, many blended in – wearing Mughal kurta-pyjamas, growing luxuriant moustaches, keeping large harems and composing Urdu poetry. Sir David Ochterlony, the Resident of Delhi from 1803, paraded down Chandni Chowk in full Indian dress, with his 13 Indian 'wives' seated behind him on elephants!

As the British Empire grew, so did racial superiority, resulting in a firm divide between British and Indian society. There were never more than 150,000 British people in India, half of whom were soldiers. They lived in a cocoon, mingling in their segregated clubs and house parties. British-style gardens bloomed around their district houses, and the vicar came to tea. The 'hill station' arose for the British to escape oppressive Indian summers – Mussoorie, Nainital and, of course, Shimla, which became the summer capital of India!

British people in India lived well, far better than back home. Food was cheap, and there were loads of servants. However, they often died within a few years of coming

David Ochterlony in Mughal-style clothes

over, due to heat, disease and overeating!

Imperial Civil Servants were very powerful and well-paid – district collectors got the equivalent of 2,500 dollars per year. As they had passed the notoriously difficult examinations, they were known as the 'Competition-Wallahs'.

A typical British bungalow of the Raj

A British traveller, George Otto Trevelyan wrote in the 1860s that an average rural district collector 'rises at daybreak and gallops across fields bright with dew to visit the scene of the late dacoit robbery... then adjourns to the swimming-bath, where servants are ready with clothes, razors, and brushes. After a "chota hasree" the collector returns to the hard business of the day'.

'Seated under a punkah in his verandah,' he writes reports and 'letters of explanation, of remonstrance, of commendation'. After lunch, 'he sets off in his buggy to Cutcherry, where he spends the afternoon in hearings'.

If the caseload is light, 'he may have time for three or four games at rackets. Otherwise, he drives with his wife on the race-course; or plays at billiards with the inspector of police... Then follows dinner, and an hour of reading or music.'

FUN FACT! Queen Victoria used to learn Urdu from her own khidmatgar Abdul Karim, although she never visited India!

Life in Calcutta was a round of galas. The most exclusive had strict guest lists, while others were open to

A British Entourage

British people living in India usually had many attendants. A British lady, A. Deare, describes her incredible entourage while travelling from Agra to Poona (spellings follow the original text):

– Two palankeens. Twenty-four bearers. One sirdar, or head bearer, and his assistant. Two elephants with their drivers, and two attendants. One of these carried a tent. One gig. Eight horses. Eight grooms. Eight grass-cutters for the horses. One coachman.

– Six clashies, or men to pitch tents. Twenty coolies—(people hired per diem, to carry furniture which is transported upon their heads.)

– One washerman and his family. One baker and his assistant. One khansomer, or house steward. Two footmen. Two tailors. One mashalchi, to clean knives and carry the lantern and run errands.

– Two women servants. One cook and assistant. One sweeper to each tent.

– Seventy sheep. Thirty-five goats. Two shepherds. Nine camels. Three camel drivers. Fourteen bullocks. Five waggons. Seven drivers. Twenty-four fowls, forty ducks, twelve geese, twelve rabbits, twelve turkeys. Two men to take care of the poultry.

– Besides the families of all these servants, with their horses, bullocks, and attendants, which may be computed upon an average of three to one.

A memsahib in transit

all British people... 'something or other serves as a peg to hang a public dinner or a public ball upon. Then there are the races, and the amateur theatre, and concerts, and fancy fairs...'

TRAVEL

Before the railways came, travel was on horseback or by palanquin, with servants sent ahead to prepare the tents

Food in British India

The British ate really well in India and British tables became bywords for gluttony! The author Aldous Huxley was stunned by the sheer amount eaten, saying, 'Five meals a day – two breakfasts, luncheon, afternoon tea and dinner – are standard throughout India.' These included:

- **Chhota Hazri:** (small breakfast): Served early (6 a.m.), with tea and perhaps a piece of fruit.
- **Burra Hazri:** A few hours later came an enormous breakfast, with a selection of 'crumbled chops, brain cutlets, beef rissoles, devilled kidneys, whole spatchcocks, duck stews, Irish stews, mutton hashes, brawns of sheep's heads and trotters, not to mention an assortment of Indian dishes such as jhal frazie, prawn dopiaza, chicken malai and beef Hussainee'.
- **A light tiffin lunch:** ... at 1 p.m. would be European-style soup, roast meat or grilled fowl, pie, cheese, dessert and wine.
- **Dinner:** ... was huge again: mulligatawny soup, 'an overgrown turkey (the fatter the better)... an enormous ham... beef, a saddle of mutton, fowls in a dish, geese, ducks, tongues, humps, pigeon pies... mutton chops and chicken cutlets, devilled bones and stews and curries of any game the sportsmen amongst them had shot during the day'.

Note: Spellings follow the original text.

THE EMPIRE CHRISTMAS PUDDING

according to the recipe supplied by the King's Chef Mr. CEDARD, with Their Majesties' Gracious Consent

Ingredient	Origin
1 lb Currants	Australia
1 lb Sultanas	Australia or South Africa
1 lb Stoned Raisins	Australia or South Africa
5 ozs Minced Apple	United Kingdom or Canada
1 lb Bread Crumbs	United Kingdom
1 lb Beef Suet	United Kingdom
6 ozs Cut Candied Peel	South Africa
8 ozs Flour	United Kingdom
8 ozs Demerara Sugar	British West Indies or British Guiana
5 Eggs	United Kingdom or Irish Free State
$\frac{1}{4}$ oz Ground Cinnamon	India or Ceylon
$\frac{1}{4}$ oz Ground Cloves	Zanzibar
$\frac{1}{4}$ oz Ground Nutmegs	British West Indies
$\frac{1}{4}$ teaspoon Pudding Spice	India or British West Indies
$\frac{1}{4}$ gill Brandy	Australia · S. Africa Cyprus or Palestine
$\frac{1}{4}$ gill Rum	Jamaica or British Guiana
1 pint Beer	England · Wales · Scotland or Ireland

This recipe (first version in 1925) drew on ingredients from various parts of the British Empire

and food. A *Handbook of India* cautions the English traveller to be 'scrupulously careful of violating… caste or religion. Though the people are… timid, they will not scruple to assault an individual, if provoked… Injury done to a cow, the death of a monkey or a peacock, or entrance into a temple booted, are amongst the outrages of which the Hindoo is peculiarly intolerant.'

British authors wrote detailed descriptions about the heavily trafficked Ganga and Indus rivers. The journey between Calcutta and Allahabad took three weeks with frequent stops along the way.

The Western Viewpoint

The long-held idea of India as an exotic, contradictory land was described by writer Mark Twain when he visited India in 1896:

'This is indeed India! …

With her, everything is on a giant scale. She has been used to wealth so vast that she describes 100,000 with one word — a lakh; she describes ten millions with one word—a crore…

India has many names…the Land of Contradictions, the Land of Superstition, the Land of Wealth and Poverty, the Land of the Thug and the Poisoner, the Land of the Suttee, the Land of the Unreinstatable Widow, the Land where All Life is Holy, the Land of Cremation, the Land where the Vulture is a Grave and a Monument, the Land of the Multitudinous Gods…'

However, once Europeans began colonizing the world, Western scientists started claiming that White Europeans were a superior race. Even Voltaire, the sage of the Enlightenment in Europe, wrote in 1734 that 'Whites…

Negroes... the yellow races are not descended from the same man...'

According to race theory, each race had natural features, proved by so-called 'scientific' publications. The 'black' African was a strong beast of burden who barely felt pain or emotions. The Native American was stubborn and had (literally) thick skin. The 'yellow' Chinese was sly and crafty. The 'brown' Hindoo was cowardly and deceitful, and needed a firm hand. The 'white' man, was, (of course!) noble, brave, hard-working and patient!

The general sense across Europe was that it was the white man's God-given Duty to bring Christianity, Civilization, Conscience and Clarity – the four Cs – to the fifth, the Coloured masses. Ideas of race coloured people's very outlook to life, and casual British references to the weakness, laziness and deceit of Indians were common and accepted.

A disgruntled English observer said: 'The ordinary Hindoo... no sense of shame in the matter of laziness, and considers himself horribly ill-used if he is kept to his duty. I learnt this fact during my first night on these shores. After half an hour's sleep the atmosphere was hot, very hot; ... I awoke... to see the punkah hanging motionless... the bearer fast asleep.'

Anglo-Indians

Many British initially married local Indian women. Gradually, such marriages became unacceptable, but by then there was already an important minority of people with mixed heritage, today called Anglo-Indians.

After the Uprising of 1857, the British deliberately gave Anglo-Indians many privileges (thinking they would be more loyal), including reserved government jobs and better pay than Indians... but still less than 'pure' British people. The Indian Railways became very Anglo-Indian, with special Anglo 'railway towns', as did the postal, telegraph and customs departments.

Socially, Anglo-Indians lived in a bit of a no man's land. They wouldn't mix socially with Indians, and the British wouldn't mix with them. They forged a unique identity for themselves.

Their names were pure British vintage like Philomena, Edith and Sybil. They wore Western dress and spoke with crisp British accents, learning only smatterings of 'native' languages. This fun-loving community enjoyed social evenings of foxtrot, waltzing and jiving, and prided themselves on their 'civilized' social graces (like eating with fork and knife).

A British Indian being waited upon

In 1947, there were up to 500,000 Anglo-Indians. Looming Indian independence seemed disastrous for them, and many mass-migrated to Britain, Canada, Australia and New Zealand.

Explore More

English Words from Indian Ones: A Quiz

1. British people used the phrase 'There was a cold day' to remember this Hindi command.
2. The phrase 'There was a banker' was used to remember another Hindi command.
3. This word for washing your hair comes from the Indian word for head massage, 'champi'.
4. This popular party drink is named after an Indian drink with five ingredients.
5. This bed, used for babies, is named after an Indian portable bed.
6. This colour, popular for uniforms, is named after the Urdu word for 'dust'.
7. This popular nightwear item literally means 'leg garment' in Urdu.
8. This word, meaning short note, comes from the Hindi word for 'letter'.
9. This word, meaning a kerchief tied around the head comes from the Hindi word for 'tying'.
10. This colour is named after an Indian fruit.

Find out about more such words of Indian origin that are now included in English dictionaries.

* RESEARCH official and public buildings and monuments built during the British period and note their distinctive features, such as the Chhatrapati Shivaji Maharaj Terminus (earlier Victoria Terminus), Mumbai (see pic, left).

ANSWERS: 1. *Darwaza khol de* – Open the door; 2. *Darwaza band kar* – Close the door; 3. Shampoo; 4. Punch from *panch* (five); 5. Cot after *khaat*; 6. Khaki, after *khak*; 7. Pyjama from *pai-jama*; 8. Chit from *chitthi*; 9. Bandana from *bandhana*; 10. Orange from the Portuguese *naranja* (which was from Hindi *narangi*)

11

The Rise of Nationalism

[1858–1914 CE]

'Freedom is my birthright. So long as it is awake within me, I am not old. No weapon can cut this spirit, no fire can burn it, no water can wet it, no wind can dry it.'
— 'Lokmanya' Bal Gangadhar Tilak

11

A People Find their Voice

As Indians got closer to the world through newspapers, trains and steamers, they saw for themselves the rising democracy and liberalism in the West. Indians began to consider India as one country, bound by centuries of history and culture. They wanted the British government to grant Indians the same fundamental rights that British citizens got at home.

They also compared the equality in the West to the racial scorn and second-class treatment meted out to Indians, who were denied entrance to first-class carriages and white-only clubs.

Political History

The British Parliament claimed to have Indians' interests at heart and Queen Victoria's 1858 Proclamation said, '… our subjects, of whatever race, should be freely and impartially admitted to offices in our service.' When Canada was granted Dominion Status in 1867 – self-rule with continuing allegiance to the British Crown – Indians also became hopeful. Realizing the importance of lobbying the government and building public awareness, Indians set up early political organizations like the Indian Association in Bengal and Poona Sarvajanik Sabha.

LORD LYTTON

Viceroy Lord Lytton was faced with the Great Famine on his arrival in 1876. His swift actions to control the budget ended in six million deaths. (This spirit of thrift did not extend to the extravagant Delhi Durbar of 1877.) After the futile Second Afghan War, he hastily forced through the draconian Vernacular Press Act, which let the government fine, seize or close down non-English newspapers on flimsy excuses. He also reduced the maximum age for the Imperial (Indian) Civil Service entrance examinations in London from 21 to 19 years, making it almost impossible for Indians to appear. Indians began loathing him (but the British made him an earl!).

LORD RIPON

Viceroy Lord Ripon (in office: 1880–84) was a breath of fresh air to beleaguered Indians. He ended the expensive Afghan War, repealed the Press Act, and said he wanted to 'govern India for herself and not for Englishmen'.

He improved labour conditions, organized forest conservation and focused on woefully ignored primary education. However, when the 1883 Ilbert Bill let Europeans be tried by Indian judges, the backlash by European planters and businessmen (and the newly formed English Defence Association)

Lord Ripon, a rare humane and just viceroy

resulted in the bill being watered down and Ripon's resignation. Masses of Indians came to bid farewell to that 'large-hearted nobleman'.

EARLY NATIONALIST LEADERS
The fire of nationalism was lit by educated Indians.

Dadabhai Naoroji was a professor, activist and educationist, who moved to London and founded the East India Association. He was a founding member of the Indian National Congress (INC), and wrote an explosive and influential book on India's wealth drain, *Poverty and un-British Rule in India*. The 'Grand Old Man' became one of Britain's earliest non-white Members of Parliament (MP) from the Liberal Party in July 1892!

Surendranath Banerjea successfully passed the Civil Service examination, but was rejected for being overage. He sued the Company in London and won, but was soon dismissed on flimsy grounds. His Indian National Association organized a pan-India agitation against Lord Lytton's policies. The British began calling him 'Surrender Not Banerjea'!

Sir Pherozeshah Mehta studied law in England, and was influenced by Naoroji. 'Ferocious Mehta' was a member of the Bombay Legislative Council, and in a rare achievement, was appointed to the Supreme Legislative Council in 1893. He became vice chancellor of the University of Bombay and helped found the Central Bank of India.

W.C. Bonnerjee fled his traditional brahmin family with his child bride to England where he named his first son Kamal Krishna Shelley, after the poet Percy Bysshe Shelley! Despite his utter Britishness, he was a keen Indian nationalist.

Born in 1866 to a Maharashtrian brahmin family, Gopal Krishna Gokhale became a professor and a member of the Bombay Legislative Council at a young age. He founded the influential Servants of India Society, which trained young people for public service. He was one of the main leaders of the early Indian National Congress. A mentor to Gandhi, Gokhale convinced him to return to India from South Africa.

Top: Gopal Krishna Gokhale; above: Indophile A.O. Hume

As an Englishman in the Imperial Civil Service, Allan Octavian Hume was an unlikely star of Indian nationalism. He started a large network of free elementary schools, an English High School, and organized college scholarships. His proposals for agricultural reforms to help farmers were 'stabbed to death... in the India Office.' He wanted Indians to form a united body to lobby the government. The genesis of the Indian National Congress came from his letter urging educated Indians to take the lead, saying: '... the real work must be done by the people of the country'.

INDIAN NATIONAL CONGRESS (INC)

Indian nationalists organized the first session of the INC in December 1885 in Bombay, with Hume (now retired) as general secretary, and W.C. Bonnerjee as president. There were regional committees at Karachi, Ahmedabad, Surat, Bombay, Poona, Madras, Calcutta, Benares, Allahabad, Lucknow, Agra and Lahore.

The first session of the Indian National Congress in 1885

The INC aimed to be a united pan-Indian body with 'unswerving loyalty to the British Crown', which would constitutionally oppose 'all acts opposed to principles laid down by the British Parliament...' It met annually in a different city with a new elected president. The INC was 'moderate' for its initial 20 years, with presidents like Dadabhai Naoroji, Pherozeshah Mehta, Surendranath Banerjea, Gopal Krishna Gokhale and Justice Mahadev Govind Ranade, who believed the British would agree to reasonable demands. They asked for more Indians in the Legislative Councils and Civil Service, and simultaneous Civil Service examinations in England and India. They wanted press freedom, more schools and hospitals, and Indian-owned industry.

As the INC quickly grew from 72 delegates to the thousands, British reaction was mixed. Bureaucrats were hostile, the English press in India dismissive. The viceroys listened to the demands but did not act. All insisted that the INC represented a 'microscopic minority' of India.

After years with no results, INC began constitutional agitation, rousing public opinion through pamphlets, and meetings in India and Britain. The Indian Councils Act of

1892 included more Indians in the councils, but gave no real power. An Extremist section of the Congress started vocally opposing the 'mendicant policy' of the Moderates; they wanted to demand change, not plead for it.

LORD CURZON

Into this simmering discontent came the new viceroy Lord Curzon (in office: 1899–1905), a conservative-minded Englishman – talented, arrogant and insensitive. His classmates had composed a ditty about him:

> My name is George Nathaniel Curzon,
> I am a most superior person.
> My cheek is pink, my hair is sleek,
> I dine at Blenheim once a week.

Curzon was a great scholar, who became a fierce protector of India's shabbily treated historical monuments. However, he considered Indians 'less than schoolchildren'. In 1903, he announced the partition of the Bengal province. The idea was not new nor without merit – with 78 million people across 489,500 sq km, the sprawling province was too large to be efficiently governed as one unit. However, he chose to divide it by religion – Hindu-majority West Bengal versus Muslim-majority East Bengal. Confidential British reports said, 'Bengal united is a power, Bengal divided will pull in different ways... and weaken

Viceroy Curzon's partition of Bengal led the masses to protest

opponents to our rule...' Curzon promised Muslims in Dacca (Dhaka) 'unity which they have not enjoyed since the days of the old Mussulman king...' The scathing Indian press denounced British 'divide and rule' policy.

SWADESHI AND BOYCOTT

Curzon expected Indians 'to howl until a thing is settled, then accept it', but for the first time, Indian masses protested strongly, thronging the streets crying 'Bande Mataram', vowing to use only swadeshi (Indian manufactured) goods and boycott all British goods (which would have a disastrous impact on British trade).

Rabindranath Tagore wrote *Banglar Mati, Banglar Jal* (Soil of Bengal, Water of Bengal), and *Amar Sonar Bangla*.

On Partition day, 16 October 1905, thousands of Hindus and Muslims took a dip in the Ganga, tied rakhi (friendship) bands to one another and marched down the streets, singing 'Bande Mataram'. The boycott and swadeshi movement spread to Poona, Bombay, Punjab, Delhi and Madras, disapproved of by the Moderates.

THE EXTREMISTS RISE

The Moderates thought the Extremists were asking for too much too soon, and the Extremists believed that the British government was giving too little too late. Leaders like 'Lal, Bal, and Pal' – Lala Lajpat Rai, Bal Gangadhar Tilak and Bipin Chandra Pal – started talking of mass agitation to gain Swaraj, or Indian self-rule.

By the 1906 Calcutta Congress, there was open hostility. Extremists stormed out of the pandal when outmanoeuvred in their choice of Congress president. Tilak's public speech drew 25,000 people and thunderous applause when he said that appeals were 'hopeless' and 'the remedy was boycott'. The following year, the Moderates abruptly shifted the INC session to Surat from Tilak's stronghold of Nagpur. When Dr Rashbehari Ghose was nominated as president over Lala Lajpat Rai, the Extremists disrupted speeches. Soon both sides were crying 'Shame! Shame!' and the session was suspended. The next day descended into pandemonium, as shoes, chairs and tables were flung about! The English press smugly claimed that this only proved that Indians were unfit for representative institutions.

The Surat split was formalized in 1908. The Moderates, who controlled the leadership, finalized a Congress constitution enshrining their beliefs. The government came down hard on the Extremists, who scattered.

LOKMANYA TILAK

As a student, Bal Gangadhar Tilak (1856–1920) came to understand the explosive power of the pen, which led him to set up newspapers: the *Kesari* ('The Lion') and *The Mahratta*, which harshly criticized British policies. A man of fierce intellect, he was an advocate of modern English education. His New English School and Deccan Education Society provided inexpensive education. He became very popular after his 1897 trial and imprisonment for sedition, and became known as 'Lokmanya' (respected by the people).

Tilak vehemently defended Hindu traditions and started popular mass festivals like Shiva Jayanti (Shivaji's birthday) and Ganesh Chaturthi to rouse Indian cultural pride.

He joined the INC, but found it too appeasing. He believed that the rulers and the ruled could never be friends.

FUN FACT! Sri Aurobindo, the saint of Pondicherry, originally fled to that French territory because he was wanted by the British for a bomb conspiracy.

After the Surat split, he was jailed in Burma for six years. Released in 1914, he began the All India Home Rule League, adopting the slogan, 'Swaraj is my birthright and I will have it.' He reconciled with the INC and worked for Hindu–Muslim unity through the Lucknow Pact with Muhammad Ali Jinnah.

LALA LAJPAT RAI

From a humble background, Lala Lajpat Rai (1865–1928) earned his law degree through scholarships. A follower of Dayanand Saraswati, he started the DAV

Lal, Bal and Pal: the iconic nationalist trio

(Dayanand Anglo-Vedic) school in Lahore, with Lala Hansraj. He quickly became a fiery orator of the INC. This 'Punjab Kesri' (Lion of Punjab) spent much time on social work, such as famine and earthquake relief. Frustrated with the Moderates, 'Lalaji' organized the boycott and swadeshi agitation in Punjab, where he had a large following. In the USA during the First World War, he started the Indian Home Rule League and the *Young India Magazine* to spread awareness about India's plight. He returned to India in 1920 and reunited with the INC. Often jailed, he died in 1928 due to police brutality during a protest.

BIPIN CHANDRA PAL

An ardent nationalist and a prolific Bengali journalist, Bipin Chandra Pal (1858–1932) wrote for, or started, many journals like *Tribune, New India, Bande Mataram* and *Amrita Bazaar Patrika.* He encouraged passive resistance to 'compel the submission of any power that set itself against us'. The British called him 'the chief purveyor of seditious ideas who promulgated the doctrine of Swaraj'.

REVOLUTIONARIES

Political assassinations spread across the West in the late 19th century, including those of generals (Spanish), presidents (French and USA) and monarchs (Italian and Austrian). A revolutionary movement sparked in India too as young Bengali bhadralok formed underground cells and targeted high-profile government officials.

Aurobindo and his brother Barin Ghose provided martial training through the Anushilan Samiti, and launched the radical newspapers *Jugantar* and *Bande Mataram.* They even sent someone to Paris to learn bomb making from exiled Russian radicals. Revolutionaries distributed pamphlets to build public sympathy and emphasize that civilian deaths were by accident not design. They wanted to show personal courage and sacrifice to inspire other Indians and shatter the myth of British invincibility.

In 1907, the Bengal Lieutenant Governor's train was derailed. Two Englishwomen were killed from a mis-targeted bomb, and a munitions factory discovered in the Ghose garden. London was stunned when Madanlal

Dhingra gunned down an official on its streets in 1909. The authorities started a severe crackdown on underground cells and the 'Indian Reign of Terror'.

SRI AUROBINDO
Well-off Aurobindo Ghose (1872–1950) studied at Cambridge and came 11th in the Civil Service exam, but moved to Calcutta during agitation against the partition of Bengal. A major voice in the swadeshi and boycott movements, he also secretly helped revolutionaries like 'Bagha' Jatin. He was arrested by the British in the Alipore Bomb case. When released due to lack of evidence, he went to French-ruled Pondicherry and became the spiritual guru Sri Aurobindo.

MORLEY–MINTO REFORMS
Lord Curzon was succeeded by Lord Minto (in office: 1905–1910). Britain's new government agreed to address Indian demands through the Morley–Minto reforms in 1909 (John Morley was the new Secretary of State for India), which increased Indian numbers across the government, and allowed for their election (rather than nomination). However, they introduced separate electorates for Muslims.

King George, in India for the 1911 Delhi Durbar, reversed the partition of Bengal, but also abruptly switched British India's capital from Calcutta to Delhi, in view of the agitations and revolutionary activity in Bengal.

FUN FACT! When the British made Delhi the new capital, just 100,000 people lived in the devastated city. A hundred years later, it is touching 25 million!

In 1912, a bomb was thrown into Viceroy Lord Hardinge's elephant howdah during a procession,

seriously injuring him. The fires for
freedom were smouldering away.

THE MUSLIM LEAGUE

By the 1870s, Britain began
projecting British India as the largest
'Mohammedan' power in the
world and claimed that Britain was
'protecting' the Ottoman Empire
against Russia. It also started
claiming that all Indian Muslims

*Sir Syed Ahmad Khan did
not see eye to eye with the
Indian National Congress*

were a united class that needed 'exceptional assistance' like
scholarships and reserved government positions.

The National Muhammadan Association was founded
in 1877. The Anjuman-i-Islam came up in different
cities to promote Muslim culture and Western
knowledge. Indian Muslims began developing a distinct
political identity.

When the pan-Indian INC was formed in 1885, Muslim
delegates attended its second session, and the lawyer
Badruddin Tyabji was invited to be the next Congress
president. However, Muslim leaders like Syed Amir Ali
and Sir Syed Ahmad Khan were convinced that Hindu
'numerical superiority' would work against 'Muslim
interests'. Muslim upper classes largely stayed away.

When the INC was credited for the Morley–Minto
reforms, a group of prominent Muslims met the new
viceroy, Lord Minto, requesting that Muslims should
get a 'fair share' of the increased native representation.
They wanted a minimum fixed proportion of Muslims
in government and separate electorates (Muslim voters
would vote for reserved Muslim seats). Lord Minto

The First World War

In 1914, tensions between European countries escalated into the First World War. Germany, Austria and Turkey were allied against Great Britain, France, Russia and, later, the USA. Nine million soldiers and 13 million civilians died in this Great War as modern technology showed its dark side through planes, submarines and chemical weapons.

Indians supported Britain and nationalists toned down anti-British rhetoric. The British Indian Army provided 10 per cent of British manpower, almost 1.25 million soldiers and support staff. Nearly 75,000 Indians died. The princely states funded millions of pounds worth of supplies. Indians hoped that their generous contribution in Britain in lives, supplies and money would be rewarded, but they faced only freshly broken promises after the war.

Above: Indian soldiers at war; right: Khuda Dad Khan became the first Indian to win a Victoria Cross in a war that proved futile for Indians

happily accepted this and the British congratulated themselves as this prevented '62 millions [Muslims] from joining the ranks of the seditious opposition'.

The Morley–Minto reforms bolstered the idea that people would vote for co-religionists rather than the best candidate, and that a candidate would work for co-religionists, rather than all the voters.

The All India Muslim League was formed in Dacca (now Dhaka) in 1906 to protect the interests of Indian Muslims, support the Bengal partition and remain loyal to the British. Its first president was the Aga Khan, and the founders were the aristocracy of the United Provinces.

The majestic Raj Bhavan (Government House), Kolkata

Culture

Elements of British culture became part of Indian life. Art, architecture and literature were influenced by Western aesthetics. The novel and modern theatre prospered.

ARCHITECTURE

British buildings were initially built in the neoclassical style, imitating ancient Roman architecture in their grandeur of scale and simplicity of form, seen in the Raj Bhavan in Kolkata. By the mid-19th century, the Gothic Revival style was the rage in Britain, with medieval elements like pointed arches, window tracery and spires. Bombay has many examples in the Chhatrapati Shivaji Maharaj Terminus, the Bombay High Court and Bombay University, whose Rajabhai Clock Tower strongly resembles London's Big Ben! The new Indo-Saracenic style saw Mughal domes and arches with classical European styles, such as in the Rashtrapati Bhavan and the Parliament House in Delhi.

In private life, the British lived in bungalows (derived from 'bangla', or house in the Bengal style), typically with a raised platform, high ceilings, large windows and covered verandahs.

Top: Paluskar, saviour of Hindustani classical music; below: Rukmini Arundale, dance pioneer

PERFORMING ARTS

Indian classical dance and music had languished without royal patronage. With renewed pride in India's heritage, educated Indians re-popularized them.

Pandit Vishnu Digambar Paluskar 'saved' Indian classical music through his Gandharva Mahavidyalaya, which taught classical music in a college format. He also started ticketed public performances. Pandit Vishnu Narayan Bhatkhande classified the Indian ragas into the still-used *thaat* system. He also wrote the first modern textbooks on Hindustani classical music.

Rukmini Devi, a Tamil brahmin, defied convention to marry an older British theosophist, Dr George Arundale. Inspired by the famous Russian ballerina, Anna Pavlova, she popularized the obscure Sadhir dance of the temple devadasis as Bharatanatyam.

The gramophone reached India in 1901 and the first Indian recording was released in 1902 by Gauhar Jaan. Born Angelina Yeoward of Armenian and Anglo-Indian descent, and a famous singer and courtesan in Calcutta, she became the first recording star of India, with 600 short records in 10 languages. She popularized Hindustani classical thumris, *dadra*s, bhajans and *tarana*s.

THEATRE

Distinct styles came up in Hindi, Bengali, Marathi, Tamil and other languages, influenced by Western-style theatre.

Tagore's Tales

The leading light of the illustrious Tagore family, Rabindranath Tagore wrote the national anthems of two countries (India and Bangladesh) and contributed to Sri Lanka's! Born in 1861, Rabindranath was raised in the vibrant Tagore mansion in Jorasanko and was a polymath.

The Indian peasant's miserable existence in rural East Bengal sparked a lifelong compassion for humanity, and a strong nationalist and reformist spirit in him.

Rabindranath (right) on stage

He created an accessible Bengali through hundreds of poems, novels, plays, dance dramas and short stories. His songs, for which he also composed the music, the wonderful Rabindra Sangeet, are still sung widely. In 1901, he founded an ashram at Santiniketan. A great traveller, he became an ambassador for Indian culture and was the first Asian to win the Nobel Prize for Literature in 1913 for his *Gitanjali*.

An excerpt from a poem:

'Who are you, reader, reading my poems in wonder an hundred years hence?

... From your blossoming garden gather fragrant memories of the vanished flowers of an hundred years before.

In the joy of your heart may you feel the living joy that sang one spring morning, sending its glad voice across an hundred years.'

Theatre also became a way of social protest, both against the British and social evils. A famous example is the Bengali *Nil Darpan*, written in 1860 by Dinabandhu Mitra, which highlighted the slave-like conditions of indigo labourers under European plantation owners. Ishwar Chandra Vidyasagar got so involved while watching the play that he threw a shoe at the villain! When indignant European planters sued the British publisher for libel, his

1,000-rupee fine was paid on the spot by Kaliprasanna Singha, the great Bengali patron of arts.

The Parsi Natak Mandali started Parsi theatre in 1853. Their first play was *Rustom and Sohrab* from the Persian *Shahnama*. Theatre groups travelled around. Their painted backdrops, stage effects, dialogue and songs would later morph into Indian films! Early themes included Indianized Shakespeare and Indian mythology.

CINEMA

In 1895, the Lumière brothers unveiled their first 'living photographic pictures' in Paris. A special screening soon came to Bombay. An Indian photographer, H.S. Bhatavadekar, promptly imported a movie camera and shot a 1899 documentary of a wrestling match in Bombay, and the 1903 Delhi Durbar.

The first Indian movie was Dadasaheb Phalke's 1913 *Raja Harishchandra*, which he wrote, directed, printed and edited! Dadasaheb Torney had released *Shree Pundalik* earlier in 1912, but it had a British cameraman. Dadasaheb Phalke, a Sanskrit scholar and friend of Tilak, wanted his films to inspire nationalism.

About 1,300 silent films were made between 1912 and 1934. Barely 25 survive! The film was prone to decay and fire; many were destroyed for their silver content.

Poet-nationalist
Subramania Bharati

LITERATURE AND LANGUAGE

With regional language presses, adventure and detective novels became popular, especially in Bengali and Hindi. Serialized novels in magazines attracted many readers. Devaki Nandan Khatri's serialized adventure novel *Chandrakanta* (1892) was a runaway success. Thousands of Indians learned to read Hindi to follow it!

A leading Tamil poet was Subramania Bharati who was an active INC member. He wrote thousands of poems with patriotic, religious, social and children's themes, and criticized the blind following of convention.

Born in Bombay, Rudyard Kipling (a Nobel laureate in 1907), after studying in England, returned to India for seven years as a reporter in 'a joyous homecoming'. His next 40 years in England were spent writing about India! *Kim* and *The Jungle Book* are beloved classics. Though he loved India, he supported British rule for the country.

Industrialization in India

After British deindustrialization of traditional Indian industries, modern industry slowly began under the managing agency system (*see next section*). In textiles, jute and coal mining, but also British-controlled ones like leather tanneries and sugar mills, India became a major exporter of raw materials, especially jute, which was exported to Dundee in Scotland.

The first textile mill was started in Bombay by Cowasjee Nanabhoy in 1853. Cotton textiles remained mainly with Parsis and Gujaratis. By 1947, more than 200 mills were concentrated around Bombay and Ahmedabad. The first Indian jute mill was a Scottish experiment in 1855, but by 1900, Calcutta had surpassed Dundee in jute production.

THE MANAGING AGENCY

Managing agencies were private companies that ran public companies on legal contract. Managing agents were usually British people living in India, who raised capital from European investors. One called Andrew Yule managed a staggering 37 companies including tea gardens, power utilities, jute mills, coal mines, a railway and a steamship company! The powerful agents dominated the Calcutta area and were paid handsomely whether or not the companies did well. They worked for their own benefit, not the sharehholders'!

INDIAN BUSINESS COMMUNITIES

The first to work with the British, the Parsis became wealthy philanthropists, prominent in education and industry.

Sir Jamsetjee Jeejeebhoy became rich in the China opium trade and funded hospitals, schools and charitable homes in Bombay. He was the first Indian to be knighted.

Pioneering industrialist Jamsetji Nusserwanji Tata was a global visionary who founded the Tata Group, India's biggest conglomerate to date. Devoted to India, he built a unique hotel (the Taj Mahal Hotel at Colaba), and his descendants fulfilled his dreams of building an iron and steel company, a hydroelectric plant and a world-class university.

Pioneering industrialist Jamsetjee Jeejeebhoy

The Marwaris or Rajasthani merchant class, migrated to Bombay and Calcutta in the late 19th century and became traders, brokers and distributors for British goods.

Many set up capital-intensive industries in the 1920s, such as jute, cotton and sugar mills. G.D. Birla started many industries including car manufacturing. His Ambassador dominated Indian roads for the next 50 years! He was closely associated with Gandhi and the freedom struggle.

The Tamil Chettiars were mainly involved in moneylending and financing export crops. They became a major part of the Tamil diaspora in Ceylon, Burma, Malaya, Singapore, Java, Thailand and Indo-China, with rubber, sugar cane, tea and coffee plantations.

What in the World Was Happening! (1858-1914 CE)

Asia
- CHINA: Europeans gain many concessions. In 1900, the Boxer rebellion breaks out. In 1911, Dr Sun Yat Sen overthrows the Qing dynasty.
- JAPAN: Meiji Restoration industrializes and modernizes Japan.

Europe
- The Industrial Revolution spreads. Powered ships, internal combustion engine cars and powered flight are invented.
- Germany and Italy unify into nations.
- Much of Asia and Africa is divided up among European imperial powers. The Suez Canal shortens distances.
- Queen Victoria rules (1837–1901) in England's greatest hour.
- The First World War breaks out in 1914.

Americas
- The American Civil War (1860–65) emancipates black slaves. American capitalism flourishes.
- The USA gains control of Cuba, Puerto Rico, and the Philippines after the Spanish–American War.

Africa
- European exploration and colonization.

Australia and New Zealand
- In 1893, New Zealand is the first to enact women's suffrage.

Explore More

• FIND out about similarities between British and Indian buildings of the period. For starters, see left: one of the clock towers is Indian and the other one, British!

• RESEARCH the theatre and films of the period covered in the chapter and note the difference between the two.

• COLLECT information about the etchings and postcards of the period and make a scrapbook with photos or photocopies.

CORONATION CINEMATOGRAPH
AND VARIETY HALL

SANDHURST ROAD, GIRGAUM.

BEAU IDEAL PROGRAMME.

1½ Hours Show   Throughout   1½ Hours Show
                       this week

RAJA HARISCHANDRA.

A powerfully instructive subject from the Indian mythology. First film of Indian manufacture. Specially prepared at enormous cost. Original scenes from the sacred city of Benares. Sure to appeal to our Hindu patrons.

Miss IRENE DELMAR.
(Duette and Dance)

THE McCLEMENTS.
(Comical Sketch)

ALEXANDROFF.
THE WONDERFUL FOOT-JUGGLER

TIP-TOP COMICS.

Time :—6 to 7-30 ; 8 to 9-30 ; 10 to 11-30
and 11-45 to 1-15.

Note   Double Rates of Admission

Above: A poster for the play Raja Harishchandra; left: A postcard of Taj Mahal Hotel in Mumbai

Independence at Last

[1914-1947 CE]

'Generations to come, it may well be, will scarce believe that such a man as this one ever in flesh and blood walked upon this Earth... Mahatma Gandhi's life achievement stands unique in political history. He has invented a completely new and humane means for the liberation war of an oppressed country, and practised it with greatest energy and devotion.'
—Albert Einstein

12
A New Path for the World

India now struggled for her independence in a unique, never-before-seen way, peacefully and with the reluctant consent of her occupiers. Mahatma Gandhi's new method of non-violent satyagraha would shine like a beacon across the world, an inspiration for future leaders like Martin Luther King and Nelson Mandela.

India enthusiastically supported Britain during the First World War with men, money and materials, and Delhi's iconic India Gate was built to honour the 75,000 Indian soldiers who died. After the war, Indians looked forward to the new rights that they had been promised by the British (but got Jallianwala Bagh instead).

The Montague–Chelmsford Reforms

What with new-found Congress unity as the Extremists and the Moderates made up, the recent bonhomie between the Congress and the Muslim League through the Lucknow Pact, the dangerously popular Home Rule movements and the revolutionaries, the British felt the pressure to concede some political reforms to India.

Through the 1919 reforms, led by the liberal Secretary of State Montagu and the rather less liberal viceroy Lord Chelmsford (in office: 1916–1921), a new 200-seat lawmaking body was formed, and more people were given the right to vote. However, now even Sikhs, Christians, Anglo-Indians and Europeans got separate electorates. Provinces took over some portfolios like agriculture, education and public works, but the viceroy still kept the real power!

Viceroy Lord Chelmsford said, '*Festina Lente*' (make haste slowly). The INC thought that the 'haste' was too slow, and the British were creating social divisions too rapidly, and so boycotted the elections.

The Rowlatt Act

When the First World War began, a new 'Defence of the Realm Act' gave the government great power within Britain – during wartime. The government could use private property, replace trials with court martials and restrict freedom of speech. A more drastic Indian version gave them almost unlimited powers to jail suspected revolutionaries – as long as Britain remained at war. Soon, an American newspaper wrote, 'The whole country is seething… 300 Indians have been hanged, 700 transported and 10,000 interned without trial.'

After the war, British judge Justice Rowlatt made suggestions about political terrorism in India. The 1919 Rowlatt Act gave the government permanent powers to gag the press, make arrests without warrants, jail people without trial and even hand death sentences without appeal! India exploded in disbelief. Lawyer and Congress leader Motilal Nehru called the government a 'mad bull that goes about attacking all who dare stand up against it'.

Agitations were stronger in Punjab, already simmering with unrest under its imperialist lieutenant governor, Sir Michael O'Dwyer. Punjab had sent far too many of its boys to fight in the war, food was becoming unaffordable and new unpopular taxes made people resentful.

Jallianwala Bagh

Amritsar sparked with riots when two Congress leaders were jailed for anti-Rowlatt speeches. Public assemblies were promptly banned. However, 13 April 1919 was the public holiday of Baisakhi, and 20,000 people gathered in a totally enclosed ground called Jallianwala Bagh. Many were out celebrating while others were peacefully protesting the Rowlatt Bill.

In marched Brigadier General Reginald Dyer. Without asking the people to leave, his 90 Indian soldiers fired 1,600 bullets at the unarmed men, women and children, aiming specifically at the narrow exits. Many jumped into a well and drowned. Between 370–1,000 people died and around 1,200 were injured. Dyer openly admitted that he 'had made up his mind to punish them for having assembled'.

In the following days, Indians were made to crawl on the street and public cages were set up. A crowd in Gujranwala was machine-gunned by an airplane!

As public outrage grew in India, both Dyer and O'Dwyer were dismissed. However, there was a shocking outpouring of British support. Dyer was hailed as the 'Hero of

FUN FACT! The 'Butcher' of Jallianwala Bagh, General Dyer, was called the 'Saviour of India' by British newspapers. The British public raised today's equivalent of a million pounds for his legal defence.

the Amritsar Shooting', and 26,000 pounds collected for his legal defence.

Rabindranath Tagore returned his knighthood (which he had received in 1915), claiming this 'revealed our helplessness ... praised by most papers, which have brutally made fun of our sufferings'.

Jallianwala Bagh became a critical turning point, as it showed Indians that most British had a contemptuous disregard for Indian lives.

Gandhi

Mohandas Karamchand Gandhi (1869–1948) was born on 2 October, the youngest child of the diwan of the small princely state of Porbandar in Gujarat. Young 'Moniya' was greatly influenced by his mother's austere religious fasts. He studied law in London, where he was involved with the small, but thriving, vegetarian movement. He made close British friends and even studied dancing, violin, French, and English diction!

In 1893, Gandhi was invited to legally represent Indian merchants in South Africa, which had a large

From top: A young Mohandas (left) with his brother; in South Africa; at the Kheda protests in 1918; spinning in the late 1940s

population of formerly indentured Indian labour. Here he got a shocking lesson in imperial arrogance. Despite his valid ticket and smart Western apparel, he was thrown out of a first-class carriage, just because a white passenger objected to having an 'Asiatic' in there.

Gandhi stayed on in South Africa to fight for the rights of Indians – launching the Natal Indian Congress, petitioning officials, and creating public support through speeches, pamphlets and newspapers. The South Africans got very annoyed, and once, an angry white mob pelted him with stones and rotten eggs! However, Gandhi still considered himself a loyal British subject and raised 1,100 Indian volunteer ambulance-men during the Boer War there.

He was influenced by the anti-capitalist and anti-war writings of John Ruskin and Leo Tolstoy, and started the Phoenix Settlement and Tolstoy Farm, communes where people lived and worked together as equals.

Gandhi gradually began leading peaceful civil resistance, which he called 'satyagraha', for Indian rights. He was jailed a few times as he went on long marches, which included women, and got masses of Indians in South Africa involved, until all his demands were finally agreed to in 1914.

In 1915, Gandhi was persuaded to leave to work for the Indian cause. A British official wrote, 'The saint has left our shores... I sincerely hope forever!'

Gandhi returned to India, switched to wearing a dhoti and turban, and spent some years relearning his country. He found the INC too placid and westernized, and it found him too radical! He founded a satyagraha ashram on the banks of the Sabarmati in Ahmedabad, where he and his followers did manual work like farming and spinning, and worked passionately for women's rights, vegetarianism and against untouchability.

His small regional successes made him famous – the Champaran satyagraha for miserable indigo farmers, and his fast unto death in Ahmedabad, against his own friend, the textile mill owner Ambalal Sarabhai!

Gandhi gradually became the undisputed leader of the Congress and reorganized it – creating a Working Committee for daily operations, strengthening regional branches and making it affordable even for the poorest. A great fundraiser, Gandhi lifted the Congress out of near-bankruptcy to an annual income of millions of rupees.

Sardar Vallabhbhai Patel

Born in Gujarat to a farming family, Vallabhbhai Patel (1875–1950) studied law. He was finally able to go to England at the age of 36, where he topped his law course.

He returned and became a suave, successful, bridge-playing lawyer, who dressed in

Vallabhbhai Patel and Gandhi during the Bardoli satyagraha

natty Western suits. He was initially sceptical of Gandhi's ways and methods, but soon dedicated himself to the freedom struggle.

In 1928, his leadership of the Bardoli satyagraha was a great success. He grew close to Gandhi when they were together in Yerawada jail, and became the main organizer and fund-raiser for the Congress. He was known as Gandhi's 'blind follower', one of the few to support him even when he suspended the non-cooperation movement.

Gandhi named Jawaharlal his successor

He was one of the first Congress leaders to realize the inevitability of Partition, and convince other leaders.

Jawaharlal Nehru

The son of the influential Allahabad lawyer Motilal Nehru was brought up in affluence. 'Joe' went to Harrow and Cambridge, and became a lawyer, returning to India in 1912. Jawaharlal Nehru (1889–1964) eventually became a loyal follower of Gandhi, but also a fiery, committed socialist. He was the first to push for Purna Swaraj (total independence) in the Congress, and after the 1929 Lahore session, emerged as one of the main leaders of the Indian independence movement.

After the 1937 provincial elections that swept Congress to power, Nehru's popularity with the common masses was unmatched. On 15 January 1941, Gandhi said, 'I have said for some years and say so now that not Rajaji [C. Rajagopalachari] but Jawaharlal will be my successor.'

Bhimrao Ambedkar

'Babasaheb' Ambedkar as a young man

Bhimrao Ramji Ambedkar (1891–1956) was born in the 'untouchable' Maharashtrian Mahar caste, and had to sit outside his classroom on a special sack and wait for the peon to give him drinking water. A very bright student, he was the first Dalit to attend Elphinstone College in Bombay, and was sponsored to go abroad. He got (two!) doctorates from Columbia University in New York and the London School of Economics.

He worked as a lawyer in Bombay and began agitating unceasingly for Dalit rights, like the right to use village wells and enter temples. In 1935, Ambedkar became principal of the Government Law College in Bombay and settled there with a personal library of more than 50,000 books. He declared, 'Though I was born a Hindu, I solemnly assure you, I will not die as a Hindu', and after much study, became Buddhist (along with 500,000 followers) in 1956.

Khilafat and Non-cooperation Movements

In 1920, Gandhi launched a mass non-cooperation movement together with the brothers Maulana Shaukat Ali and Maulana Mohammad Ali, who wanted to restore the caliph to the Ottoman throne. The Congress wanted the repeal of the Rowlatt Act and Swaraj (self-rule) all within one year!

Gandhi travelled widely, asking ordinary Indians to boycott foreign goods, government schools and courts, to spin swadeshi Indian cotton themselves, and most importantly, to stay completely peaceful through it all.

It was a huge success. Cloth imports plunged, people started burning foreign cloth publicly, and around 100,000 students left colleges.

PUBLIC MEETING
AND
BONFIRE OF FOREIGN CLOTHES

Will take place at the Maidan near Elphinstone Mills, Opp. Elphinstone Road Station

On SUNDAY the 9th Inst. at 6-30 P. M.

When the Resolution of the Karachi Khilafat Conference and another Congratulating Ali Brothers and others will be passed.

All are requested to attend in Swadeshi Clothes of Khadi. Those who have not yet given away their Foreign Clothes are requested to send them to their respective Ward Congress Committees for inclusion in the GREAT BONFIRE.

A public notice exhorting people to join the swadeshi and boycott movement

Even as prisons were stuffed with peaceful protestors, Indians flocked to join the Congress. Gandhi became the 'sole executive authority' for Congress, with all the power.

In February 1922, Gandhi's nightmare was realized when some agitators burnt down a police station in the small town of Chauri-Chaura, killing 22 policemen. Gandhi immediately suspended the civil disobedience movement at its peak, to the horror of jailed Congress leaders, who began to deeply doubt his political wisdom.

Gandhi was soon jailed for sedition, but released after 22 months due to illness. The Khilafat movement too floundered, when the Turkish nationalists were victorious after all, but abolished the very post of caliph!

Bardoli
In 1928, Gandhi asked Vallabhbhai Patel to lead a small satyagraha out of Bardoli in Gujarat to protest an increase in taxes. It went off beautifully. Not a single farmer paid tax, and when the British auctioned off their land, no one bought it! They were forced to cancel the tax increase.

The Simon Commission
The 1919 reforms required a ten-year review. A 1927 British parliamentary mission, headed by Sir John Simon, arrived to a national boycott, as it had no Indians. British MPs touring India were greeted by thousands of black flags and protestors crying, 'Simon, Go Back! Simon, Go Back!' The chant became so popular that some Indians in Assam called Sir John 'Simon Go-Back sahib'! Lala Lajpat Rai died of police brutality during protests, saying, '... the blows struck at me today will be the last nails in the coffin of British rule.' The Simon Commission

recommended Dominion Status that Indians had been clamouring for, but younger leaders like Jawaharlal now wanted complete independence.

Purna Swaraj
At the 1929 INC session at Lahore, led by Jawaharlal Nehru, Purna Swaraj became the official goal, and 26 January 1930 was fixed as India's freedom day.

Dandi March
That day came and went, with no Swaraj in sight. Gandhi decided to agitate against the unfair Salt Tax. Congress leaders were sceptical! Gandhi and his followers set off

The famous Dandi March, which ended in Gandhi making salt against the law

on foot, walking 300 km to the seaside town of Dandi.

On 6 April 1930, in the full glare of international press, Gandhi made sea salt 'illegally'. This simple act of publicly defying the all-powerful British government, and their cruel reprisal – beating and injuring unarmed, peaceful protestors – electrified the nation. There were general strikes, and men, women and children all came out to protest British rule. The British responded heavily, and 100,000 people were jailed in short order. Soon, most of the Congress leadership was arrested, including Gandhi and the Nehrus. The press was gagged and protests banned.

First Round Table Conference

To show that they did care about Indians, the British hosted the First Round Table Conference in London in November 1930, inviting important princes, Muhammad Ali Jinnah (leader of the All-India Muslim League) and B.R. Ambedkar. As Gandhi was in jail, the Congress refused to go, claiming it was like 'performing Hamlet without the Prince of Denmark'! Ambedkar's demand for separate electorates for the Depressed Classes (Dalits) sent out ripples of shock and the conference closed a failure.

Gandhi–Irwin Pact

The world watched the Dandi March (and judged) as 'The British beat the Indians with batons and rifle butts. The Indians neither cringed nor complained nor retreated. That made England powerless and India invincible.' The frustrated British released Gandhi in January 1931 and announced a Second Round Table Conference – with

him this time! Future British PM Winston Churchill was outraged when Gandhi and Viceroy Irwin met beforehand, '... at the nauseating and humiliating spectacle of this seditious fakir, striding half-naked to negotiate on equal terms'.

Irwin agreed to abolish the Salt Tax and release Congress prisoners, while Gandhi suspended his civil disobedience, and made a public appeal for violent revolutionaries to lay down arms.

Gandhi in Darwen, Lancashire, England, with mill workers

Churchill's Hysteria

British prime minister Winston Churchill (in office: 1940–45 & 1951–55) openly declared, 'I hate Indians. They are a beastly people with a beastly religion.' Viceroy Lord Wavell muttered into his diary that 'He knows as much of the Indian problem as George III did of the American colonies.'

Sir Winston Churchill

When Gandhi fasted (again) at the end of the Second World War, PM Churchill 'worked himself into one of his states of indignation over India, at how this, 'our hour of triumph everywhere in the world, was not the time to cringe before a miserable little old man.'

Churchill wrote, 'I do not think Gandhi has the slightest intention of dying, and I imagine he has been eating better meals than I have...' Churchill hampered all the viceroy's attempts to agree terms with the Congress, and the latter wrote: 'The Prime Minister passionately hopes that the fulfilment of our pledges can still somehow be prevented... and makes difficulties at every stage....'

Gandhi in England

Gandhi sailed to London with two goats and a collapsible charkha. European and American newspapers were full of his strange habits – his goats, loincloth, peculiar diet and weekly days of silence. Huge crowds gathered to hear him in England. When invited to tea with the king, he wore only his dhoti and a shawl, and when asked if he had worn enough clothing, he replied, 'The King had enough on for both of us!'

The conference itself failed disastrously again.

Viceroy Lord Willingdon began another harsh round of jailings, and Gandhi and

Gandhi was quick with a quip – when asked by a English journalist what he thought about Western Civilization, he said he thought it was a good idea!

FUN FACT!

Congress leaders were soon back in. British PM Ramsay Macdonald's Communal Award divided Indian society even more by giving separate electorates to Forward Castes, Lower Castes, Muslims, Buddhists, Sikhs, Christians and Anglo-Indians.

With his demand for separate electorates for Dalits, B.R. Ambedkar clashed fiercely with Gandhi, who wanted reform in Hinduism, not division. From inside Yerawada jail, Gandhi began a deadly serious fast, scaring Hindus into coming together and giving Dalits access to temples, wells and roads. Ambedkar called this a 'political stunt', but his will was broken by immense public pressure. Eventually, under the Poona Pact, a single Hindu electorate was agreed to, with reserved seats for Dalits.

The Revolutionary Movement

Revolutionary movements picked up, imbued with a new spirit of socialism.

The US-based Ghadar Party published a weekly newspaper with the slogan '*Angrezi Raj ka Dushman*' ('Enemy of the British Raj')!

Jatindranath Mukherjee (known as 'Bagha' Jatin for his having killed an attacking tiger) headed the revolutionary outfit Jugantar with the motto '*Amra marbo, jagat jagbe*' ('We shall die to awaken the world').

Ram Prasad Bismil composed powerful revolutionary poetry. He formed the Hindustan Republican Association

From left:
Revolutionaries Bhagat
Singh, Sukhdev and
Rajguru

(HRA), and was hanged for the Kakori train robbery. He wrote:

> *Sarfaroshi ki tamanna ab hamare dil mein hai*
> *Dekhana hai zor kitna bazu-e-katil mein hai*
> (Our hearts are filled with the desire to get our heads cut off/ Now let's see how strong the killer's arms are.)

Chandrashekhar Azad, who gave the HRA a socialist direction, was betrayed and killed in a shootout.

Bhagat Singh was attracted to Marxism. He was involved in the murder of British police officer John Saunders and was hanged on 23 March 1931, along with Sukhdev and Rajguru.

GOVERNMENT OF INDIA ACT, 1935

The Government of India Act, 1935, gave more power to Indians. Provinces became self-ruled by elected ministers, under British-appointed Governors. In the 1937 provincial elections, the INC swept seven of 11 provinces and formed coalitions in another two.

The Muslim League lost badly and now wanted to form coalitions with the Congress. When rebuffed, Jinnah became upset, claiming (rather unfairly!): 'Muslims can expect neither justice nor fair play under the Congress'.

CONGRESS RULE

Once in power, the INC improved education and healthcare, and increased press freedom. Its membership quickly grew by 10 times, to five million people!

However, in 1939, when the Second World War broke out and Britain declared war on Germany, it announced

India as a 'belligerent' (fighting on its side) without discussion. Congress ministries resigned in outrage.

Jinnah and the Muslim League

Born to a prosperous Gujarati Ismaili family in Karachi, Muhammad Ali Jinnah (1876–1948) studied law in London, where he developed a reputation for never repeating a silk tie. The English said, 'Do not forget... Jinnah is a pure Englishman by education, outlook and affection.'

Jinnah was extremely successful in Bombay, where he joined the Congress and was strictly against the Muslim League's demand for separate electorates, claiming it would 'divide the nation against itself'. In fact, he left the Congress in 1920 because he disliked Gandhi's free use of religion! He left India, but was coaxed back by Muslim League leaders in 1934.

Now, when the Muslim League failed in the 1937 provincial elections, and could not form coalitions either, Jinnah started to believe that Indian Muslims would be powerless in independent, democratic India. Of course, this conveniently ignored the regional Punjabi and Bengali Muslim parties that had won, and INC's Muslim candidates, who had swept their reserved seats!

Jinnah (front, second from left) with other leaders of the Muslim League

Jinnah now changed course completely. He positioned the Muslim League as a 'national' spokesperson of Indian Muslims by allying with regional Muslim parties. He then systematically

Netaji Subhash Chandra Bose

Born in 1897, Subhash Chandra Bose qualified for the Imperial Civil Service, but chose to fight for India's freedom after the Jallianwala Bagh massacre. He worked with the Congress, was jailed 11 times and deported and exiled periodically, before being pushed out of the Congress due to differences with Gandhi.

During the Second World War, Bose escaped house arrest in Calcutta (disguised as an Afghan Pathan) and escaped to Germany, pursued by murderous British secret agents! In 1943, he went secretly to Singapore by submarine and formed the Indian National Army (INA) from the Indian Army prisoners of war captured by Japan. The INA had the first all-female Rani of Jhansi regiment, which included Tamil-origin women from Malaysia.

The INA marched from Rangoon with a cry of 'Chalo Dilli' ('Let's Go to Delhi'!) and briefly captured some parts of north-east India, and the Andaman and Nicobar Islands. After the Japanese surrender in September 1945, Bose reportedly disappeared in a plane crash.

The notorious Red Fort trials of high-profile INA 'traitors' caused a great upsurge of public sympathy and inflamed the Indian armed forces, the backbone of British colonial strength. A peaceful air force mutiny in January 1946 was followed by a Royal Indian Navy mutiny in February, where 78 of 88 ships mutinied. This really shook the British.

Netaji at a Congress meeting in 1939

travelled across India, convincing Muslims that they needed 'organized protection' from the Congress 'Hindu Raj', claiming that Congress Muslim legislators were just stooges. It was incendiary and it worked.

Muslim League membership jumped to over two million – at the cost of widespread distrust between the Muslims and the rest of India. In 1940, Jinnah claimed Muslims needed a separate country, Pakistan ('Land of the Pure') – from P(unjab), A(fghania), K(ashmir), S(ind), and (Baluchis)TAN.

Jinnah's agitation seems cynical. He always knew that his new country would have less than half of all Indian Muslims. If he truly believed in a horrific Hindu Raj, was he happy for the Muslims left behind to be so 'oppressed'?

The Second World War

The Second World War was in many ways a continuation of the First, where Germany had been so badly humiliated. Adolf Hitler promised to restore Germany to military greatness, and whipped up anger against its wealthy Jewish minority. The Axis powers – Germany, Italy and Japan – fought the Allies – Britain, France, USA and USSR.

The Congress offered to cooperate if power was transferred to them; they refused promises of changes after the war. By March 1942, the Japanese were nearly in India.

Cripps Mission

The British desperately needed Indian support for the war, and their PM Churchill needed to show his vital ally, president Roosevelt of the USA, that the British were moving towards Indian autonomy.

Britain sent over the liberal Sir Stafford Cripps (Nehru's friend) to India in 1942, who eventually still promised Dominion Status only after the war. The mission ended a failure, and Gandhi called the offer 'a post-dated cheque', to which a journalist added, 'on a failing bank'.

'Leave India to God'

In May 1942, Gandhi wrote, 'The British cannot suddenly change their nature; racial superiority is treated as virtue

Noor Inayat Khan

Born in Russia in 1914 to an Indian father and an American mother, Noor Inayat Khan grew up across Russia, Britain and France. In London, she published *Twenty Jataka Tales* for children.

When the Second World War broke out, she wanted Indians to win 'high military distinction' and became a British spy. She travelled to occupied Paris as a wireless operator called Jeanne-Marie Regnier. Despite Nazi arrests of her fellow underground resisters, she remained to transmit important messages under perilous conditions, becoming the most wanted British agent in Paris, actively hunted by the Nazis!

She was betrayed for 100,000 francs but managed to escape with some other agents. Soon recaptured, she was classified as 'highly dangerous' and kept shackled in chains in solitary confinement in Germany. She was later shot at the notorious Dachau concentration camp. Her last, extraordinarily courageous word was '*Liberté*'. She was thirty.

in India, Africa, Burma and Ceylon. This drastic disease requires… immediate withdrawal from India…'

In August 1942, the INC launched another mass struggle, demanding that the British 'Quit India' immediately, under the slogan '*Karenge ya Marenge*' (Do or Die). The British government quickly (and secretly) jailed Congress leaders. Inflamed crowds burned buses, pelted stones and looted public buildings. Strikes and boycotts spread. The government retaliated with mass jailings, floggings and machine-gunning from planes.

Meanwhile, the Muslim League successfully gathered mass support for a separate Muslim nation.

The Bengal Famine

The 1943 Bengal Famine witnessed the greatest British atrocities in India. Wartime demand and reduced imports from Burma drove up food prices steeply (the cost of rice became fourfold!). Neither rice hoarding nor exports were stopped. Starving villagers started migrating, and millions died right on the streets of Calcutta.

America and Canada offered to donate grain. Churchill said casually, 'We simply cannot find the shipping...' even as he kept six million tonnes of wheat as 'emergency' rations in the Indian Ocean.

The Final Push

An ill Gandhi was released from jail in 1944, as the British were worried that India's saint would die in their custody. However, Gandhi stumped them (again) with a remarkable recovery!

Churchill appointed a military general as the next Indian viceroy, and was stunned when Field Marshall Wavell wanted to resolve matters through talks, not troops! However, Wavell was frustrated in his attempts by what he called the 'Aged Trinity' – Churchill, Gandhi and Jinnah who were all around 70 years old!

In the 1945 British elections, popular wartime PM Churchill was shockingly displaced by Labour PM Clement Attlee, whom he had contemptuously called 'the sheep in sheep's clothing'. Attlee openly accepted that Britain's days in India were over. Relentless Indian agitation was getting Britain bad press worldwide, the USA (whose money Britain badly needed), wanted them out, and the Indian armed forces had begun mutinying.

But to whom should the British hand over?

Jinnah's Stand

In 1946, a group of British MPs came over as the Cabinet Mission, but were unable to get the Congress and Muslim

Women in Front

During the independence struggle, many women emerged from seclusion and became satyagrahis, marching side by side with men.

Sarojini Naidu, the nightingale of India, was a poet and freedom fighter. A child prodigy from Hyderabad, she studied

at Cambridge. She joined the Indian national movement and became the voice of Indian women freedom fighters. She was Congress president, represented women at the Second Round table Conference and became India's first woman governor after Independence.

Wealthy **Bhikaji Rustom Cama** became 'seditionist' when in London for medical care in 1901. She founded the Indian Home Rule Society in 1905. Barred from India, she relocated to Paris, where she wrote for India's cause. She designed one of the first Indian flags in 1907.

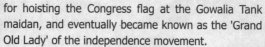

Aruna Ganguly married Congress leader Asaf Ali in 1928 despite staunch opposition (he was Muslim and older by 20+ years). **Aruna Asaf Ali** became famous during the Quit India movement for hoisting the Congress flag at the Gowalia Tank maidan, and eventually became known as the 'Grand Old Lady' of the independence movement.

League to agree. They finally proposed three groups: the princely states; Muslim-majority provinces; and Hindu-majority provinces, all ruled by a weak central government that looked after only defence and foreign relations.

A Constituent Assembly would be formed – a group of freshly elected representatives to frame a constitution for an independent India. The British also planned to hand over most power to the Indians through an interim government (until elections could be held).

Jinnah stubbornly insisted that the Muslim League and the Congress should have exactly the same number of people in this temporary government. He also offensively demanded that Congress remove all Muslim delegates – whom he called showcase Muslims – as only he could speak for Indian Muslims. He was rebuffed and absolutely refused to join the Interim Government.

A Deadly Gamble

Jinnah declared a 'direct action day' to be held on 1 August 1946, asking Muslim League supporters 'to sacrifice for winning their goal of Pakistan.' Direct action day became direct killing day in Calcutta, as Muslim League supporters pillaged, looted and killed for four days while the government led by the Muslim League stood by.

This carnage convinced the Congress that there could be no cooperation with the Muslim League. It also resulted in

horrific Hindu mob violence against Muslims in Bihar, prompting mass migration. An endless cycle of revenge and retaliation now spread across north India.

As it became clear that the British were in retreat mode, Indians working for

Indian National Congress leader C. Rajagopalachari or 'Rajaji' (standing) favoured talks with Jinnah and the Muslim League

the government started openly siding with either the Congress or the Muslim League.

A dangerous situation started forming, as countless militias came up. Young men armed themselves with steel-tipped rods, spears and swords, and created a ruckus while marching aggressively down streets, or driving around in open jeeps. Many organized themselves into formal groups – like the Muslim Khaksars and National Guard, the Hindu Rashtriya Swayamsevak Sangh (RSS), and the Sikh Akali Fauj.

A Hollow Victory

In February 1947, the British announced they would leave India by June 1948. In the same month, the king's cousin, Lord Louis Mountbatten (in office: 1947–1948), was sent over as viceroy to find a solution, and also keep official ties between India and Britain cordial.

Mountbatten had two months of intense one-on-one discussions with all parties, until eventually, the Congress reluctantly agreed to the partition of India, much to everyone's shock. Jinnah insisted on '… the whole of Punjab, Sind and NWFP and Bengal and Assam, and… a corridor to unite them.' When Mountbatten refused, citing the 50 per cent non-Muslims in Punjab and Bengal, Jinnah said bitterly, 'You insist on giving me a moth-eaten Pakistan.'

The British were now in a tearing hurry to leave India and Mountbatten impulsively announced 15 August 1947 as India's independence day, a full year ahead of the original deadline. Pakistan celebrated its independence on 14 August and India on 15 August. The joyous celebrations were marred by vicious Hindu–Muslim violence, which no one had anticipated.

Refugee trains and uprooted millions: tragic scenes of the Partition

Partition Is Announced

Sir Cyril Radcliffe, a stranger to India, was made to partition Bengal and Punjab in strict secrecy within five weeks (he had asked for two years!). He fled India before the announcement, claiming, 'there will be 80 million people with a grievance… I do not want them to find me.'

The Story of a Flag

Did you know India had many, many flags? There was a Company flag, and a British Indian flag after 1857, resembling those of Canada and Australia.

There were many flags used during the independence struggle – from the Vande Mataram flag to the Home Rule flag. The Congress started a flag design competition and many designs were submitted – including thunderbolts, diyas and the cow. Gandhi proposed a striped white, green and red flag with a large charkha in the middle.

The Congress chose the Swaraj flag, designed by Pingali Venkayya, using it to start a 'flag satyagraha' where people agitated for the right to publicly carry the Swaraj flag. As many as 1,500 people were arrested.

The Swaraj flag, modified by changing the charkha to the Ashoka Chakra, was eventually adopted as free India's national flag.

From bottom to top: The British East India Company flag; the Bande Mataram flag designed by Bhikaji Cama (1907); the Home Rule flag (1917); Gandhiji's flag (1921); Swaraj flag (1931); Netaji's flag (1939); and independent India's flag (1947)

The boundaries were finally announced on 17 August, two days *after* Indian and Pakistan's independence, and many found themselves in the wrong country!

Midnight Transfer of Power

The Constituent Assembly met at night on 14 August 1947. 'Vande Mataram' was sung and Nehru read out his famous 'Tryst with Destiny' speech. At the stroke of midnight, a conch was sounded and each member took a pledge. The national flag was presented and Nehru informed Viceroy Mountbatten that India was independent!

15 August 1947

At 8:30 a.m., the Government was sworn in at the Viceroy's House (Rashtrapati Bhavan). They then drove to Parliament House amidst crazy crowds, where people had climbed on to every rooftop. The crowds kept shouting 'Mahatma Gandhi *ki jai*', 'Pandit Nehru *ki jai*', and also, 'Mountbatten *ki jai*'!

Villagers swarmed Delhi, decked out in their finest garb, by foot, car and bullock cart! In the evening, the Mountbattens made their way in a gilded six-horse carriage, accompanied by hundreds of horse-mounted guards. Nehru sat at the front.

At the Red Fort, there were just too many people! All speeches and parades were abandoned. As the Indian flag was hoisted there for the first time by Prime Minister Nehru, a brilliant, unexpected rainbow appeared, causing wild cheering at this 'good omen'.

Punjab exploded in vengeful communal violence. The police were totally inadequate as groups of all communities were unbelievably brutal. Trains pulled in full of dead bodies and many women were harmed or kidnapped.

A Mahatma Is Snatched Away

Gandhi had spent Independence Day in Calcutta trying to keep peace. Still, many Hindu nationalists remained very angry about his placation of Jinnah and Muslims.

Nathuram Godse developed great hatred towards Gandhi, calling him the 'Father of Pakistan'. He had even tried to stab him and bomb him before. Finally, on 30 January 1948, Godse shot Gandhi at Birla House in Delhi.

Godse did not try to escape and was executed, without once expressing remorse. A stunned India grieved deeply. Nehru said, 'The light has gone out of our lives and there is darkness everywhere...'

What in the World Was Happening! (1915–47)

Asia
- JAPAN: industrializes; conquers Asia and loses; two atom bombs are dropped on it at the end of the Second World War.
- CHINA: The country is racked by internal warfare, and then by conquest by Japan.

Europe
- The First World War rages between 1914–18, forever changing the world. The Great Depression crashes the global economy from 1929–32.
- GERMANY: Hitler and his Nazi Party rise.
- The Second World War rages from 1939 to 1945.

America
- The US becomes the premier world power, along with the USSR.

Africa
- The continent is colonized and divided up among imperial powers.

Explore More

* COLLECT your favourite
quotes from what freedom
fighters said and wrote. Some
memorable words of Mahatma
Gandhi are:

— 'Be the change you want to see
in the world.'
— 'An eye for an eye will only
make the whole world blind.'
— 'Whenever you are in doubt, recall the face of the
poorest and weakest man whom you have seen and
ask yourself if the step you contemplate will help him.'

* MAKE a list of, and visit, historical sites associated
with the freedom struggle in your city.

* FIND out how India's independence inspired other
colonies to fight against, and throw off, colonial rule.

* LISTEN to the 'Tryst with Destiny' speech by
Jawaharlal Nehru and analyze how many of the aims and
dreams mentioned in the speech have been achieved.

Coins and Currency

Bars or round-shaped, of gold, copper or silver, the hundreds of types of coins tell the history of India.

For centuries commodities were used as the means of exchange. The Indo-Europeans measured wealth in cows; the word 'pecuniary' comes from *pecus*, which means cow in Latin (the similar Sanskrit word is *pashu*). Cowrie shells were used as legal tender in India right until the 18th century.

The earliest coins found were minted in Lydia (in modern Turkey) in the seventh century BCE, The earliest metal coinage found in India is from the sixth century BCE, from the *mahajanapada*s. They may have picked up the concept from the Persians who ruled western India, but the shape of Gandhara coins are stamped bars, while Persian coins were round.

The Mauryans minted silver and copper coins, called *pana* and *karshapana*. Goods were called *panya* (what is bought with *pana*), and dealers in goods, i.e., merchants were called *panik*, which morphed to *vanik*, then *vania*, and then 'bania'.

Roman gold coins poured into India in the first century BCE, giving rise to bitter complaints by Roman politicians like Pliny. They were especially popular for coin necklaces. After supply fell by the fourth century because of the decline of the Roman Empire, Roman-style real gold coins and fake-gold-covered terracotta coins, were made in India for jewellery.

Coins with portraits were first introduced by the Indo-Greek Kings. A coin of Agathocles of Bactria (Balkh in Afghanistan) of 186 BCE, has the earliest known depiction of Krishna (in Greek dress!). Rulers like Menander issued the earliest Indian gold coins.

Kanishka the Kushan minted the gold coins called *dinar* after the Roman coin *denarius*. Artistic gold coins were minted by the Imperial Guptas. During the Delhi Sultanate, coins called *tanka* and *jital* were used (think: Bangladeshi *taka!*).

The first rupee was minted by Sher Shah Suri. It was named after the Sanskrit *raupya* meaning 'of silver'.

The Mughals had a trimetallic currency. One gold mohur was equal to nine silver rupees, and a rupee equalled 40 copper *dam*s. The names reflect Indian multiculturalism: mohur is from Persian *muhr*, meaning seal; *rupiya* is of Sanskrit origin, *dam* from the Greek *drachma*! Incidentally, the English phrase 'I don't give a damn' – refers to the low-valued Indian coin, *dam*.

Each kingdom, and even merchant guilds, minted their own coins, and there were specialized moneychangers in every town called *saraf*s, who could value and exchange hundreds of currencies.

The first paper currency in India was introduced by the British in the 18th century. Till independence, 64 paise made 1 rupee. Smaller denominations were 256 *damri* = 192 *pie* = 128 *dhela* = 64 paisa = 16 *anna* = 1 *rupiya*. The currency was decimalized in 1957; 100 new paise were now equivalent to a rupee.

Sweeping Changes ···· 13

'In ancient times, do you think that there were not the
ignorant, and the shallow-minded? And why after all should
you embrace so fondly a carcass of dead thoughts. Live
in the present and shape the future, do not be casting
lingering looks to the distant past...'
— Subramania Bharati, poet, independence activist and
social reformer

13
East and West: The Twain Do Meet

India was becoming part of the greater world, and new trends in clothes, sports, movies and art came here too. Cities modernized rapidly, caste taboos slowly (very slowly!) got diluted, foreign travel started and Indians began mingling with the British, especially once they were accepted into higher levels of government.

Social Organization

The First World War changed the role of women around the world. They became far more independent and free – in their fashion, lifestyles and demands (for the right to vote, for one!). Life for Indian women started opening up in the early 20th century – in the cities, anyway! Girls from wealthy, especially royal families, started going to study in England and attended Swiss finishing schools. Some women became pilots, movie stars, film-makers, business owners, lawyers, doctors and politicians. Many broke long-held taboos against wearing Western dresses, partying and dancing in public.

Women participated in the Indian freedom struggle at every level. For the first time, they came out of their seclusion to boldly march in protest on the streets, and even go to jail. Many women voted in the 1937 provincial elections. From Gandhi to B.R. Ambedkar, Indian leaders wanted equal rights for women in all fields – including inheritance. The Indian National Congress had many women as annual presidents, and Vijayalakshmi Pandit became the first woman cabinet minister in the United Provinces. However, the vast majority of Indian women still led traditional, secluded lives.

This was a time of strong social movements against untouchability. Gandhi and the nationalist movement condemned it, and called the Dalits – Harijans (people of Hari/God). Consumed with anger about the centuries of oppression the Dalits had faced, Ambedkar became their voice and wanted to dissociate them from Hinduism altogether!

Demand for Dravida Nadu

In the early 20th century, a new movement gathered steam in the Madras Presidency, as protests started against the lopsided power of brahmins. In 1916, the anti-Brahmin Justice Party was formed. It won local elections in 1920 and stayed (more or less) in power until 1937, becoming a permanent fixture of Tamil politics.

E.V. Ramasamy Naicker (also called Periyar, 'the Respected One'), quit the Congress party as he thought it was too 'Brahmin dominated', and became a big promoter of 'Dravidians', who he claimed were a different race from north Indians. He also wanted people to reject rituals, superstitions, caste and even God! Periyar started a 'Self

*A painting of E.V.
Ramasamy Naicker
'Periyar'*

Respect' movement for backward castes, marked by weddings without brahmin priests, and widow remarriage. He also worked with the Justice Party to strongly agitate against Hindi, made compulsory across the Madras Presidency by the Congress in 1937. The Justice Party morphed into the Dravida Kazhagam in 1944, which demanded a separate country of Dravida Nadu or Dravidistan, and wanted to remove the very concept of caste.

The Economy

Modern factories slowly came up, mainly to make cotton textiles and jute fabric (fibres of the native jute plant were used for strong, coarse – and cheap! – fabric for packaging, rugs, twine and so on). India had the world's largest jute manufacturing industry, mainly controlled by Europeans and mostly for export. Cotton cloth, however, was largely for domestic use, and most textile mills were in Bombay Presidency. Other industries like iron, steel, paper, sugar and cement came up but were not well-developed.

Indian industry grew slowly, with countless obstacles – borrowing money from banks was difficult and costly; machines had to be imported; fuel and transport were pricey; it was hard to get well-trained workers and managers. Indian factory owners found it tough to export goods without strong connections to foreign markets, while most Indians were too poor to buy their products.

Overall, India's economy hardly grew, and the average income per person remained very low.

How Tea Became Indian

Tea was foreign to India. Though there was a native variety in Assam, locals cooked it as a vegetable with garlic and oil! So even as India became a major tea grower and exporter in the 19th century, Indians themselves did not drink tea... only using it as medicine sometimes! Slowly, British-style tea – with a drop of milk and a dash of sugar – became popular with Indian upper classes.

In the 1920s, the Tea Association started campaigns to get ordinary Indians to start drinking tea. Tea canteens were started in factories, and tea vendors were put to work on the great railway network. Cries of '*Chai! Garam chai!*' (Tea! Hot tea!) started on train stations across the country. Although European tea instructors kept showing vendors how to make tea the correct – British – way, local stall-keepers ignored them and brewed it strongly with a lot of milk and sugar, resembling other hot milky drinks! However, the campaign was a big success and this brewed tea became the quintessential Indian drink!

Science and Technology

As the world grew smaller, Indian scientists started making their mark.

Sir M. Visvesvaraya was one of the great Indian engineers. He initially worked for the British government, designed irrigation projects and dams, such as the Krishna Raja Sagara Dam, and even patented a system of automatic floodgates! He became the diwan of Mysore in 1912 and started many industries and institutions. His birthday (15 September) is celebrated as Engineer's Day in India.

Srinivas Ramanujan was a childhood mathematics prodigy, who taught himself and filled entire notebooks with theorems he had proved! When some of these reached the brilliant mathematician G.H. Hardy in

From top: M. Visvesvaraya, S. Ramanujan and C.V. Raman

England, he was amazed, and coaxed a reluctant Ramanujan to ignore the Hindu prohibition on foreign travel and visit Cambridge in 1914. Together, they came up with brilliant mathematical work. Ramanujan was made the first Indian Fellow of Trinity College at Cambridge! However, he suffered from malnutrition – he was vegetarian, refused to eat out and could not cook – and later got tuberculosis. He died young at 32 in Madras.

Sir C.V. Raman became the first Asian to win the Nobel Prize in a science, with his Nobel Prize in Physics in 1930, for discovering the Raman Effect about the scattering of light. He became the first Indian director of the prestigious Indian Institute of Science in Bangalore.

Aviation

The Wright brothers flew the first airplane in 1903 in the USA. By 1910, the flamboyant maharaja of Patiala had bought India's first plane. In 1911, in the first Indian flight, a Frenchman flew 6,500 mails between Allahabad and Naini across just six miles! Planes were used in the First World War, and the British air force had Indian pilots like Indra Lal Roy, who shot down ten German planes.

The tycoon J.R.D. Tata claimed he was 'hopelessly hooked on aeroplanes' and got the first pilot's licence issued in India! In 1932, he started Tata Airlines, India's first commercial airline, and was the pilot of its very first flight from Karachi to Bombay, which carried 25 kg of letters.

Today, we know his airline better as Air India! The Indian Air Force was also launched in 1932.

Sarla Thakral, an early – sari-clad – Indian pilot

Not far behind, Urmila K. Parikh was the first Indian woman to get a pilot's licence in 1932 and Sarla Thakral got hers in 1936.

Sports

Badminton was invented by the British within India and was initially called 'Poona', because it was so popular with the British Regiment there! It is still very popular, and one of the games where India has produced world champions.

India started competing in the modern Olympics from 1920, in a handful of sports. Field hockey, an English school sport, was brought to India by the British army. The Indian hockey team debuted in the 1928 Olympics and won the gold medal... and kept on winning it at every Olympics until 1960! Much credit for this went to Major Dhyanchand (1905–79), who is considered the greatest hockey player ever. His hockey stick was once broken open in the Netherlands to check if there was a magnet inside! The great cricketer Don Bradman, after watching Dhyanchand, said that '... he scores goals like runs in cricket.' In those days, hockey was far more popular than cricket, and became independent India's national game!

Cricket was a quintessentially British game that came to India in the 18th century. Wealthy Indians started playing it gradually. Bombay Presidency was an important centre, with pentangular tournaments between teams of Europeans, Parsis, Hindus, Sikhs and Muslims.

Ranjitsinhji ('Ranji'), ruler of Jamnagar (Gujarat), became the first non-white person to play for the English team in 1896, after much difficulty! His nephew Duleepsinhji was also a leading player, as were Lala Amarnath and the nawab of Pataudi.

The Indian cricket team played its first Test match at Lord's in London in 1932, captained by India's best batsman of the time, C.K. Nayudu (who kept playing until he was sixty-eight!). Its first test in India was held against England in 1934 at Eden Gardens, Calcutta.

A favourite royal Indian game, British army officers first picked up polo from Manipuri royals, and called it 'Pulu' after the Tibetan word for ball! The Calcutta Polo Club was established in 1862, and polo became a glamorous society game where nobles and royals

From top:
Hockey magician
Dhyanchand;
Ranjitsinhji

went to be seen. Sir Pratap Singh of Jodhpur took one of the earliest polo teams abroad in 1897 – his style of breeches became very popular and were called 'jodhpurs'! Jaipur's Raja Sawai Man Singh II was so obsessed with polo that when he got married in 1930 to (two!) Jodhpur princesses, he asked for the Jodhpur polo team as dowry!

Culture

The last decades before Indian independence were a time of self-sacrifice, of rising pride in India, her history and her heroes, and a time of reform – improving the treatment of women and lower castes.

This spirit spread through all aspects of art. Indian classical music and dance was revived and brought to the public stage and recording studios. New novels and plays were written – about legendary heroes who had also fought for freedom, and also about, for and by women!

LITERATURE

A great body of modern Hindi literature came up – some in the commonly spoken 'Urduized' form, and some that was highly Sankritized.

Hindi poetry entered the Chhayavad era, with themes of love, nature and individualism. Its *char stambh* (four pillars) were Jaishankar Prasad, Mahadevi Varma, Sumitranandan Pant and Suryakant Tripathi Nirala. Jaishankar Prasad's Sanskritized poems, such as the epic *Kamayani*, and plays, such as *Chandragupta*, ranged from the romantic to the nationalistic.

Munshi Premchand was one of the era's great writers. His short stories, novels and plays had a stark, searing realism expressing the problems of poor people, colonialism, corruption, and often, just human relationships. *Nirmala* and *Godan* are two of his famous novels, and hundreds of his stories are compiled in *Mansarovar*.

Sarat Chandra Chattopadhyay was a Bengali novelist and short-story writer, who often wrote about women. More than 50 movies in different Indian languages have

From top: Literary lights: Mahadevi Varma, Mulk Raj Anand, Sarat Chandra and Premchand

been made from his works, like *Parineeta* and *Devdas* (which has 16 movie versions so far!).

Indian writing in English was pioneered by authors like Mulk Raj Anand, R.K. Narayan and Raja Rao.

Though he had a PhD from Cambridge, Mulk Raj Anand wrote about the troubled lives of Dalits and the poor. His 1935 novel, *Untouchable*, was inspired by real life, and made him a leading English author.

Jim Corbett was born and raised in the Himalayas. A crack shot, he gave up hunting for pleasure, and fearlessly hunted man-eating tigers and leopards (on request by the government and villagers). His books about his hunts were a worldwide success, especially the 1944 *Man-Eaters of Kumaon*. He convinced the United Provinces to open India's first wildlife sanctuary in 1936 (renamed Jim Corbett National Park in 1957). He even has a tiger subspecies – *Panthera tigris corbetti* – named after him.

ARCHITECTURE

Indian princes started building fanciful palaces. Blending the 'English gentleman with the Indian prince', they had Western features like dining and drawing rooms, ballrooms, and even fireplaces! French beaux arts were seen in Kapurthala, Italian Renaissance in Gwalior, Classical British in Kashmir and, of course, classic Indian styles everywhere. The Viceroy's House (now the Rashtrapati Bhavan) blended Western styles with Indian details.

In the 1920s, Jodhpur's lavish sandstone-and-marble Umaid Bhawan Palace was built to give work to farmers during a severe famine, while the maharaja of Mysore built the Lalitha Mahal to resemble St Paul's Cathedral in London, especially to host the visiting viceroy!

The grand Umaid Bhawan Palace, Jodhpur

ART

Indian art reflected global moods and changes. Western techniques became popular, as did new Western trends like cubism! Local and nationalist themes were also common. Independent India declared the painting of nine artists as national treasures. Besides Raja Ravi Varma and Abanindranath, Gaganendranath and Rabindranath Tagore, these included Nandalal Bose, Jamini Roy, Amrita Sher-Gil, Sailoz Mookherjea and Nikolas Roerich.

Nandalal Bose was influenced by the Ajanta frescoes and mentor Abanindranath Tagore. A founder of modern Indian art, his thousands of works cover Indian and mythological themes. His 1930 black-and-white linocut print (made by carving with a knife) of Mahatma Gandhi became an iconic symbol of the freedom struggle. Later, he and his students beautifully illustrated the Indian Constitution with gold leaf and colours ground from stones! He also created emblems for national awards like the Bharat Ratna.

Jamini Roy was also from the Bengal school and Abanindranath's student. Starting off with Western impressionistic styles, he moved to folk and tribal art, and Kalighat painting, calling himself a *patua*, a village painter of Kalighat Pat!

Amrita Sher-Gil's painting found its real essence after she returned to India from abroad

Amrita Sher-Gil had a Sikh father and a Hungarian mother. She learned painting in Shimla, and went to Paris at 16 to train. Her earliest paintings are very Western, but after travelling around India in 1934, she started showing the life of Indian people, especially women. Her work became famous after her untimely death at just 28 years.

RADIO

The first public radio broadcasts began in 1920 in England and the USA. In India, the Radio Club of Bombay started in 1923, and the Indian Broadcasting Company opened stations in Bombay and Calcutta by 1927. It soon went bankrupt as it was only in English and did not get many listeners! The government took it over in 1930, later renaming it All India Radio. It started broadcasting in many regional languages, becoming hugely popular!

MOVIES

Ardeshir Irani produced India's first 'talkie' called *Alam Ara* in 1931, and the era of silent movies was over. Tamil and Telugu talkies soon followed. With sound, songs

> **Bollywood's original movie star was an Australian stunt girl called Hunterwali Nadia, known for her daredevil acts on screen** FUN FACT!

and dance became a must for Indian movies! The film *Indra Sabha* from 1932 still holds the record with a whopping 71 songs. Studios came up in Madras, Calcutta and Bombay. Movies about the freedom movement often got censored, but those about social injustice, like *Achhut Kanya*, *Aurat* and *Ek Hi Rasta* did very well. K.L. Saigal became India's first superstar, after his 1935 film *Devdas*!

MUSIC AND DANCE

Film music became very popular, and singers like K.L. Saigal, Shamshad Begum and Noor Jehan became stars. The Carnatic classical singer M.S.

Uday Shankar and Anna Pavlova in Radha–Krishna

Heroines of Yesteryear

When movies first came to India, it was a big taboo for Indian women to perform in public.

As the first movies were silent, many of the earliest Indian female actors were Baghdadi Jews who did not speak any Indian languages! Ruby Myers from Poona became the highly paid Sulochana, appearing in movies like *Anarkali* and *Madhuri*! One single Baghdadi family had the actor–producer Pramila (Esther Victoria Abraham), her sister, the actor Romila (Sophie Abraham), and her cousin, the starlet Rose!

The first Indian stuntwoman, the swashbuckling *Hunterwali* Fearless Nadia, was actually an Australian actress called Mary Evans!

However, Devika Rani was Indian cinema's first lady. From the Tagore family, she was educated at an English boarding school, and studied architecture and textile design. Together with her barrister-turned-film-maker husband Himanshu Rai, Devika started a movie studio called Bombay Talkies in 1934 and became a famous actor. After Rai's death in 1940, she ran the studio herself, successfully producing many films. Another legend was Shobhana Samarth, whose daughters Nutan and Tanuja became stars, as did her grandchildren, like Kajol!

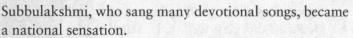

Top: A poster of Hunterwali *with 'Fearless Nadia';*
(right) superstar Devika Rani

Subbulakshmi, who sang many devotional songs, became a national sensation.

Uday Shankar came from a well-off Bengali family, and at nineteen, got into Indian dance and music, even performing dances like *Radha–Krishna* with the famous Russian ballerina Anna Pavlova! Though not formally trained, he and his troupe toured Europe and the USA as 'Uday Shankar and his Hindu Ballet', blending Indian classical and folk dance with ballet. Incidentally, he was the elder brother of famous sitar player Ravi Shankar.

Lifestyle

Indian royalty partied hard, with summers in England, autumns on the Continent and winters at home. They wore Western dress, and their wives came out of purdah. A part of the world's jet-setting aristocracy, they bought the latest cars and planes. Among the rich, it became fashionable to keep two kitchens, one Indian and one Western!

The maharaja of Alwar was not treated royally enough in a Rolls Royce showroom, so he bought two cars and used them at home in Alwar as garbage vans.

FUN FACT!

Sarees draped in the 'Nivi style' (the most common today) were a style statement, specially of new man-made fabrics like chiffon.

Foreign vegetables, especially 'English' ones like carrots, cauliflower and string beans, became a part of Indian food! British-style bread, biscuits and cakes also became popular with ordinary Indians.

Apples in India

Though the British tried growing some apples in India, they were sour and not very popular. Imported apples were a real luxury.

In 1904, a 22-year-old American, Samuel Stokes, heir to an elevator fortune, came to work among lepers in India, much against his parents' wishes. He lived in the Shimla hills and married Agnes, a first-generation Rajput Christian girl. He later imported and planted saplings of Red Delicious and Golden Delicious apples. An instant hit, apple-growing took off and the Himachal Pradesh region became a major producer of (delicious) apples!

Stokes also became a freedom fighter and became the only American to go to jail for it. In 1932, he converted to Hinduism through the Arya Samaj and became Satyanand Stokes. His daughter-in-law, Vidya Stokes, became an active politician in Himachal Pradesh.

Explore More

The intricate and beautiful ceiling at Mysore Palace, Mysuru, Karnataka

* FIND out about the palaces built by the Indian royals during this period. What are their richest and rarest treasures? Many of these palaces, which imported many items such as Belgian glass and Italian marble, are now heritage hotels.

* LOOK at painting to the right, by iconic artist Nandalal Bose. Research the art movements in India at the time and who their leading proponents were.

* CHOOSE any topic you like — science, technology, music, dance, art or architecture — and write a short biography of the most fascinating (in your view) Indian personality from that field.

Forging of a Nation

14

[1947–1950 CE]

'I ...dedicate... myself... to the end that this ancient
land attain its rightful and honoured place in the world
and make its full and willing contribution to the promotion
of world peace and the welfare of mankind.'
— Pledge by the members of the Constituent Assembly

14
The Making of a Country

Countless challenges awaited newly independent India – the princely states had to be brought on board and a constitution had to be agreed on. Poverty, illiteracy and immense inequality had to be reduced. Many did not even believe that India could survive without the British – expecting India to starve, fall to dictatorship or splinter messily into bits. But survive India did, against incredible odds. The Indian Constitution gave all her citizens many rights, like freedom of speech, movement and religion.

The First Government

Everyone knew that the 1946 Congress president would become independent India's first prime minister. In internal Congress elections, most regional committees proposed Sardar Patel's name, while Jawaharlal Nehru received not a single nomination.

However, Mahatma Gandhi absolutely wanted Nehru, because '... Jawahar will not take second place. He is better known abroad than Sardar and will make India play a role in international affairs. Sardar will look after the country's affairs. They will be like two oxen yoked to the governmental cart.' Upon Gandhi's gentle insistence, Patel withdrew and Nehru was 'elected' (unopposed).

Amazingly, Nehru invited the viceroy, Lord Mountbatten, to stay on as independent India's first Governor General. When Mountbatten offered to become a common Governor General for India and Pakistan, Jinnah coldly declared that he himself would become Pakistan's first Governor General, and that the Pakistani 'Prime Minister will do what I tell him'.

Dealing with Partition

India's Partition caused suffering to millions, especially women. Between one and two million people were killed and countless injured. Many were abducted by the other 'side' and had to accept a new country and religion.

Ten million homeless, helpless refugees poured in an endless stream, especially in Punjab. The farmlands of those who had gone over to Pakistan were redistributed. Millions fled to Delhi. The refugees worked hard and soon came to dominate Delhi's trade. More than 500,000 refugees came to Bombay from Sindh, North-West Frontier Province and Punjab. The Sindhis became an important business community there. More than two million refugees came into West Bengal by 1950, many of whom lived on the streets of Calcutta. They were not given much land and could not settle in like Punjabi refugees.

A Messy Separation

Like a divorced couple, India and Pakistan had to decide how to divide their assets. A Partition Council held endless meetings to decide the division of everything – from mints to military to museums! Pakistan got around one-fifth of government assets.

Even typewriters, cars and stationery were divided, and both sides kept accusing each other of unfair treatment. There were even some hysterical demands to ship the Taj Mahal to Pakistan! In one case, 60 ducks ordered from England caused a fierce controversy between East Pakistan and West Bengal as they fought over how many each side would keep. In fact, Pakistan still owes India three billion rupees, which shows up in its annual budget.

Accession of the Princely States

At Independence, India's map looked quite different from today. There were 14 large provinces and 70 small and large groups of 'princely states'. The largest were Madras, Bihar and the United Provinces. Today's Rajasthan was actually lots of Rajput princely states, and Gujarat was part of Bombay province!

India's privileged princes started getting concerned about their fate – 565 princely states controlled 40 per cent of India's land and a fourth of her people. Some were larger than European countries, but most were hardly even cities. They voiced their concerns to the colonial government through a forum called the Chamber of Princes.

On 3 June 1947, Lord Mountbatten announced that India would be free, Pakistan would be created, and the British would leave – all within two-and-a-half months! The British insisted that the princely states could 'choose' to join India, Pakistan, or neither.

It suited Jinnah to have a smaller, weaker Hindustan (which would be more equal to Pakistan), and publicly said that the states were 'free to remain independent'. However, the princely states were geographically entangled with British provinces and their independence would mean a moth-eaten India. Besides, their people had fought just as vigorously for independence!

Still, rulers of larger states like Hyderabad, Jammu and Kashmir, and Travancore began to dream of becoming independent countries. This was a disaster in the making!

Sardar Patel quickly took charge of a new States Department in June 1947, asking the viceroy's constitutional adviser, V.P. Menon, to join him. He went to work, assuring the princes that the Congress was no enemy of the princely order, but wished them all prosperity. He hoped that by 'common endeavour we can raise the country to a new greatness'.

The two also got Lord Mountbatten, friend of many princes, to secretly lobby them to join India! Mountbatten, at his most persuasive, even held a glittering reception to convince the reluctant ones.

Baroda and Bikaner were the first to agree and convinced many others. They signed the Standstill Agreement, in which they agreed for either India or Pakistan to take over the running of things from the British; and also the Instrument of Accession, which permanently joined princely states to one of the two countries.

Some created a fuss. Travancore, which had

Sardar Patel literally strung the states into a country

rich natural resources like thorium, resisted until an assassination attempt on its diwan by socialists! Bhopal was very troublesome, but finally joined India at the last minute. Jinnah wooed Jodhpur and signed a blank paper, saying, 'You can fill in all your conditions.' The maharaja eventually acceded to India.

Astoundingly, Sardar Patel and Menon got all the princely states to sign over to India before 15 August, barring just three – Junagadh, Hyderabad, and Jammu and Kashmir! Patel was skilful in his handling – unfailingly respectful towards the princes, who trusted him to be fair.

JUNAGADH

The nawab of Junagadh (Gujarat) was a famous (and eccentric) animal lover who saved the Asiatic lions at Gir, kept 300 dogs and held lavish 'weddings' for them. He suddenly acceded to Pakistan to save 'the honour of Islam and the Muslims of Kathiawar', stunning India when the news appeared in newspapers! A popular revolt sparked as most people were Hindu, and India put soldiers around (but not in) Junagadh. The panicked nawab fled with his favourite wives and dogs, asking India to take over via letter! Junagadh held a vote in 1948 – fewer than 100 people voted to join Pakistan.

FUN FACT! Sardar Patel miraculously managed to convince 550+ Indian princes to peacefully hand over to the Indian Union their countries that their ancestors had defended to death for hundreds of years.

HYDERABAD

Probably the richest man in the world at the time, Hyderabad's Nizam was determined to form his own country. With its 16 million population, the 'Nizam's Dominions' had their own currency, army, railway, and radio and postal networks. The Nizam even offered to buy Goa from the Portuguese to get sea access!

The Nizam of Hyderabad greeting Nehru

However, local Congress and communist leaders had other ideas and started agitating. The Nizam started propping up the violent *razakar*s, the militia arm of the Islamist Majlis-e-Ittehadul Muslimeen (MIM), who wanted Hyderabad to become a Muslim nation state. The Nizam also drummed up support from Winston Churchill and got Syria to speak for him at the United Nations!

In November 1947, the Nizam signed a Standstill Agreement with India, but not the Instrument of Accession. The *razakar*s kept creating murderous havoc, and Hindus started fleeing in masses. Uneasy talks continued, but as violence persisted, in September 1948, Indian troops entered Hyderabad, gaining control in four days. The Nizam quickly acceded to India, claiming that he had been pressured 'against his will' all along!

KASHMIR

The story of Kashmir remains an open wound. The large princely state comprised Hindu-majority Jammu,

Buddhist Ladakh, and Muslim-majority Kashmir Valley and the Northern Areas (Gilgit Agency).

Its Dogra Rajput ruler, Hari Singh, wanted Kashmir to become a neutral 'Switzerland of the East', unwilling to join Pakistan or India. His long-time opponent (whom he often jailed!), the socialist Sheikh Abdullah wanted a secular, democratic government in Kashmir, with its accession to be decided by a popular vote.

In October 1947, Kabaili tribesmen poured into Kashmir from Pakistan, who claimed it was a 'spontaneous movement' to aid 'oppressed fellow Muslims' – but tribals are not known for their easy access to rifles, mortars, grenades and lorries! The Kabailis swept through, looting and killing before pausing at Baramulla, close to Srinagar… to send truckfuls of loot back to Waziristan.

A panicked Hari Singh hurriedly signed the Instrument of Accession in return for Indian military help. Indian soldiers were airlifted in, and began pushing back the tribals, but had to stop at the onset of the bitter winter. Pakistan's army chief was still British, and flatly refused Jinnah's order to enter Kashmir. Meanwhile, a British-led paramilitary group called the Gilgit Scouts, mutinied and 'acceded' the large region of Gilgit-Baltistan to Pakistan!

In January 1948, Prime Minister Nehru took the Kashmir issue to the UN despite Sardar Patel's strong opposition to 'internationalizing' the issue. As Patel had feared, Britain and the USA took Pakistan's side.

A ceasefire was declared on 1 January 1949, and the Line of Control has stayed there since, with a small sliver of the Valley called 'Azad Kashmir' controlled by Pakistan. Sheikh Abdullah was appointed the 'Prime Minister' of Jammu and Kashmir and began to govern it as part of India.

NORTH-WEST FRONTIER PROVINCES

A staunch follower of the Mahatma, Khan Abdul Ghaffar Khan led his Pashtun Khudai Khidmatgar in many non-violent protests, and was called 'Frontier Gandhi'. When he learned that the INC had accepted Partition, he was heartbroken and accused them, 'You have thrown us to

Khan Abdul Ghaffar Khan with Gandhi

the wolves.' NWFP was absorbed into Pakistan.

Full Integration of the Princely States

The Instrument of Accession let India manage only the external affairs, defence and communication of the princely states, which still ran their own state governments.

By November 1947, some small princely states in Odisha requested the Indian government's help in policing. Patel now asked these states to fully integrate with India, that is, dissolve the kingdoms altogether. The government reasoned that locals were agitating for full democracy with strikes and protests anyway. In return for losing their kingdoms, rulers could keep their titles and palaces, and would get a tax-free privy purse of about 15 per cent of their revenue (with a maximum of a million rupees a year). By December, Odisha and Chhattisgarh states signed merger agreements.

Mountbatten soothed the apprehension of other princes, saying that the mergers of smaller states were purely for easier administration. However, Patel and Menon worked

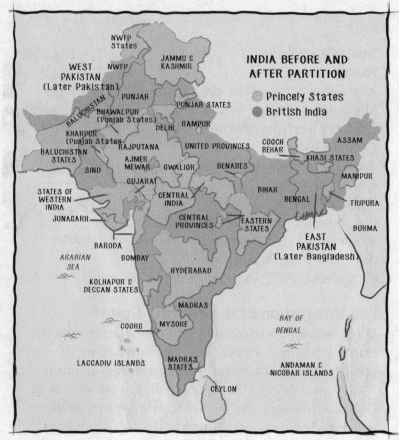

India in 1947

flat out for the next two-and-a-half years and merged all the princely states fully into India – using all the means mentioned in Chanakya's *Arthashastra – sama, dama, danda, bhed* (persuasion, money, force and division!).

Getting hundreds upon hundreds of states to merge with India – without bloodshed – will remain one of the most amazing feats of 'Iron Man' Sardar Patel. Like a magician, he convinced dynasties who had ruled for centuries to give up their kingdoms with barely a whimper.

Taking Back the Foreign Colonies

At independence, the Portuguese and French still held small outposts in India. Nehru wanted them back through friendly discussions!

The French Comptoirs de l'Inde were Chandernagore (present-day Chandannagar in West Bengal), and Pondicherry, Yanam, Mahe and Karaikal in the south. Their residents had agitated against European rule, but when referendums were held in 1948, only Chandernagore voted to join India.

In Pondicherry, the French India Socialist Party led by Edouard Goubert swept the 1948 municipal elections, but when the French accused Goubert of corruption in 1954, he began a civil disobedience movement against them! The French soon signed over all four territories – which together created the Union Territory of Pondicherry, even though they are far apart.

The Portuguese Estado da India were all on India's western coast – Daman, Diu, Dadra and Nagar Haveli and of course, Goa, which had an active local Congress committee. Portuguese dictator Antonio Salazar blankly refused to yield any Portuguese Overseas Territories. India even imposed visa restrictions between Goa and India!

In 1954, local activists took over Dadra and Nagar Haveli, seizing (lightly manned) police stations and hoisting the Indian flag. In 1955, over 5,000 unarmed protestors tried to enter Goa, but faced violent police action. The furious Indian government blockaded Goa and cut ties with Portugal.

From late 1961, things got tense, as Portuguese troops fired at a passenger boat and at Indian villagers near Goa's border. The Indian government sent in 30,000 troops, and quickly ended 450 years of Portuguese rule. The West criticized this as hypocrisy by a 'non-violent' nation, but Asian countries defended it.

Debating the Constitution

Once the British agreed to free India, elections were held in 1946 to select 296 members for a Constituent Assembly, which would debate and frame the Indian constitution.

Another 93 members came from the princely states. The Congress won most seats, and formed a government to take over the running of the country from the British.

The Constituent Assembly

The Constituent Assembly was diverse and had men, women, capitalists, socialists, landlords, lawyers, atheists and monks from across India. On Gandhi's request, Nehru and Patel (somewhat reluctantly) asked their fierce critic Dr Ambedkar to chair the Constitutional drafting committee for the Constitution. The Assembly met for 11 two-week sessions between 1946 and 1949. When India became free on 15 August 1947, it became the first Parliament of India.

As the Assembly began its humungous task, Nehru eloquently described the Indian Constitution as a pledge and a promise to Indians and the rest of the world, assuring minorities, women and Dalits that they would be well-protected.

FUN FACT!

While working on the draft Constitution, the assembly considered as many as 2,473 amendments from a total of 7,635 tabled.

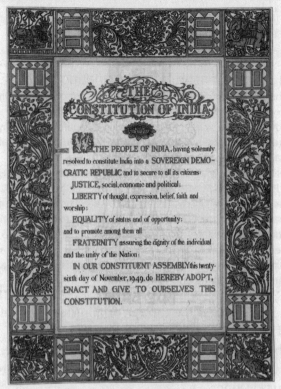

The Preamble to India's Constitution

Each clause was debated fiercely, and freely reported by the press. Pandit Nehru made stirring speeches, while Sardar Patel did the back-room work, smoothing over the inevitable arguments and making compromises.

India eventually decided on the British bicameral system of parliamentary democracy, debating and rejecting European proportional representation and the American presidential system. Every adult citizen got a vote. They would elect members to the Lok Sabha, who would then choose a prime minister. The Rajya Sabha would be elected by the state assemblies. These elected houses would make laws and thus be the legislative wing. The president would be elected by the Parliament and the state assemblies. The

The Indian Constitution: Fascinating Facts

- The Indian Constitution is the longest written constitution in the world. It has two official versions – in English and Hindi.
- Both versions were hand-scripted in beautiful calligraphy by Prem Behari Narain Raizada, and exquisitely illustrated by painter Nandalal Bose and his students.
- Aside from many aspects of the British Constitution, the concept of a Preamble and Fundamental Rights was taken from the USA, and the concepts of Liberty, Equality and Fraternity were taken from France. The concept of Directive Principles was taken from Ireland.
- The Preamble states that India is a Sovereign Socialist Secular Democratic Republic. The terms 'socialist' and 'secular' were actually added in 1976 by the then prime minister Indira Gandhi through a Constitutional amendment.

prime minister and the cabinet of ministers s/he selected would be the executive wing of the government.

To balance the power of Parliament was an independent judiciary and a strong Election Commission to ensure free and fair elections.

Every adult citizen got a vote. Separate electorates for women and Muslims were debated and rejected. However, there were reservations for Dalits and tribals to help correct centuries of discrimination.

Dr Ambedkar presenting the Draft of the Constitution to President Rajendra Prasad on 25 November 1949

Six Fundamental Rights were guaranteed, including the right to Equality, Freedom of Religion, and Freedom of Speech and Expression. The Directive Principles were not rights, but rather goals for the government to work towards to make a more equal, fairer society.

The national language excited debate. Many southern members refused to accept Hindi as the national language. Finally, it was made an official language, but for the next 15 years, English would continue to be used. It has already been many more years, though!

The constitution came into effect on 26 January 1950, which is celebrated as India's Republic Day.

Tale of Three Constitutions

Pakistan's 69-member Constituent Assembly had been elected before Independence. The first question they debated was how big a role religion should play. Jinnah had envisioned Pakistan as a secular country with content minorities, but he died soon after Independence.

Prime Minister Liaquat Ali Khan took a year and a half to release the Objectives Resolution, which laid down 'principles of democracy, freedom, equality, tolerance and social justice, as enunciated by Islam'. Vigorous opposition from non-Muslim Assembly members, who had been promised a non-religious state, was ignored.

In 1956, a constitution was finally released after nine years! In it was the name 'Islamic Republic of Pakistan' and a law that Pakistan's head of state had to be a Muslim. Also, no law could be passed 'contrary to Islam'. In 1962, General Ayub Khan released a new constitution, which changed the system of election, so only 80,000 people could vote as he felt most Pakistanis were 'not ready' for democracy! They would choose the president, who now became more powerful than the prime minister.

Pakistan's first national general elections were finally held in 1970, twenty-three years after independence! Their outcome famously led to the 1971 Bangladesh war, when West Pakistan became just Pakistan.

Zulfikar Ali Bhutto's 1973 constitution put the power back in the prime minister's hands but greatly expanded the Islamic aspects. This is the current Pakistani Constitution. In 1977, General Zia-ul-Haq, replaced non-religious British criminal laws with aspects of Islamic sharia, which introduced stoning and whipping as punishments, and criminalized adultery and blasphemy – these exist even today.

Explore More

* LOOK at the photograph above and wonder at the number of princes and princely states in India just after Independence. The photo is of an earlier meeting of the Chamber of Princes. Choose any one princely state and make a Before and After (accession) comparison of its administration and lifestyle.

* DESIGN a float for the Republic Day parade: what would be the theme for your float? How would you construct it? What would it symbolize?

* DRAFT a short but clear 'constitution' for your home/family or your class or school — incorporating as many ideas and suggestions as possible from others in the same group. Think about how to resolve differences to arrive at the best possible rules for everyone involved, if you can!

The Nehru Years

[1950–1964 CE]

15

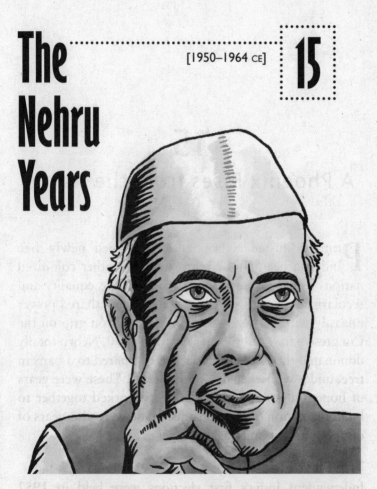

'Long years ago we made a tryst with destiny, and now the time comes when we shall redeem our pledge. At the stroke of the midnight hour, when the world sleeps, India will awake to life and freedom. A moment, which comes but rarely in history... when an age ends, and when the soul of a nation, long suppressed, finds utterance.'
— Jawaharlal Nehru, 15 August 1947

15

A Phoenix Rises from the Ashes

Prime Minister Nehru led and shaped newly free India in her first 17 years, inspiring other colonized nations as he steered it towards modernity, equality and secularism. During Nehru's early years, he shared power uneasily with Sardar Patel, who had an iron grip on the Congress party. After Patel's death in 1950, Nehru totally dominated the Congress, and was compared to a banyan tree, under whose shade nothing grew! These were years of hope and struggle when Indians worked together to build the nation of their dreams. These were also years of disappointment and dashed hopes.

The First Elections

Independent India's first elections were held in 1952 for both the central Parliament (489 seats) and state legislatures (4,000 seats), where each adult citizen of India, illiterate or educated, urban or rural, male or female, got a single vote each.

Organizing these elections was an overwhelming task – more than 200,000 voting booths were set up, voter lists prepared for 176 million people, and polling officers

The First General Elections

During the first 1952 elections, the government discovered a lot of double-voting and identity theft. As most Indians did not have birth certificates or official identification, indelible ink was used on fingernails to prevent double voting. This concept was actually replicated by many other countries. As many as 2,800,000 women were deregistered as they refused to give their own names, calling themselves wife of so and or daughter of so and so. Election officials showed great commitment, walking for days and riding on mules to attend training workshops. One voting booth near a jungle received only an elephant and some panthers on election day!

trained. As most voters could not read, each party was ingeniously assigned a visual symbol for the ballot! Popular Nehru attracted huge crowds as he campaigned vigorously. Many Indians came out to vote, and the world marvelled as a largely illiterate, underdeveloped India pulled off peaceful, free and fair elections!

Despite a robust opposition of 14 national parties and 35 regional parties, the Congress won 364 out of 489 seats (and swept the state elections). The Socialist Party won 12 seats, while the Communist Party of India (CPI) became the largest opposition party with 16 seats. In the 1957 elections the Congress won 371 seats and the CPI remained the largest opposition party. In 1962, Congress won 361 seats and a third

A typical scene from independent India's first general elections

term under Nehru, while the CPI got 29 seats, the new Swatantra Party won 18 and the Jana Sangh got 14 seats.

Political Ideologies

While fighting the British, the Congress had had members of all political views. As Congress became Nehru's party after Independence, many broke away. Other long-standing opposition included the right-leaning Jana Sangh, the leftist Communists and several breakaway parties.

COMMUNISM

After the bloody 1917 Russian Revolution, Lenin and his Bolsheviks formed the Union of Soviet Socialist Republics (USSR), becoming the motherlode of communism, which spoke of the inevitable violent 'class struggle' between the workers and owners of the world, which the workers would win. The USSR started the Comintern (Communist International) to aggressively sponsor communist activities worldwide.

Bengali revolutionary Manabendranath Roy went to the USA, and turned communist there, even starting the Communist Party of Mexico! Lenin asked to meet him in 1920, and sent him off to Tashkent with truckfuls of arms to train Indian communist revolutionaries (who were mostly caught by the British 'anti-Bolshevik' branch). The CPI was formed in 1921, but due to a general British ban on communism, it was only made legal after 20 years, when the USSR joined the Allies in the Second World War.

In 1946, the CPI fuelled a peasant guerilla rebellion in Telangana against 'feudal oppression and the Nizam's autocracy'. The government finally crushed the rebellion in 1949 and arrested 50,000 people.

In 1951, the CPI officially withdrew from violence to fight the general elections, for which it was reportedly funded by Moscow, including radio broadcasts from Tashkent! It did really well – winning 16 seats from Andhra, West Bengal and Tripura, to become the largest opposition party.

In 1957, the CPI won the Kerala state elections (to the shock of the West!) and E.M.S. Namboodiripad became India's first non-Congress chief minister, as well as the world's first democratically elected communist chief minister! Namboodiripad and his team worked with dedication and personal integrity, carrying out land reform and starting government-funded 'fair-price' shops. They even gave capitalists like the Birlas incentives to set up factories. Still, after some protests and deteriorating law and order, the Centre dismissed it in 1959. The Congress and its allies won the next election.

Political and ideological leaders of the era: (from top): E.M.S. Namboodiripad; Ram Manohar Lohia; Jayaprakash Narayan; Vinayak Damodar Savarkar; C.N. Annadurai (left) and E.V. Ramasamy Naicker 'Periyar'

SOCIALISM

Formed inside Congress in 1934, the Congress Socialist Party wanted regional socialism, with power handed to cooperatives, trade unions and local authorities.

Disillusioned by Nehru, Ram Manohar Lohia, Jayaprakash Narayan and others started the Socialist Party, and J.B. Kripalani started the Kisan Majdoor Praja Party (which won 19 seats in 1957). Mesmerizing orator Lohia became very anti-English, claiming that 'high-caste, wealth, and knowledge of English, anyone possessing two of these belong to the ruling class'.

DALITS

Ambedkar claimed that it was 'the same old tyranny, the same old oppression, the same old discrimination' for Dalits. He contested the 1952 elections under his new Scheduled Caste Federation Party, but shockingly lost to an obscure Congress candidate. Nominated to the Rajya Sabha (by the Congress!), he served until he died in 1956.

HINDUTVA

The Hindu Mahasabha was started in 1914, to politically organize Hindus, by Congress leaders like Pandit Madan Mohan Malviya and Lala Lajpat Rai, but later separated out under Veer (Vinayak Damodar) Savarkar. The atheist Savarkar coined the term 'Hindutva', and identified it with 'Hindu, Hindi, Hindustan.'

K.B. Hedgewar formed the Rashtriya Swayamsevak Sangh (RSS) in 1925, a non-political Hindutva volunteer organization. Branches called *shakha*s were opened all across India. At Independence, the RSS had about 600,000 volunteers called *swayamsevak*s. In 1951, RSS members and former Hindu Mahasabha member, Dr Shyamaprasad Mookerjee, formed the Bharatiya

Jana Sangh as a political Hindutva party. It opposed 'minority appeasement', wanted a uniform civil code and Kashmir's integration.

OTHER PARTIES
The 80-year old Congress stalwart C. Rajgopalachari started the classical-liberal Swatantra party in 1959, which stood for individual rights and opposed Nehru's 'big-government' outlook. It won 18 seats in the 1962 general elections.

Various parties were formed based on region or religion, like the Tamil nationalist Dravida Munnetra Kazhagam (DMK), and the Shiromani Akali Dal, which agitated for a Sikh-majority Punjab state.

The States Are Redrawn
The Congress had long asked the British to reorganize provinces based on language, but after Partition, decided to delay any identity-based politics, for fear of violence and riots. However, agitations started in Madras state by Telugu speakers, who felt discriminated against by Tamils. Nehru insisted that 'facts, not fasts' would prevail, but had to announce the new state of Andhra Pradesh when an old Congress worker Potti Sriramulu died due to protest fasting, and vicious rioting erupted.

The States Reorganization Act of 1956 established 14 states and three Union territories, grouped by language and culture. Madhya Bharat, Bhopal, Madhya Pradesh and Vindhya Pradesh became Madhya Pradesh. Hyderabad was dismantled, with pieces going to Bombay, Mysore and Andhra. A new Maratha state, with Bombay as its capital, was passionately opposed by Bombay communities like the Gujaratis and Parsis, but was formed in 1960 after all. Over the years, some states were further divided.

The Kashmir Problem

Nehru and his friend Sheikh Abdullah agreed to unite Kashmir with India on terms that became the Indian Constitution's Article 370. When Sardar Patel, who had been kept away, saw it, he predicted 'Jawahar *royega* (Jawahar will rue this)'. According to Article 370, Indian Parliament could only act in Kashmir on matters of defence, foreign affairs and communications, and only Kashmiris could own property in the state.

In February 1950, the UN Security Council asked both India and Pakistan to withdraw their armies from Kashmir for a plebiscite vote. Neither side agreed.

Meanwhile, the Jammu Praja Parishad began to agitate against Article 370 under the slogan '*Ek Vidhan, ek Pradhan, ek Nishan*' (One Constitution, One Head, One Flag). Formed by the RSS and Dogra Rajputs, with Shyamaprasad Mookerjee, it wanted Kashmir's complete integration. In the 1951 state elections, 45 of 49 Praja Parishad candidates were disqualified on flimsy grounds by Abdullah's government, which won all 75 seats, 73 of which were uncontested!

Following Dr Shyamaprasad Mookerjee's 1953 arrest and suspicious death in Kashmir, protestors nationwide shouted 'Kashmir *hamara hai*' (Kashmir is ours). A coup was engineered. Bakshi Ghulam Muhammad took over, and Sheikh Abdullah was jailed for 11 years. In 1964, an ill Nehru finally had the Sheikh released, who then went to Pakistan to find a joint solution to the Kashmir problem, but Nehru died during Sheikh Abdullah's trip.

Despite this churn at the top, beautiful Kashmir remained calm and teemed with tourists.

Nehru Abroad

Nehru was also India's foreign minister. Cosmopolitan and well spoken, he was already well-known around the world. Though poor and weak, India became an important international voice, especially for the dozens of newly ex-colonized countries, as Nehru urged Afro-Asian unity at Bandung (Indonesia) in 1955 and sponsored the Non-Aligned Movement in 1961, where member countries (in theory, anyway), remained neutral, without siding with either the USA-dominated Western bloc, or the USSR-dominated communist bloc.

Soviet Union

Nehru gushed about his first visit to the USSR in 1927, its economic progress, tolerance of minorities, and 'humane

Nehru at the Bandung Conference in 1955

An International Holi

Prime Minister Nehru once visited Burma. An eyewitness account by Indian diplomat B.K. Nehru: – 'The Burmese also play Holi... we were given Burmese clothes. The party consisted of the heads of India, Egypt and Burma, and sundry foreign ministers. The Burmese way of playing Holi is to receive VIPs in various pandals (tents). They are ceremoniously sprinkled with a little water from beautiful silver bowls by elegant young women. The guests, in turn, sprinkle water, delicately eat some sweets and depart to the next pandal.

'Having performed this routine twice or thrice, the Prime Minister got fed up and said he wanted to show the hosts how we played Holi in India. Nasser's enormous entourage of young men was enlisted by Jawaharlal into finding buckets and filling them with water.

'Thereafter, the Prime Minister of India upset the entire contents of these buckets on the President of Egypt, the Prime Minister of Burma, and whoever else was in sight.'

treatment of prisoners'. He loved their five-year plans, and became a great fan of state planning. Interestingly, Stalin disliked Nehru (and Gandhi) and allegedly once secretly plotted to overthrow him.

Nehru's claims of 'non-alignment' suffered a big blow when he strongly criticized the Israeli and Anglo-French invasion of Egypt during the Suez Crisis of 1956, but did not vote against the USSR at the UN when the USSR invaded Hungary in the same year.

THE USA

Socialist Nehru disapproved of America's imperialistic 'stranglehold of Central and South America'. An American official once complained that he 'talked to me as though I was a public meeting'. Nehru's criticism of America's involvement in the Korean War, and his proximity to communist Russia and China, made for tense relations.

Pakistan emerged as a key US ally, signing a military pact in 1954.

However, the USA badly wanted to keep India from turning communist, and provided a *lot* of food and loans. A real shift came after China attacked India in 1962 and Nehru asked the USA for arms. Ordinary Americans loved Nehru and newspapers compared him to one of America's founding fathers, Thomas Jefferson!

FUN FACT! American newspapers compared Jawaharlal Nehru to one of America's founding fathers, Thomas Jefferson!

PAKISTAN

India's relationship with Pakistan remained tense and conflicted over Kashmir and the division of assets – hardly like Canada and America, as Jinnah had fondly imagined! Water sharing became a major problem. West Pakistan's agriculture was heavily dependent on the Indus river system, controlled upstream by India. In 1948, India briefly stopped the waters of the Ravi and Sutlej rivers from flowing west, causing great panic in Pakistan. Water flow was restored after talks, and eventually, the World Bank brokered the Indus Water Treaty in 1960.

CHINA

The Communists took over China in 1949. Mao Zedong became 'chairman', and Zhou Enlai, 'premier'. Nehru was excited as the world's two most populous and ancient nations threw off the imperialist yoke, and looked forward to them becoming Asian leaders together – '*Hindi Chini Bhai Bhai*' ('the Indians and Chinese are brothers')!

India's ambassador to Beijing was impressed by Mao's 'dreamy and idealistic' temperament! When China

Nehru in discussion with the American ambassador at the time of the Sino-Indian conflict

occupied resource-rich Tibet in 1950, Nehru did not condemn it, despite Sardar Patel's warning that it 'was drunk with its own military strength and power' (which Nehru called 'rather naïve'). Patel died soon after and there was nobody to stop Nehru from 'helping' China – even recognizing Tibet as part of China through the idealistic 1954 Panchsheel agreement.

Soon enough, disputes began with India over two border areas – Aksai Chin, the north-eastern horn of Kashmir, a high-altitude, barren plateau, and Arunachal Pradesh, which had been handed over to the British by the Tibetans in 1914.

In 1958, India was shocked to discover Chinese maps showing Aksai Chin as part of China. Amid hostility, Zhou Enlai offered to give up claim to Arunachal if India gave up Aksai Chin (through which China wanted to build a road to Tibet!).

In March 1959, the Tibetan Dalai Lama escaped to India on horseback and was given asylum as an 'honoured guest'. Indians were loud in their anti-Chinese sentiment and the relationship deteriorated. India started an aggressive 'Forward Policy', building outposts in both Aksai Chin and Arunachal; China did not react. An overconfident India threatened 'to repeat what she did in Goa... certainly drive out the Chinese forces'. The

An Interconnected World

After the Second World War, nations realized the importance of working together through global institutions to prevent wars and help countries grow (especially poor ones).

A global peacekeeping force was set up by the newly formed United Nations. The small UN Security Council took responsibility of keeping peace. Its five permanent members, the USA, UK, France, the USSR and China could veto any action agreed by the UN.

The International Monetary Fund and World Bank gave loans and expertise to needy countries, funded by all UN member countries. As the biggest funder, the USA has the strongest vote.

After the Second World War, America gave a lot of aid (130 billion dollars today) through the Marshall Plan, to rebuild devastated western Europe... and prevent communism. (The USSR naturally refused it.) Also, rich countries started directly giving aid to poorer countries... initially as an enticement to keep away from communism.

only problem was that the Indian military was woefully underprepared for high-altitude warfare and the (very) socialist defence minister, V.K. Krishna Menon, scorned buying Western weapons.

After violent skirmishes in February 1962, China attacked simultaneously in October in Aksai Chin and Arunachal. A shocked Nehru wrote to Zhou Enlai: 'Nothing in my long political career has hurt me more.'

The Chinese advanced again, and were poised to take Leh *and* the north-east! Nehru finally swallowed his pride and asked the USA for military aircraft. On 22 November, Zhou Enlai declared a unilateral ceasefire, wanting to avoid active war with the USA, which had been busy till then with the Cuban missile crisis.

At the end of the India–China War, Aksai Chin stayed with China, and Arunachal with India after all, as Zhou

Enlai had wanted! Indians felt betrayed and Nehru's reputation took a severe beating. India started a massive modernization of her army, while China began supporting Pakistan in a proxy war against India.

Social Change

Independence and Partition changed Indian society abruptly. Almost all the British and Europeans left and most Muslim elite migrated to Pakistan.

Nehru strongly reassured minorities, particularly Muslims, that India was equally theirs, while some Congress leaders wanted 'proof' of Indian Muslims' loyalty, especially as many had voted to create Pakistan. Scheduled Castes got 15 per cent and Scheduled Tribes got 7.5 per cent reservations in government jobs, Parliament and state assemblies, giving millions employment and dignity.

FUN FACT! Before the Hindu Marriage Act of 1955, Hindu men could, by law, have as many wives as they chose.

Nehru and Ambedkar were both committed to a uniform civil code, as Indian laws about marriage and inheritance were still based on religion. However, Nehru decided to reform Hindu personal law first (which included Hindus, Sikhs, Jains and Buddhists), leaving Muslim personal law for later. They proposed the 1948 Hindu Code Bill, which gave Hindu women an equal share of inheritance, removed restrictions on inter-caste marriage, allowed women to file for divorce and, very controversially, outlawed multiple wives! It led to an explosion of public protest, but eventually Nehru pushed it through in five acts across 1955 and 1956. Hindu women have reason to be truly grateful! Nehru

Bhakra–Nangal Dam in Punjab: while inaugurating it Nehru famously said, '... these are the temples of modern India where I worship'

is still criticized for not reforming Muslim personal law then.

Trade and Economy

Newly independent India was one of the poorest countries in the world, which had to import everything from cars to cloth to needles.

Nehru wanted India to industrialize rapidly, and inspired by Soviet-style planning, created Five-Year Plans to direct both government and private investment into important sectors. However, unlike Russia, he did not ban private industry, making India a 'mixed' economy. The government built dams, power and steel plants in collaboration with other countries (like Bhilai with the Russians, Rourkela with West Germany and Durgapur with Britain), often funded by the World Bank. To make people buy Indian goods, imports were heavily taxed, yet private businesses needed many licences. (Nehru once told J.R.D. Tata: 'Never talk to me of profit, it is a dirty word.')

As the population exploded, India was perpetually short of food, and the government had to beg and borrow food. In a huge step, the ancient source of Indian revenue (from the Mauryas, to the Mughals, to the British!) – the agricultural tax – was abolished altogether, as was the zamindari system! The land of many absentee landlords was distributed to the actual farmers.

Until 1965, India's economy improved steadily without famines, and access to roads and electricity increased. However, the British Raj was replaced seamlessly by the Licence Raj – leading to corruption as officials demanded bribes for the many required permits. Also, while the state-planning model worked for projects like dams and steel plants, it slowed down India's overall growth.

Health

India's population exploded as death rates from starvation and epidemics fell dramatically – life expectancy shot up from 32 to 46 years! Mass vaccination campaigns were started, along with the World Health Organization, against malaria, smallpox, tuberculosis, leprosy and cholera. However, primary health care, especially in rural India, remained severely lacking.

Education and Science

Nehru set up world-class scientific and technical institutes in India, asking top international universities to collaborate. The Indian Institutes of Technology (IITs) were started with institutions like the Massachusetts Institute of Technology, and the Indian Institutes of Management (IIMs) were set up with universities like Harvard. The All India Institute of Medical Science combined a hospital, teaching and research.

Pioneers in science: from top: Homi Bhabha; Vikram Sarabhai

However, basic education was lacking, and nearly 70 per cent of Indians stayed illiterate.

Many Indian scientists were at Cambridge when nuclear science was taking off in the 1930s. One such, Homi Bhabha, started India's nuclear development – finding a way to use relatively plentiful thorium instead of scant uranium as raw material. In October 1965, he publicly announced that India could produce a nuclear bomb within 18 months. Within a few months, his plane crashed suspiciously in the European Alps.

Vikram Sarabhai set up many remarkable institutions. His Indian Space Research Organization had young NASA-trained scientists working from cowsheds and transporting rocket parts by bullock carts – and still managed to launch India's first rocket in 1963!

Arts, Craft and Culture

The government proudly promoted Indian heritage, culture and crafts after Independence by setting up many boards, groups and institutions like the National School of Drama, Lalit Kala Akademi and Sahitya Akademi.

The child widow and freedom fighter Kamaladevi Chattopadhyay doggedly revived Indian crafts and handloom, and started the Cottage Emporium.

The CPI had its own cultural wing (IPTA) that performed street plays against the 'oppression' of the government, with famous members like Ravi Shankar, Balraj Sahni,

The Palace of Assembly, Chandigarh, is one of the many examples of path-breaking architecture in India by Le Corbusier

Prithviraj Kapoor and Ritwik Ghatak! The Progressive Artists Group, which promoted modern painting, had iconic artists like M.F. Husain, F.N. Souza and S.H. Raza.

Famous foreign architects were invited to India and left their stamp, like the iconic Swiss–French architect Le Corbusier, who gave Punjab's new capital Chandigarh a radical design.

Writing with an Indian heart: R.K. Narayan

Nayi Kavita (New Poem) and Nayi Kahani (New Story) were modernist movements. Saadat Hasan Manto, Kaifi Azmi, Ismat Chughtai and Sahir Ludhianvi were left-leaning authors.

R.K. Narayan became famous for his English tales based in a fictional small-town, Malgudi.

Movies became the new rage, in Hindi and regional languages. Raj Kapoor took Indian cinema to the world with his socialistic movies like *Awara* and *Shree 420*. 'Evergreen' Dev Anand and Dilip Kumar became the ultimate romantic heroes. Iconic Bengali art films were made by Satyajit Ray, Ritwik Ghatak and Mrinal Sen. On the radio and gramophone, Hindi film music ruled, with Lata Mangeshkar and Mohammad Rafi as top playback singers.

End of an Era

Nehru died in May 1964 of illness. The nation grieved deeply, and even foreign ambassadors

From top: A poster for Satyajit Ray's award-winning film Pather Panchali; *the trinity of 1960s Bollywood: Dilip Kumar, Raj Kapoor and Dev Anand*

wept at his funeral. Today, his critics deride his Kashmir policy, his sometimes naïve foreign policy, his socialistic economics that held back India's growth, and his neglect of primary education and healthcare.

However, Nehru's vision, humanism and commitment to democracy inspired millions around the world. He was a secularist, modernist and patriot, who built up India's administrative, scientific and cultural institutions.

What in the World Was Happening! (1947–64)

Europe
- Countries shattered by the Second World War rebuild. The Berlin Wall is built to divide communist (East) and capitalist (West) Germany.

Asia
- Israel is formed in 1948 and is at constant war with its Arab neighbours.
- China becomes communist in 1949 under Mao Zedong.
- Many countries throw off the colonial yoke – Malaya, Burma, Indonesia, Indo-China, Philippines.
- The Korean War takes place during 1950–53, between communist North Korea (supported by China and the USSR) and capitalist South Korea (supported by the USA).
- The French are expelled from Vietnam in 1954. The USA supports South Vietnam against communist North Vietnam.

Americas
- The USA's Cold War with the USSR causes weapon pile-ups and proxy wars in other countries. The US Civil Rights movement rages through the 1960s for equal rights for the blacks.
- Latin and Central American economies are dominated by the US.

Africa
- Many countries become independent as France and the UK leave.

Explore More

* FIND out about the features of the buildings built during the Nehru years (such as the IIM Ahmedabad old campus shown above) and their architects.

* Look at the vintage photograph above. This was independent India's first cabinet. Find out who's who, and their portfolios and responsibilities.

* WATCH Haqeeqat, a film directed by Chetan Anand, and based on the 1962 Sino-Indian War.

16

The Indira Years

[1964–1984 CE]

'She suckered us. But let me
tell you she is going to pay.
She is going to pay.'

– American president
Richard Nixon on Indira
Gandhi after the Bangladesh
war, 1971

16
A Sharp Turn Left

When Prime Minister Nehru died, India was devastated and the world worried: Who would lead India? Would democracy collapse without Nehru?

For the next 20 years, Nehru's daughter Indira Gandhi shaped India just as decisively, but far more controversially. She showed extraordinary courage as she stood 'straight and tall', facing down the USA, China and Pakistan all together in 1971. However, her populist changes and dramatic increase of state control stifled economic growth. The judiciary, the press and even the Congress party became far less independent.

Political History

The grand old Congress party was straining at the seams, as rightists, leftists and centrists all pulled it in different directions. After Nehru's illness in 1963, Congress leaders of non-Hindi-speaking states got together to form the powerful 'Syndicate', and 'Kingmaker' K. Kamaraj from Madras state became the 1964 Congress president with Nehru's blessing. When Nehru died, Gulzarilal Nanda was sworn in as 'caretaker' prime minister. The Syndicate outmanoeuvred Morarji Desai, backing the centrist Lal Bahadur Shastri, who took office on 9 June 1964.

THE SHASTRI INTERLUDE

From a modest background, Lal Bahadur Shastri commanded respect as a freedom fighter and cabinet minister. Mild-mannered and with a simple lifestyle, he was a real contrast to suave Nehru. Indira Gandhi, Nehru's daughter, was made the information and broadcasting minister.

India's second prime minister, Lal Bahadur Shastri

THE INDO-PAKISTAN WAR

Everyone thought India was weak after its defeat by China. In April 1965, Pakistan surprised India in the Rann of Kutch with new American tanks, forcing Indian soldiers to withdraw 64 km. Encouraged, military dictator General Ayub Khan launched 'Operation Gibraltar' in August, when 7,000 Pakistani 'irregulars' crossed into Kashmir, blowing up bridges and buildings to spark an uprising. When that failed, their regular troops crossed the Line of Control. India marched on Lahore, forcing Pakistani troops and tanks to be rushed there from Kashmir.

On 22 September, the UN brokered a ceasefire after each side had lost about 4,000 men. Ayub and Shastri signed the 'Tashkent agreement' in January 1966, agreeing to settle the Kashmir issue bilaterally and withdraw to previous border positions. That same night, Shastri died suspiciously of a heart attack in Tashkent. His funeral was attended by millions: his call of 'Jai Jawan, Jai Kisan'

(Hail soldiers, hail farmers!) had given Indians a steely determination after the demoralizing 1962 China war.

'Goongi Gudiya'?

Gulzarilal Nanda was again sworn in as the interim prime minister. It seemed to *finally* be Morarji Desai's turn! But, in a surprise move, the Syndicate backed inexperienced Indira Gandhi, thinking she would be pliable.

Indira was Nehru's only child and had long acted as his hostess when he was prime minister. Against her family's wishes, she had married Feroze Gandhi, a Parsi, and had two sons, Rajiv and Sanjay. Nehru had been ambivalent about her entry in politics, yet she was elected Congress president in 1959. With the Syndicate's support, she swept the Congress's internal election. One of the first women leaders in the modern world, she took over during drought and a bad economy.

Called a 'goongi gudiya' (mute doll) by Congress old-timers when she first entered politics, Indira Gandhi as PM was called the Only Man in her cabinet!

The 1967 general elections were Indira's first big test. She campaigned hard, criss-crossing India, promising to reduce inequality and poverty. Stones thrown at her during a rally hurt her nose, but she finished her speech!

She formed the government, but Congress lost a whopping 80 seats, barely mustering a majority. The Swatantra Party became the largest opposition with 44 seats. The Jana Sangh rose to 35 seats. (The CPI had split.)

To the Left, to the Left

Indira Gandhi soon wanted to break free of the Syndicate. The strongly left-leaning prime minister's office (PMO), led by her trusted adviser P.N. Haksar, became all-powerful, eclipsing ministries and even her cabinet!

She made populist speeches to the poor and minorities, criticizing businessmen who 'make big profits and draw fat salaries'. In May 1967, she presented a 10-point programme to Parliament about the government taking over all banks, abolishing privy purses for the princes and guaranteeing a minimum wage. Radical members of the Congress joined her against the right-leaning faction led by Morarji Desai and the Syndicate.

The Congress Cracks Open

When the Indian President Zakir Husain died in 1969, Indira Gandhi issued a shocking executive order to nationalize the 14 largest banks and then got many Congress members to vote for her presidential candidate, V.V. Giri,

Morarji Desai

rather than the Syndicate's (and the Congress's original) candidate, Neelam Sanjiva Reddy. When expelled from the Congress Party for 'indiscipline', she formed a new party called the Indian National Congress (R) – 'R' stood for Requisitionists – which quickly became dominant!

This Great Congress Split transformed Indian politics. From a Congress that accommodated many beliefs, Indira's Congress was dominated by her and she even took over the relatively independent state units of the Congress party.

Elections 1971

Indira Gandhi now confidently called for early general elections. A 'Grand Alliance' against her included the

Swatantra Party, Jana Sangh, Socialists, Congress (O) – standing for Organization – and regional parties. They shouted 'Indira *Hatao*' (Remove Indira), claiming she was limiting individual rights. Her fiery reply, '*Garibi Hatao*' (Remove Poverty), was a bigger hit. The poor saw her as their saviour. 'The Indira wave' won her 352 of 518 seats, and a two-thirds majority in Parliament. She began giving morning 'darshans' outside her house to queues of people!

Western Disturbance

Meanwhile, civil war loomed in the neighbourhood. Bengali East Pakistan was seeing mass protests and strikes against West Pakistan, for not letting Mujibur Rahman form a government after he won the 1970 elections. Bengali Pakistanis had little funding, few army and government posts, and Urdu imposed on them as the national language.

From March 1971, the Pakistani army raged against its Bengali countrymen, killing perhaps a million. Intellectuals and leaders were arrested, violence perpetrated against women, and Bengalis were slaughtered and dumped in mass graves. Millions of panicked refugees, both Hindu and Muslim, fled to India.

With India's help, East Bengalis formed the Mukti Bahini, a guerilla troop to fight the Pakistani army. While Indira Gandhi demanded that Pakistan stop its genocide, China and the USA stood solidly behind Pakistan. In a major move away from 'Non-Alignment', India signed a Treaty of Friendship with the USSR, which included mutual aid against any threat.

On 3 December, Pakistani planes bombed Indian airfields in the west, and its army attacked Kashmir. Helped by the Mukti Bahini and the inability of Chinese troops to cross snowed-in mountain passes, Indian troops reached Dhaka in days. On 6 December, India formally recognized the new country of Bangladesh and Pakistani General Niazi surrendered in Dhaka

Pakistani General Niazi of Pakistan, signing the Instrument of Surrender, 1971

on 16 December. The USSR helped prevent the USA and China from attacking India, by its support in the UN.

The liberation of Bangladesh was a moment of joy in India, and of great anguish in Pakistan. In June 1972, Pakistani president Zulfikar Ali Bhutto signed the Shimla Agreement: India released all 93,000 Pakistani prisoners of war on assurance that Pakistan would respect the LOC (they did not)! Indira Gandhi was lauded for her strategy and decisiveness, and for coolly, courageously staring down both China and superpower USA.

Into the Emergency

By 1972, the glow of victory had faded and Indira faced sharp criticism when the permit and land to produce a new, affordable people's car was 'awarded' to her inexperienced son Sanjay Gandhi at throwaway prices.

Besides, in 1973, a sharp rise in world oil prices pushed prices of essential goods up by 35 per cent! As hoarding and black marketeering began, public anger grew. The respected, 71-year-old former freedom fighter, Jayaprakash Narayan, led a popular, peaceful protest, 'the JP movement', to build the India the freedom fighters had dreamed of. A railway strike paralysed the country for weeks. In March 1975, thousands of protesters led by JP

Mrs Gandhi earned the nickname of 'Empress of India'

marched to Parliament, chanting *'Janta ka dil bol raha hai, Indira ka singhasan dol raha hai'* (the public speaks, Indira's throne quakes). The crisis point came when Indira Gandhi was found guilty on two minor counts of electoral malpractice in the 1971 election. A million protesters gathered in Delhi, and the opposition put huge pressure on her to resign.

The Emergency

The 'Empress of India' got Indian President Fakhruddin Ali Ahmed to sign the Proclamation of Emergency on the night of 25 June 1975. Police swooped in to arrest all opposition leaders like Jayaprakash Narayan, Morarji Desai, Charan Singh, Atal Bihari Vajpayee and L.K. Advani, under the draconian MISA (Maintenance of Internal Security Act), which people renamed the 'Maintenance of Indira and Sanjay Act' ! Thousands of people were flung into jail.

Despite severe criticism from world press, for the next two years, general elections were postponed and unfriendly state governments toppled. Press freedom was suppressed and over 200 journalists were jailed. Without any official position, Sanjay Gandhi replaced ministers with his loyalists.

Indira Gandhi with sons, Rajiv (left) and Sanjay (right)

He announced that he would focus on forests, dowry, illiteracy, and city and family planning. Worthy goals as they were, his methods were horrific, especially his forced mass sterilization of men to control the population!

In January 1977, Indira Gandhi suddenly announced fresh elections, and freed all her political opponents (without consulting Sanjay!). No one quite knows why – perhaps it was global criticism, or the deeply democratic Nehru's ghost whispering in her ear!

The Country Speaks

The Jana Sangha, Bharatiya Lok Dal, Socialist Party and Congress (O) combined to form one party called the Janata Dal, with massive national support. The Congress was routed in north India. Both Indira and Sanjay lost to rivals. The world press reported that 'India clearly prefers its democracy'. There was a sense of exhilaration – for the first time, a non-Congress party would rule India!

The Janata Government

It was *finally* Morarji Ranchhodji Desai's turn to be PM! A freedom fighter, he had been chief minister, Union minister and even deputy prime minister. He was thought to be a good administrator, upright and austere, but also inflexible. The Janata government kept close ties with the USSR, but reduced hostility towards the USA, and president Jimmy Carter visited India. It computerized Indian railways. Most importantly, it re-established the battered Indian Constitution and judiciary.

However, power struggles within the Janata Party led to a split by July 1979. Morarji Desai had to resign and Chaudhary Charan Singh took over, but could not form a majority, and mid-term elections had to be called.

Erstwhile PM Chaudhary Charan Singh

Elections 1980

Amazingly, just three years after the oppressive Emergency, Indira Gandhi swept back to power in 1980 with 353 seats, even more than the 1971 elections! People had chosen stability over the Janata Dal's squabbling.

Sanjay became the prime-minister-in-waiting, choosing chief ministers and election candidates, but in June 1980, the 33-year-old recklessly crashed his two-seater plane. A devastated Indira persuaded her reluctant elder son Rajiv, an Indian Airlines pilot, to join politics. His Italian wife Sonia was dead against it, but Rajiv eventually took over Amethi, Sanjay's erstwhile seat, and became the new heir.

The States

In the 1967 state polls, hit by a national food crisis, the Congress lost in many states. Coalitions were often formed by parties bound only by a hatred for the Congress.

West Bengal

The United Front coalition came to power in 1967 in West Bengal, a combination of a breakaway Congress faction (Bangla Congress) and the Communist Party of India (Marxist) [CPI-M].

In 1967, a dispute between farmers and landlords in Naxalbari in north Bengal sparked a violent communist rebellion led by Kanu Sanyal, in which landlords were beheaded and peasants shot in retaliation by the police. Many fled to the forests and the word 'naxalite' came to mean an armed man fighting the Indian government (and the CPI-M) for the cause of the poor and oppressed. West Bengal saw hard years with labour unrest, strikes, bombings and attacks on landlords and industrialists (who

fled). In 1977, a CPI-M-led Left Front came to power, and
Jyoti Basu, an UK-educated lawyer and leader of CPI-M,
became chief minister, taking up rural agricultural reform.

THE NORTH-EAST
After the 1971 war, Meghalaya and Mizoram were carved
out of Assam state. A violent nationalist movement had
begun among the Naga tribes since the 1950s, and the
state of Nagaland was carved out in 1963.

When a periodic famine (called *mautam*), caused by the
flowering of bamboo every 48 years and the consequent
increase in the rat population, devastated Mizoram during
1959-60, protests against government apathy turned into
angry liberation movements (aided by East Pakistan!).

In Assam, there was an anti-immigrant backlash against
Bangladeshi refugees and non-Assamese industrialists,
with strikes, violence, and killing of non-Assamese people.

Sikkim, an Indian protectorate since 1947, became
disenchanted with its ruler and voted to
join India. It became the 22nd Indian state
in 1975, following a 97 per cent vote.

THE SOUTH
The south saw pro-Dravidian parties in
power, often led by film superstars!

There was some support for naxalites
in Telangana in Andhra Pradesh. Film star
N.T. Rama Rao's new Telugu Desam party
won a two-thirds majority in 1982.

In Tamil Nadu, the DMK (Dravida
Munnetra Kazhagam) finally came
to power in 1967, led by the popular

N.T. Rama Rao (top) and M.G. Ramachandran: superstar politicians

screenwriter Karunanidhi and superstar M.G. Ramachandran, and raised lower-caste reservations and food subsidies. M.G. Ramachandran formed the AIADMK (All India Anna Dravida Munnetra Kazhagam), winning the 1977 elections. His free midday meals scheme at government schools reduced dropouts and was imitated across India.

THE NORTH

The Kashmir issue simmered, with Sheikh Abdullah under house arrest or exiled until 1974. He signed an accord with Indira Gandhi, giving up the demand for a Kashmiri plebiscite, in return for state elections. His National Conference won and he was chief minister until he died in 1982. His son Farooq took over until, in 1984, he was displaced in a coup by defectors allied with the Congress.

PUNJAB

Indira Gandhi agreed to a Sikh-majority state in 1966. The Punjabi-speaking regions remained Punjab, while the rest became Haryana and Himachal Pradesh. The Akali Dal still kept agitating against the Congress, finally coming to power in the 1977 anti-Indira wave.

Meanwhile, a Sikh religious preacher called Jarnail Singh Bhindranwale began a movement to 'purify' Sikhism – initially supported by Sanjay Gandhi and former Congress chief minister Giani Zail Singh, as a counter to the troublesome Akalis. A movement for an independent Sikh country called Khalistan took off, and militant Bhindranwale launched a reign of terror against Punjabi Hindus. In October 1983, Sikh militants shot Hindus inside a bus, prompting President's Rule.

Bhindranwale moved into the Golden Temple complex and Indira Gandhi controversially launched an army blitz, 'Operation Bluestar'. The Golden Temple was damaged by tanks as 500 terrorists were killed over the two-day battle. This damage to their holiest shrine angered Sikhs.

An Assassination

Mrs Gandhi received death threats and was advised to remove the Sikh members in her personal bodyguard, but she refused on secular principles. On 31 October 1984, as she walked from her home to her office next door, two of her Sikh bodyguards shot at her 33 times at close range.

By evening, Rajiv Gandhi was sworn in as prime minister. Violence exploded against the Sikhs in Delhi. Mobs started looting, burning and killing Sikhs. The army was finally called in after three horrific days. More than 3,000 Sikhs were killed in Delhi alone, and 8,000 across India.

Trade and Economy

As death rates kept falling, India's population kept rising, reaching 550 million in 1971 and 685 million in 1981! This caused a serious food shortage. The brilliant agriculture minister, C. Subramaniam, put his full effort into the green revolution, designed by the American scientist Norman Borlaug (who had been invited by Nehru in 1962). High-yield seeds and fertilizers were developed and distributed, and loans given to farmers. By 1967, there was a bumper food crop of 95 million tonnes, ending India's food crisis.

As Indira Gandhi tightened government control, India's economic growth plummeted to just 3.6 per cent per year, mocked by economists as the 'Hindu rate of growth'. Fourteen major banks (controlling 85 per cent

The Story of Amul and the White Revolution

Even though milk, yoghurt, butter and ghee were a big part of the Indian diet, India was chronically short of milk at Independence and milk powder had to be imported.

In 1949, Verghese Kurien, a dairy engineer whose US education had been funded by the Government of India, was posted to the small town of Anand in Gujarat, to a minor farmers' cooperative for a reluctant 'forced tryst with milk'. He stayed on to help out the exploited farmers and transformed Indian dairy! He started a unique scheme where small-scale farmers sold milk to a cooperative, which sold milk and milk products under the brand name Amul. Kurien set up efficient collection systems, modern technology to process milk,

 and new technology to freeze-dry it. This was such a roaring success that Kurien was asked in 1965 to replicate this model across India through Operation Flood, and head the National Dairy Development Board. It brought about a white revolution as India crossed the target of a billion litres of milk. India is now the largest producer of milk in the world, and the cattle are owned by the poorest!

of deposits), were nationalized, maximum income tax was raised to 97.5 per cent(!), and licences, quotas and bureaucratic permissions became a truly complex maze.

As labour laws were strengthened, there was much union unrest and a two-year strike of almost 200,000 textile workers permanently finished off Bombay's textile industry. The number of poor kept increasing, and made up nearly 50 per cent of the population by the 1960s.

Religion

Even as Indira Gandhi officially added the word 'secular' to the Constitution, in the late 1960s, Hindu–Muslim riots reared their ugly heads again after a relatively peaceful 20 years, in Ranchi, Assam, Bhiwandi and across Uttar

Pradesh. Political parties were slow to act for fear of losing precious vote banks of one community or another. One of the worst riots took place in Ahmedabad in September 1969, with more than 1,000 people killed.

Arts and Culture

The support for socialism, disillusionment with the government and powerful people, the dreams of the poor and villagers, all reflected in the arts of the time.

Modern and experimental art flourished, with Paritosh Sen and Jogen Chowdhury as top Calcutta artists. Bombay's Akbar Padamsee was a pioneer of modern Indian art.

In 1965, Hindi was to become the official language, as per the drafters of the Indian Constitution. However, faced with extreme protests and immolation from non-Hindi-speaking states, especially Tamil Nadu, PM Shastri agreed that each state could use its own language and English indefinitely.

After the Emergency, there was a spectacular growth in newspapers and magazines as regional language papers, especially Hindi ones, overtook English dailies. Salman Rushdie's 1981 *Midnight's Children* ushered in a new era of Indian writing in English when it won the Booker Prize. The Jnanpith Award began honouring Indian language writers, such as Ramdhari Singh 'Dinkar', Tarashankar Bandyopadhyay, Firaq Gorakhpuri, K. Shivaram Karanth, T. Sivasankara Pillai and Amrita Pritam.

Both TV and radio were government-controlled. Radio was very popular, reaching far-flung corners of India. In 1965, the state broadcaster Doordarshan began telecasting black-and-white programmes for a few hours daily. In 1982, nationwide colour telecasts were introduced for the

Lifestyle in the Indira Years

India was the land of scarcity and permits. All brands were Indian, as even Coca-Cola was thrown out in 1977, and Indian substitutes like Campa Cola and Thums Up became popular. Everything 'imported' became exotic and desirable to young people.

There was a four-year wait for an Ambassador car, 12 years for a Fiat and hope eternal for a phone connection! One had to queue, queue, queue: for gas cylinders, for milk, for basic goods at the ration shop. Paneer was banned in the summer due to milk shortage!

To travel abroad, people needed authorization from the Reserve Bank of India, and could only get eight US dollars in foreign exchange per day! A Guest Control Order even prohibited serving meals at private social functions for more than 100 people.

Eating out became popular as food taboos started breaking. A new cuisine – Indian-Chinese – became popular along with the Punjabi-Mughlai cuisine and south Indian snacks like idli and dosa.

There was no great economic activity. As a Western journalist put it back then, 'Five thousand years of civilization – with that behind them, Indians seem to be in no hurry to go anywhere'.

Asian Games in New Delhi. Colour TV serials became the rage, like the first soap opera hit *Hum Log* in 1984.

India became the largest producer of movies in the world!

Films and film music dominated the tastes, fashion, speech and world view of millions of Indians. Cinema stars, such as Rajesh Khanna and Amitabh Bachchan, became larger-than-life celebrities. Many films focused on rural themes, like dacoits, of which *Sholay* (1975) is the biggest Indian blockbuster of all time! Many 'art' movies in Hindi and regional languages won international awards.

From top: Writers Amrita Pritam, K. Shivaram Karanth and Ramdhari Singh 'Dinkar'

Sports

After Independence, cricket overtook hockey in popularity, especially after India's dramatic wins over England and the West Indies in 1971. 'Little Master' batsman Sunil Gavaskar and Indian spinners became overnight stars. Besides that and the 1983 Cricket World Cup win, only exceptions like Prakash Padukone (badminton) and Michael Ferreira (billiards) were in international limelight. India hosted the well-organized 1982 Asian Games, in which 33 Asian countries participated. New stadiums were built, roads widened and colour broadcasting began. The face of Delhi changed.

What in the World Was Happening! (1964-1984)

The cold war rages between the USA and USSR, with the world divided into 'blocs'.

Europe
- Colonial powers like Britain and France gradually surrender all their colonies; Europe is divided into the Western bloc and the Eastern bloc, which was behind the (Soviet) Iron Curtain.

Americas
- The USA is embroiled in the Vietnam War. It finally withdraws in 1973, after raging domestic opposition and loss of prestige.
- Neil Armstrong becomes the first man on the moon in 1969.
- American culture, music and movies dominate the world; many Indians start emigrating to America.

Africa
- European powers exit Africa, replaced by local governments, sometimes democratically elected, often dictatorships.
- Indians settled in countries like Uganda get forcefully expelled.

Explore More

* FIND out about what happens when a state of Emergency is declared in the country: Who can declare an Emergency? Under what circumstances can the Emergency be declared? How does it affect public life? What are the freedoms and constitutional rights that can be curtailed as a result of this? Think about why it was, and is, considered a step against democracy.

* LIST a selection of films that were made between 1964 and 1984. You could also ask older members of your family to recall a few and tell you about them. Analyse the popular and bestselling themes of those times and work out the social concerns that different movies reflect and express.

* READ about Project Tiger that was launched in 1971 to save tigers, whose population was declining sharply. Find out what this project is called now, how it progressed and what its achievements are.

Indian Scripts
Reading between the lines of Indian language scripts
reveals fascinating facts.

Writing evolved independently in many cultures like the Sumerian, Egyptian, Mayan and Chinese. All these used symbols to mean words, which needed the knowledge of a large number of symbols – Chinese uses more than 50,000 symbols today!

The great change came when the Egyptians began using symbols for sounds. This gave rise to a semi-'phonetic' script.

The Phoenicians, traders from the Middle East, created the first true alphabet, early forms of which were in use by 1500 BCE. It had simple symbols that could be learnt in days instead of years. All cultures coming in contact with this soon adopted the idea, and created their own alphabets (except the Chinese)! This was the parent of all phonetic scripts in use now.

The Greeks and Romans created scripts from the Phoenician, which formed the base for European language scripts. The Hebrews and Arabs modified it into their own scripts. The Persian Empire adopted this alphabet as the Aramaic alphabet (replacing the cuneiform) and brought it to India with the Persian conquests of the Indus region in the sixth century BCE.

In India, (except Harappan writing) the earliest complete inscriptions appear in the Mauryan period, in the Hathi Gumpha in Odisha, and the Ashokan edicts in the third century in a script called Brahmi. Some earlier potsherds and stones were found with some letters inscribed, like one at Adichanallur in Tamil Nadu, dated to about 500 BCE.

Many believe that Brahmi was derived from the Aramaic script. Of its many variations, one became the Gupta Brahmi over the next 500 years.

Brahmi is the ancestor script of all South Asian writing systems and many South-East Asian scripts such as Burmese, Thai and Javanese.

All ancient and modern Indian scripts, north and south Indian, are also derived from Brahmi. This, of course, does not include the Harappan script. An example of how one letter evolved is below:

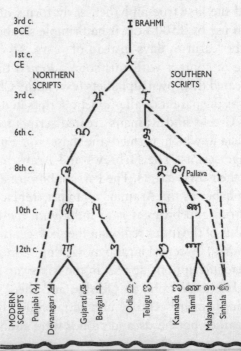

17 Liberalization
[1984–2000s]

'Where the mind is without fear and the head is held high,
Where knowledge is free,
Where words come out from the depth of truth,
Where the clear stream of reason has not lost its way
Into the dreary desert sand of dead habit,
Where the mind is led forward by thee
Into ever-widening thought and action,
Into that heaven of freedom,
My Father, let my country awake.'
– Rabindranath Tagore, writer, composer, painter,
polymath, social reformer

17
Breaking the Shackles

Over the last 30 years, India has grown at a rapid pace economically and its clout in the world has increased. From being thought a basket case, which always needed foreign aid, it has become the third largest economy in the world after the USA and China! Power has, however, kept changing hands between the Congress, BJP and coalitions of other parties.

Political History

Rajiv Gandhi swept the 1984 elections on a sympathy wave, winning 401 seats, the highest ever for the Congress. India was heady with optimism and change, bowled over by this softer, friendlier Gandhi who promised a 'clean and efficient government' to take India into the 21st century.

Rajiv signed peace agreements with the many groups agitating for separation, in Assam, Mizoram, Darjeeling, Tripura, Nagaland and Manipur. Militant activities by ULFA (United Liberation Front of Assam) continued in Assam, as did insurgencies in Tripura, Manipur and Nagaland.

PUNJAB

Rajiv Gandhi also signed a peace treaty in Punjab in 1985, but Khalistani Sikh militants continued a reign of terror, killing thousands of innocent people (including the former army chief who had planned Operation Bluestar). Director General of Police K.P.S. Gill's crackdown between 1988 and 1995 was key in ending the militancy.

KASHMIR

A National Conference–Congress alliance came to power after the 1987 elections in Kashmir. Meanwhile, *mehmani* mujahideen (guest jihadis) trained in urban guerrilla warfare, turned to Kashmir after Russia left Afghanistan in 1989. They and their newly trained Kashmiri separatist brothers unleashed a bloodbath. Kashmir, long considered paradise on earth, which had maintained communal peace through 1947, 1965 and 1971, now exploded with Kalashnikovs, bomb blasts and grenade attacks. Around 80,000 Indian troops were sent in.

Militant diktats appeared on city walls, cinema halls and bars were closed, and women ordered to wear burqas. From January 1990, militants demanded that the 'infidels' and 'occupiers' – the minority local Hindus called Kashmiri Pandits – leave. When they began torturing and killing them, 200,000 Kashmiri Pandits had to flee overnight to refugee camps in Jammu and Delhi. Today, fewer than 3,000 Hindus remain in Kashmir Valley. Despite elected governments, army presence and public unrest continues.

TURMOIL AT THE CENTRE

Rajiv Gandhi began his reforms by loosening telecom restrictions – Indians no longer had to wait for years for a telephone line! Personal computers could be imported and quickly became popular. But his 'Mr Clean' image soon took a severe beating in 1987 with the exposure of bribes worth 640 million rupees given by a Swedish company Bofors to Indian politicians for military purchases.

Rajiv Gandhi's finance minister, V.P. Singh (who was sacked for investigating these murky defence deals),

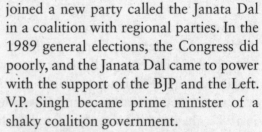

joined a new party called the Janata Dal in a coalition with regional parties. In the 1989 general elections, the Congress did poorly, and the Janata Dal came to power with the support of the BJP and the Left. V.P. Singh became prime minister of a shaky coalition government.

He suddenly declared high reservations in government jobs for OBCs (Other Backward Castes) based on the long-ago Mandal Commission recommendations (from 1980). As now nearly 50 per cent of jobs were reserved, forward-caste students began violent agitations, striking, rioting and even setting themselves on fire. Meanwhile, after BJP leader L.K. Advani's arrest during a road rally to make a Ram temple in Ayodhya, the BJP withdrew its support and V.P. Singh's government fell after just a year.

Indian prime ministers (from top): Rajiv Gandhi, V.P. Singh, Chandra Shekhar, P.V. Narasimha Rao, H.D. Deve Gowda; (facing page from top): I.K. Gujral, Atal Bihari Vajpayee, Manmohan Singh, Narendra Modi

After him his rival, the veteran Janata leader, Chandra Shekhar, became PM with Congress support, for just four months!

New elections were called in mid-1991, but while campaigning vigorously in Tamil Nadu, Rajiv Gandhi was killed by a female LTTE suicide bomber. The Congress won 244 seats on a sympathy wave and formed a minority government headed by the ageing, almost-retired Congress veteran P.V. Narasimha Rao. Despite his precarious position, Rao stayed for the full five years, even as he quietly dismantled India's long-standing licence raj and ushered in India's economic boom!

In 1996, a new coalition government had H.D. Deve Gowda as prime minister for ten months followed by a brief spell under I.K. Gujral.

After fresh elections in 1999, the BJP and its coalition, the National Democratic Alliance (NDA), finally formed a stable government, with a prosperous five years under Prime Minister Atal Bihari Vajpayee. With 'India Shining', everyone expected the BJP to win a second term in 2004, but shockingly, the Congress (with only 145 seats) formed the government with a coalition, called the United Progressive Alliance (UPA).

Sonia Gandhi (Rajiv's Italian-born widow) had been convinced to become Congress president in 1998. She declined the post of PM, appointing the well-respected economist Dr Manmohan Singh instead. India saw fast growth, and people began to dream of 'superpower' India.

The UPA won a second term in 2009, but the government was plagued with large-scale corruption scandals, high debt and slowing growth.

In 2014, after 30 years, a party won a clear majority – the BJP and its allies got 282 seats under Narendra Modi, who promised 'achchhe din' (good days) and economic growth. The Congress was reduced to its lowest ever 44 seats.

The Rise and Rise of the Bharatiya Janata Party

The Bharatiya Janata Party was founded in 1980 as the heir of the Bharatiya Jana Sangh, winning just two seats in the 1984 elections. It has steadily gained ground since then. In 1992, the Babri Masjid–Ram Mandir issue polarized the country, and Hindutva politics entered the mainstream. Since 1984, voters have steadily switched from the Congress to the BJP. From 8 per cent in 1984, it got 31 per cent of votes in 2014, while the Congress went from 49 per cent to 19 per cent in the same period.

India and the World

India is active in international forums including the United Nations, though its periodic bids for a place in the UN Security Council are ironically always blocked by China. India contributes many soldiers to UN Peacekeeping Forces who are sent to different troubled spots across the world. India is an important member of SAARC (South Asian Association of Regional Cooperation) launched in 1985, BRICS (Brazil, Russia, India, China and South Africa), and the G20 (the 20 largest economies).

Sri Lanka

Sri Lanka was plagued by civil war between the Buddhist Sinhalese and its Hindu Tamil minority. India initially sided with Tamil separatist movements, but after terrorist acts by the militant Liberation Tigers of Tamil Eelam (LTTE), Rajiv Gandhi sent an Indian Peace Keeping Force (IPKF) in 1987 to Sri Lanka. It failed disastrously and an LTTE suicide bomber later killed Rajiv Gandhi. The Sri Lankan government finally quelled the LTTE by 2009.

CHINA

China's economy grew phenomenally after Deng Xiaoping opened it up in the 1978. China has become India's largest trading partner, though India imports far more, mostly in electronics. The world has been predicting that India and China will rise to dominate the world economies, as they did historically. Both countries are trying to create rival spheres of influence in Asia. China is encircling India with military bases, called the 'String of Pearls', in the Indian Ocean, and investing in India's neighbours, like Myanmar, Sri Lanka, Maldives, and of course, Pakistan. In turn, India is allying with the USA, Japan, Australia, Afghanistan and Iran.

PAKISTAN

The India-Pakistan reel plays in an endless troubled loop: Relations gradually thaw, and peace talks start. Pakistan demands to resolve the 'Kashmir Issue' with international refereeing, while India insists Pakistan stop sponsoring terrorists before any bilateral discussions. Kashmiri separatists (allegedly funded by Pakistan) act up, resulting in a pushback by the Indian army. There is a terrorist attack somewhere in India. And repeat.

When India tested a nuclear bomb in 1998, Pakistan followed quickly with its 'Islamic Bomb', using Chinese

The Kargil Conflict

In Kargil, a high-altitude region on the Line of Control between Pakistan and India, Indian and Pakistani troops would vacate their outposts in the bitter winter, returning after the spring thaw.

In the spring of 1999, the Indian army found that Pakistani 'militants' had occupied many Indian outposts that overlooked the strategic highway connecting Leh to Srinagar. All this, while peace agreements were being signed between prime ministers Nawaz Sharif and Atal Bihari Vajpayee. Pakistan initially claimed this was the work of 'Kashmiri Independence fighters'. India started retaking the posts one by one. Some were 5,000-m high and had to be taken by soldiers attacking uphill, often involving hand-to-hand combat, in tremendous shows of bravery.

Once India presented evidence that the militants were Pakistani army officers in disguise, the USA, which usually sided with Pakistan, told Pakistan to withdraw, which it did. General Musharraf soon engineered a coup and the military took control of Pakistan.

help. India and Pakistan's 1999 war over the Kargil region alarmed the world as both countries had nuclear arms.

The USA

In the past three decades, India's relationship with the USA has transformed, especially after the USSR collapsed in 1991. India's opening up to foreign trade created an important market for American goods! The USA looks upon India as a natural ally (especially versus China), as both are democracies (unlike China!).

Terrorism

Terrorism became the world's problem after the shocking 9/11 attacks, where Islamic terrorists crashed passenger planes into New York's World Trade Center.

India has faced frequent terrorist attacks since the early 1990s, and still suffers nearly 10 per cent of all terror incidents in the world every year! Terrorism comes in three forms in India. Attacks by ethnic separatists, like Khalistanis and ULFA, have reduced. Maoist terror remains a big problem, carried out by violent left-wing militias hiding out in the forest areas of India, but the situation is slowly improving. Islamic terrorism is carried out by terror groups like Lashkar-e-Taiba (LeT) and the Jaish-e-Mohammed (JeM), which are reportedly sheltered by Pakistan and nurtured by international outfits like ISIS or Al Qaeda.

Besides intermittent bomb blasts in markets, major attacks like the one on the Indian Parliament in 2001 and the 26/11 attack on Mumbai in 2008 spread shock and terror. In fact, some of the terrorists involved in 26/11 had been released earlier by the Indian government in 1999 in exchange for hostages on a hijacked plane. Ajmal Kasab, the only terrorist captured alive during the four-day Mumbai attack, revealed the support of the Pakistani secret service, the ISI.

Religion

Rajiv Gandhi's secular halo vanished with the Shahbano case. When Muslims protested a Supreme Court judgment giving alimony of 179 rupees a month to a 75-year old woman (because they deemed alimony as un-Islamic), worried about alienating their Muslim voters, Rajiv Gandhi's government passed a law that denied all Muslim women divorce maintenance beyond three months!

Another cause of social polarization came with the Babri Masjid dispute. In 1986, when a district court opened this Ayodhya site (locked up since British times) for Hindu worshippers who believe this site to be the birthplace of Rama, groups like the Vishwa Hindu Parishad and the RSS began mass agitations to build a temple there. Hindu–Muslim clashes and bloody riots kept exploding across north India over the next few years.

In 1990, after L.K. Advani's arrest by the Bihar government, as many as 150,000 *kar sevaks* (Hindutva volunteers) heading to Ayodhya were also arrested. Ensuing clashes sparked more Hindu-Muslim riots across Uttar Pradesh.

Meanwhile, the VHP announced that 6 December 1992 would be the day to start building the temple. With only unarmed police around, there was a mass surge of Hindu *kar sevak*s towards the Babri Masjid, many of whom climbed up the mosque and started battering it with hammers. The mood turned ugly, the mosque started crumbling and was demolished in a few hours.

The country was shocked, including the BJP in power in Uttar Pradesh. The BJP-led Uttar Pradesh government was dismissed and President's Rule imposed. This violent demolition led to horrific riots across India. In March 1993, Bombay experienced 'revenge' in a series of bomb blasts, killing 300 and injuring more than 1,000 people.

The Babri Masjid is under government custody, while the cases continue in courts.

Gujarat

Gujarat suffered regular Hindu–Muslim clashes. In a major riot in 1969, as many as 2,000 lives were lost, besides arson and loot. Violence kept bubbling up, especially in the 1985 and 1993 riots.

In February 2002, a large group of *kar sevaks* was returning from Ayodhya. At a small station called Godhra (near Ahmedabad), coaches were locked by a Muslim mob, petrol poured in, and set ablaze, burning alive 58 people. Violent riots erupted, especially in Ahmedabad and Vadodara. Many men, women, children and police officers were killed; official figures cite the death of 790 Muslims and 254 Hindus. Amid claims that the government did not do enough to stop the riots, Gujarat's then chief minister, Narendra Modi, was questioned by an investigation team appointed by the Supreme Court, and cleared of all charges in 2012.

In 2009, a Muslim president swore in a Sikh PM of a party led by a Catholic in a Hindu Majority country — now that is multiculturalism!

FUN FACT!

Meanwhile, he was elected chief minister thrice, and became the Indian prime minister in 2014.

India's Achievements and Contradictions

Indian infrastructure remains a study in contrasts. The many smooth multi-lane highways vie with potholed barely-there rural roads. There are superb metro systems in many cities, and places where bullock carts amble along. Hundreds of millions of mobile phones connect Indians in the most remote locations, but many homes do not yet have electricity or potable water!

Sports

India has become the world's hub of cricket due to its large fan base, topped by its two World Cup wins in 1983 and 2011. With the new, popular 20-over match format seen in the Indian Premier League (IPL, started in 2008), cricketers became even bigger superstars. New premier leagues have sprung up for kabaddi, football and hockey.

Abhinav Bindra won the first individual gold for India in shooting in the 2008 Beijing Olympics! Wrestlers and weightlifters have been winning international medals and boxer Mary Kom has won the world championship many times as well as an Olympic medal. In badminton, India has world champions like Saina Nehwal, P.V. Sindhu and K. Srikanth, all coached by Pullela Gopichand, a former Indian badminton player.

CULTURE

The international profile of India has risen tremendously in the last few decades – officially by government initiatives like the 'Incredible India' campaigns, and unofficially by the film industry – seen (dubbed or subtitled) around the world. Movies like *Dangal* made more money in China than in India! India is now the largest producer of movies in the world, beating American Hollywood, with nearly four billion viewers.

Indian TV serials have become very popular, especially since private TV channels were allowed in the 1990s. In fact, India boasts more than 800 channels, in English, Hindi and regional languages. Indian serials are dubbed and watched around the world! However, in general, English has become more prized, as the language of study, work and fun, for the upwardly mobile.

SOCIAL ORGANIZATION

DALITS AND OBCs: Independent India's founders wanted to remove the concept of caste, and expected reservation to last for 10–15 years until historically deprived groups caught up. In fact, with more new caste-based reservations and voting, caste is becoming more important in modern

India. In the 1980s, distinct Dalit parties like the Bahujan Samaj Party (BSP) were started by Kanshi Ram and later led by Mayawati.

WOMEN: In 30 years, women have come a long way, as ministers, entrepreneurs and CEOs. In fact, India has many women CEOs heading major banks, almost unheard of in the West. There are now millions of women in rural government too, after the government reserved 50 per cent of seats for women in the local Panchayati Raj institutions.

However, alarmingly, at 940 women per 1,000 men, the number of Indian women around compared to men is far lower than in developed countries. A simple calculation tells us that there are about 60 million missing women who have died either in the womb, or due to malnutrition, or lack of medical care. The government had to make it illegal for doctors to reveal the sex of the child before birth to prevent female foeticide, but it still goes on. Dowry remains a social ill. In some states, there are so few women, they have to be 'imported' from other far-flung areas.

THE RISE OF THE NRI

With more than 30 million Indians living overseas, Indians have increased their visibility abroad. In the USA, Indian entrepreneurs have been significant in the IT industry, and the heads of Google, Sundar Pichai, and Microsoft, Satya Nadella, are of Indian origin. Many other CEOs of major US multinationals are Indians born and educated in India! Indian companies too are investing abroad and becoming multinationals, like the Tata and ArcelorMittal groups.

One interesting Indian cultural export is yoga, which is becoming very popular across the world, with hundreds of millions of non-Indian practitioners.

ECONOMY

Rajiv Gandhi slightly loosened rigid government controls, and there was higher growth in the 1980s. However, the real leap came under Prime Minister Narasimha Rao and his finance minister, Dr Manmohan Singh, in 1991, after India faced a severe foreign exchange crisis.

Major steps were (quietly) taken – including opening up government-reserved sectors like insurance, banking and air travel to private business. Still, labour laws were not eased up and the bureaucracy remains fearsome. Despite that, from 1984 to 2014, India's total income, according to World Bank data, increased by almost nine times, while the population grew only 1.7 times. This means each person became six times better off – that is a lot!

There was great growth in areas like software exports, which became a huge foreign exchange earner, with companies like Infosys, Wipro and TCS. Another industry moving to India is business process outsourcing (BPO). India also now manufactures and exports garments, medicines, cars and engineering products.

Many new private airlines now ply hundreds of flights, at prices that compare with the railways. The number of passengers travelling by air in a year has risen from 260,000 in 1970 to 119 million in 2016!

Cities like Hyderabad are symbolic of growing modern Indian cities

Retail has exploded and a vast array of Indian and foreign brands is available both in stores and online. The Indian middle class (loosely defined) now stands at about 250 million! We are finally being perceived internationally as the land of computers and technology and Bollywood rather than the land of snake charmers and starving children.

Still, the number of poor remains far too high. Even though the people living 'below the poverty line' (BPL) has reduced from 40 per cent to about 25 per cent – that is still 300 million people. There are millions who do not get enough to eat, who do not go to school, who lack toilets, healthcare and drinking water. Even as the rich get richer, the Indian state has not ensured these basics for all.

EDUCATION AND HEALTH

There is an endless demand for education. New private colleges attract foreign students from regions like Bhutan and Africa, but basic primary education is still not available to many Indians. Many girls still drop out of school in their teens, due to many reasons, including a lack of toilets in schools.

India has many private hospitals that offer world-class healthcare. Their rates (reasonable compared to the West) attract medical tourists from all over, but are unaffordable for many Indians. Public healthcare is scarce and of poor quality. While polio eradication has been a success, TB and HIV remain major issues. Life expectancy is about 68 years, against 80 years in developed countries – of 200 countries, our rank is about 126. Infant mortality is about 35 per 100,000 as against 2 to 5 in developed countries.

SCIENCE, TECHNOLOGY AND DEFENCE

India has stunned the world with its space technology –
homegrown and cheap! On 5 November 2013, it
successfully launched the Mangalyaan probe at a small
budget of 750 million rupees, becoming the first Asian
nation to orbit Mars. It also launched 104 satellites at one
go in 2017, setting a world record.

India also developed world-class indigenous defence
technology, testing its first missile in 1988. A prime mover
of this was the scientist Dr A.P.J Abdul Kalam, who
became one of the most popular presidents of India.

LIFESTYLE

The great consumer revolution has finally arrived in India.
A visitor to India in the early 1980s would not recognize
a large metro like Delhi today.

Our visitor would land in a modern, award-winning
airport, bustling with many airlines and hundreds of
flights, instead of a small, rundown building with a few
Indian Airlines and Air India flights. He would see many
Indians popping over to Thailand and Sri Lanka for
weekends, and to Europe and America for longer breaks.

Multi-lane highway-style roads would be full (choked,
really) of international cars instead of single-lane roads
plying lazily with Ambassadors and Fiats. He would pass
gleaming glass buildings, glossy modern hospitals and
educational institutions, and shop at world-class malls with
major international brands, instead of small retail shops
with a limited choice of local goods. He could stay at fancy
resorts and watch one of hundreds of Indian or foreign
channels on a flat-screen HD TV, or visit a swanky multiplex
cinema, or maybe catch the cricket IPL tournament in action.

He would see young men and women in smart clothing busily going to work on the metro, punching away on their smartphones. He would think India has totally transformed.

However, if he went into India's rural interiors, he would find an India that has changed little. People would have mobiles, and may be more educated, but still be plagued by poverty, caste discrimination, bad housing, low-quality education, the absence of electricity, and even a lack of toilets. Change has come to India. A lot in some places, and little in others.

That's a good amount of history behind us.

Now, for the future.

What in the World Was Happening! (1984–2000s)

Asia
- China rises to become the largest economy in the world.
- Islamic fundamentalist organizations, such as Al Qaeda, ISIS and Boko Haram, wreak havoc across the world.

Americas
- USA: Al Qaeda crashes planes into American buildings on 9 September 2001.
- The USA enters into wars in Afghanistan and Iraq.
- The USA elects its first black president, Barack Obama, in 2008.

Africa
- Nelson Mandela helps end apartheid in South Africa.
- Many Arab countries overthrow military dictators in a movement called the Arab Spring.

Europe
- The Cold War ends in 1991; the USSR splinters into many nations.
- Eastern Europe abandons communism.
- Europe comes together under the European Union (EU) with a common currency. In 2016, the UK votes to exit from the EU.

Explore More

* TALK to your grandparents and other older family members, or neighbours and other people you know and ask them about their life and times, especially their childhoods. How different were their growing-up years from yours? Make a timeline of when common products that you use now (and they did not!) came to be and how did they ever manage without them!

* VISIT modern 'monuments' such as buildings connected to the government, or institutions connected to culture, sports, science and technology in your own city.

* MAKE a time capsule! Using a plastic bottle or jar, put in objects and photographs relevant to the present times. A time capsule is a historic cache or store of things and information. You can add your personal details and some of your favourite things, and own observations about India today.

* CHOOSE any one personality whom you are impressed or inspired by from the past 30 years and make a 'biography' scrapbook or chart about that person. Gather material from online sources and books in libraries, but make sure you also visit at least one place connected to the person.

Epoch	The Mughals	The Mughals	The Beginning of British Colonialism
Pan India	*Establishment of Mughal rule *Europeans trade with India by the sea route	Mughal Empire's apogee	*Mughal Empire fragments *Rise of the Marathas *Establishment of British Raj *British rule: transfer of wealth from India to Britain
North-western India	*Babur raids Punjab *Guru Nanak *Fall of Chittor *Mughal rule: Lahore is a major Mughal city	*Mughal Empire's apogee *Sikhs gain prominence: Guru Gobind Singh	*Raids of Ahmad Shah Abdali *Sikh chieftains become powerful *Maratha raids across Rajasthan and Punjab
Indo-Gangetic Plain	*Babar conquers Delhi *Foundation of Mughal Empire *Akbar creates a glittering secular court *City of Dinpanah built at Delhi	* Jahangir, Nur Jahan *Shah Jahan builds Taj Mahal; shifts capital to a new city at Delhi *Aurangzeb	*Nadir Shah of Iran loots Delhi *Ahmad Shah Abdali raids India, defeats Marathas at Panipat *Mughal empire breaks apart into Awadh, Rohillas and others
Eastern India	Sher Shah Suri takes over Sultanate of Bengal; conquered by Akbar to become part of the Mughal Empire	*Assam resists conquest by the Mughals *Founding of Calcutta (Kolkata) *European traders set up outposts	*British defeat Nawab of Bengal in the Battle of Plassey; allotted Diwani of Bengal *Great Bengal famine in 1760s *Establishment of the British Raj
	1500–1600 CE	**1600–1700 CE**	**1700–1800 CE**
Central India	* Rana Sanga defeated by Babur *Conquest of Gujarat and Malwa by the Mughals	Rise of the Marathas under Shivaji	Establishment of the Maratha kingdoms of the Scindias, Gaekwads, Holkars and Bhonsles
Southern India	*Portuguese rule Indian Ocean *Bahmani Sultanate breaks up into Bijapur, Golconda, Ahmadnagar, Berar, Bidar *Vijayanagar falls at Talikota	*Bijapur and Golconda finally conquered by Aurangzeb *Marathas start dominating the south *European trade picks up	*The British and French fight for dominance; the British win and acquire substantial territories from Indian kings *Tipu Sultan defeated by British
Elsewhere in the world	*Expansion of the Ottoman Empire to Europe *Age of Exploration for the Europeans *Conquest of the Americas	*East India Company founded *Europeans begin colonizing the world	*Industrial Revolution begins *Europeans colonize the world due to technological superiority *The United States of America is the first modern democracy
Cultural Highlights	*Fatehpur Sikri *Humayun's tomb *Meera Bai *Tulsidas *Rahim *Purandara Das *Abul Fazl	*Taj Mahal *Red Fort *Mughal miniatures	*Hawa Mahal *Mir Taqi Mir *Sadarang

British Raj	India Gains Independence	Liberalization	Epoch
*Great Uprising of 1857 *The crown takes over from East India Company *India becomes one of the poorest countries in the world	*India becomes independent *Partition of the country *Emergency imposed 1975-1977 *Liberalization in 1991 *Rapid economic growth	*India becomes the third largest economy in the world *Narendra Modi becomes Prime Minister	Pan India
*The Sikhs under Ranjit Singh set up an empire in Punjab; conquered by the British after his death *The British-Afghan Wars	*New country of Pakistan; >10 million migrate; 1 million die in Hindu–Muslim riots *Green Revolution in Punjab *Khalistan separatist movement quelled	Kashmir insurgency continues	North Western India
*British win Battle of Patparganj and take over many kingdoms *Uprising in 1857: millions die; Delhi destroyed; Mughal emperor deposed	*British capital shifts to Delhi, which becomes capital of independent India *Anti-Sikh riots in 1984 *Delhi grows exponentially	Delhi is second most populous city in the world	Indo Gangetic Plain India
*Bengal Renaissance in education and the arts *Social reform *Tea plantations in Assam *Opium	*Partition of Bengal; capital shifts to Delhi *Partition of India; new nation of Bangladesh *Insurgencies in the North-East	Regional parties dominate in most states	Eastern India

1800–1900 CE	1900–2000	2000–	
*British win the Maratha wars *Treaties with some princely states; others taken over *Major centre for Uprising of 1857; Rani of Jhansi	Princely states absorbed into the Union of India	Gujarat becomes model of development under Chief Minister Narendra Modi	Central India
*Southern famine *Foundation of Presidency College in Madras *British rule deepens	*Reorganization of states on linguistic lines *Anti-brahmin movement *Regional parties dominate	Rise of infotech Industry	Southern India
*Age of Colonialism: The British Empire is the largest in the world *The USA spreads to the Pacific	*First World War *Second World War: Colonies become independent *Rise and fall of communism *USA becomes most powerful nation	*Rise of China *Rise of India *Rise of Islamic fundamentalism *European Union	Elsewhere in the world
*Chhatrapati Shivaji Maharaj Terminus (earlier Victoria Terminus) *Bharatendu Harishchandra *Bankimchandra *Mirza Ghalib	*Constitution of India *Rashtrapati Bhavan *Parliament House *Gitanjali *Pather Panchali	*Akshardham temple *Dalit Chetna Sthal *Dangal	Cultural Highlights

Index

Abdali, Ahmad Shah 91, 92, 96, 98, 103, 159, 161, 386
Accession, Instrument of 316-18
Act, Government of India 1935
Act, Rowlatt 267
Advani, L.K. 354, 370, 376
Adyar, Battle of 147
Afghan War, First 163-65
Agra 12, 13, 15, 16, 18, 20, 31-35, 48, 49, 52, 57, 80, 91, 110, 116-118, 120, 128, 176, 237, 247
Agreement, Standstill 315, 317
Ain-i-Akbari 43, 49, 113, 125
Akbar, Jalauddin Muhammad 40- 68, 70, 78, 85, 114-116, 118, 120, 122, 123, 125, 130-31, 183, 188, 197
Ali, Aruna Asaf 285
Ali, Hyder 148-49
Ali, Maulana Mohammad 273
Ali, Maulana Shaukat 273
Aliwal, Battle of 163
Ambar, Malik 59-60
Ambedkar, Bhimrao Ramji 272-73, 276, 278, 297, 322, 324, 332, 340
Aminchand 144
Anand, Mulk Raj 303-04
Anglicists 185
Anglo-Indians 240-41, 267, 278
Anglo-Mysore War, First 148
Anglo-Mysore War, Fourth 150
Anglo-Mysore War, Second 148
Anglo-Mysore War, Third 150
Annadurai, C.N. 331
Arjan Dev, Guru 55
Arya Samaj 192-93, 309
Assaye, Battle of 153
Aurangzeb 51, 54, 61-79, 83, 87, 94, 95, 98, 99, 101, 115, 119, 123, 125, 131-32, 143, 155, 159, 386
Awadh 32, 88, 90-96, 98, 99, 103, 125-

27, 145, 154, 167, 168, 172, 177, 180, 386
Azad, Chandrashekhar 279

Babur, Zahiruddin Muhammad 15, 20, 28-30, 46, 112, 386
Baburnama 5, 10, 13
Badauni, Mulla 17, 50
Bahini, Mukti 352
Baji Rao I 100, 102-03
Balaji Baji Rao II 100, 151, 154, 166
Banda Bahadur 84, 95, 97
Banerjea, Surendranath 246
Bangladesh 196, 201, 259, 294, 325, 347, 353, 357, 383
Banks 223, 351, 360, 361, 379
Baz Bahadur 32, 33
Bengal 212-216, 218, 220, 221, 223, 245, 249-50, 253-60, 283, 287, 288, 303, 305, 308, 313,
Bengal, Asiatic Society of 184
Bentinck, William 169, 186, 210
Bernier, Francois 2, 67, 68, 121, 127
Bharati, Subramania 260, 261, 295
Bharatiya Janata Party 368, 370-76
Bhavan, Rashtrapati 257, 290, 304, 387
Bijapur 68, 72-74, 77, 124, 138, 386
Birbal 47, 48, 52, 126
Birla, G.D. 263
Bismil, Ram Prasad 278
Black Hole of Calcutta 144
Bombay 138, 142, 143, 166, 175, 184, 193, 203, 217, 218, 220, 223, 246-47, 250, 257, 260, 261-62, 272, 298-302, 307-08, 333, 360, 313-14, 361, 376
Bonnerjee, W.C. 246, 247
Bose, Nandalal 200, 304, 305, 310, 324
Bose, Netaji Subhash Chandra 281
Boycott 250-52, 254, 273, 274
Brahmo Samaj 187, 189, 194, 202

British 103, 104-7, 115, 137-289, 294,
    296, 299-304, 309, 312, 315, 318,
    322, 330-33, 338-40, 342, 375
Bundela, Raja Bir Singh 49, 63
Bundelkhand 63, 174
Buxar, Battle of 92, 145

Calendars 205-206
Cama, Bhikaji Rustom 285, 289
Canning, Governor General 175, 178
Chandernagore 12, 147, 321
Chandrashekhar 371
Chattopadhyay, Bankimchandra 197
Chauri-Chaura 274
Chauth 76, 99, 100
Chhatrasal, Raja 102
Chillianwallah, Battle of 163
China 1-8, 51, 56, 118-21, 134-35, 179,
    208, 212, 214, 233, 262-63, 291,
    337-40, 345, 348-53, 368, 372-73
Chittor/fort 18, 33, 126, 386
Christianity 39, 63, 169, 171, 195, 196,
    202, 234, 240
Churchill, Winston 277, 282, 284, 317
Clement, Attlee 284
Clive, Robert 133, 144-45, 147
College, Fort William 184, 186
College, Hindu 190-92, 196, 227
Commission, Mandal 370
Commission, Simon 274
Communications 222, 334
Communist Party of India (CPI) 329-31,
    343, 350, 356-57
Communist Party of India (Marxist)
    (CPI-M) 356, 357
Conference, Bandung 335
Conference, First Round Table 275
Conference, Second Round Table 276, 285
Conflict, Kargil 374
Congress (Party) 322, 328-33, 340, 348,
    350-352, 355-56, 358, 368-72
Constitution, Indian 324-25, 334, 355,
    360, 361, 364, 387

Currency 22, 76, 223-24, 293-94, 317
Curzon, Lord 230, 249-50, 254

Dalhousie, Lord 165-68
Dalits 272, 276, 278, 279, 297, 304, 322,
    324, 332, 378, 379, 387
Daniyal 36, 57, 61
Dara Shikoh 61, 64-68, 70
Denmark 140, 276
Derozio, Henry Louis Vivian 191
Desai, Morarji 349-51, 354-55
Dhyanchand, Major 301-02
Din-i-Ilahi 38, 51
Discovery, Age of 137
Diu, Battle of 138
Dominion Status 244, 274, 282
Dravida Nadu 297-98
Durbar, Imperial/Delhi 200, 229, 231,
    245, 254, 260
Durgavati, Rani 32, 33
Dutch East India Company/Dutch 79,
    115-17, 124, 137, 140-41, 145, 179
Dyer, General 268

East India Company 74, 78, 79, 86, 104,
    140-45, 148, 155-58, 164, 168, 176,
    183, 185, 187, 195, 212, 223, 289
Eknath 127
Elections, First General 328, 329
Emergency 353-56, 387
Enlai, Zhou 337-39
Extremists 249, 251, 266

Faizi 47, 49, 50, 125
Famines 82, 115, 210, 214-16, 217, 342
Farrukhsiyar 84-86, 92, 97, 100, 143
Fatehpur Sikri 11, 35, 39, 52, 55, 116,
    120, 123, 131, 386
Fazl, Abul 37, 47, 49, 50, 130, 386
Flag 289, 290
French (The) 82, 107, 115, 137, 140,
    147-48, 150, 152, 156, 160, 179,
    254, 321

Gama, Vasco da 136, 138
Gandhi, Indira 324, 347-63
Gandhi, Mahatma/Mohandas
    Karamchand 233, 247, 263, 265,
    266, 269-84, 289-92, 297, 305, 312,
    313, 319, 322,
Gandhi, Rajiv 350, 354, 356, 359, 368-71,
    373, 375, 380
Gandhi, Sanjay 350, 353-358
Gandhi, Sonia 356, 371
Gazette, Hicky's Bengal 220
George V, King 231, 254
Ghaghra, Battle of 12
Ghalib, Mirza 127, 132, 167, 180, 387
Ghat, Satichaura 172
Ghazni 8, 91, 164, 165
Ghose, Aurobindo 252, 253, 254
Ghose, Barin 253
Gobind Singh, Guru 72, 95, 159, 386
Godse, Nathuram 291
Gokhale, Gopal Krishna 181, 246-48
Gol Gumbaz 124
Golconda 60, 68, 76, 124, 161, 386
Golden Temple 97, 122, 159, 359
Gowda, H.D. Deve 370, 371
Grand Trunk Road 22
Gujral, I.K. 370, 371
Gujrat, Battle of 163

Habibullah, Haji 45
Hakim, Mirza 34
Hargobind, Guru 71
Hastings, Warren 149, 153-54, 183-84,
    197
Holkar, Ahilyabai 106, 108
Holkar, Jaswant Rao 152
Hossain, Begum Rokeya Sakhawat
    201
Humayun 12-21, 26, 28-30, 120, 132
Hume, A.O. 247
Hyderabad 92, 94, 103, 124, 127, 147-50,
    154, 175, 227, 228, 231, 285, 315-
    17, 333, 378

Imperial/Indian Civil Service 219-20,
    223, 245-48, 254, 281
Indian National Congress/INC 246,
    247-252, 255, 261, 266-89, 297-98,
    312-321. See also Congress Party.
Indigo 118, 142, 213, 215, 259, 271,
Industrialization 261-63
Iqtadari 41
Irrigation 118, 166, 222, 299
Itmad-ud-Daulah 58, 120

Jafar, Mir 144-45
Jahanara 61, 62, 64, 66, 67, 115
Jahangir 14, 44, 49, 50, 54-61, 63, 64, 70,
    71, 78, 80, 95, 118-120, 123, 125,
    129-31, 142
Jallianwala Bagh 266, 268-69, 281
Jama Masjid 62, 121
Jana Sangh 330, 333, 350, 352, 357, 372
Jeejeebhoy, Sir Jamsetjee 262
Jews 37, 140, 234, 308
Jhansi 166, 173, 174, 180, 281,
Jhansi, Rani of / Lakshmibai 174
Jijabai 72, 73
Jinnah, Muhammad Ali 252, 276, 279-87,
    291, 313, 315-18, 325, 337,
Jizya 37, 68
Junagadh 316
Jung, Muzzafar 147

Kabul 8, 10-11, 13-16, 19, 29, 34, 88, 164
Kabuliyat 22
Kachhwaha, Ram Singh 72
Kalanaur 29
Kamran 15-17, 19
Kandahar 15, 19, 21, 29, 34, 38, 60, 64,
    88, 164
Kannauj, Battle of 16, 26
Karkhana 42, 45, 116, 117
Karnavati, Rani 18
Kashmir 34, 80, 104, 116, 121, 128, 139,
    160-63, 227, 304, 315-18, 333-38,
    345, 349, 352, 358, 369, 373-74,

Khalsa, Sikh 72, 95, 159,
Khan, Bairam 29, 30, 31, 32, 50
Khan, Genghis 7
Khan, Hasan Ali 85
Khan, Hussain Ali 85
Khan, Khan Abdul Ghaffar 319
Khan, Noor Inayat 283
Khan, Saadat 88, 89, 90, 95
Khan, Sir Syed Ahmad 195-96, 255
Khan, Zulfikar 85
Khan-i-Khana 30, 31, 50
Khanua, Battle of 11, 12
Khurram, prince 58, 60-61
Kipling, Rudyard 176
Koh-i-Noor 10, 13, 90, 161, 162

Labour, indentured 190, 230, 232, 270
Lahore 8, 15, 16, 21, 60, 80, 88, 91, 97,
    116, 122, 128, 159, 160, 247, 252,
    272, 275, 349
Lahori, Abdul Hamid 65, 125
Lang, Timur 2, 6, 7
Lapse, Doctrine of 165-68, 174
League, All-India Muslim 255-56, 266,
    276, 279-81, 283, 286-87
Lebedev, Gerasim 203
Lenin 330
Literature 13, 106, 186, 191, 196-98,
    260, 303
Lodi, Ibrahim 9, 10, 11, 12
Lohia, Ram Manohar 331, 332
Lytton, Lord 229-30, 245-46

Macaulay, Lord Thomas Babington 185,
    186, 226
Mahal, Begum Hazrat 172, 176
Mangalore, Treaty of 149
Manohar 44, 122
Mansabdari 41, 51, 98, 99, 125, 129
Manucci, Niccolao 57, 77, 78, 79, 129, 131
Marathas 59, 64, 68, 72-77, 82, 86, 91-96,
    98, 103-106, 108, 113, 148-154, 166,
    211, 333, 386

March, Dandi 275-76
Mariamma 136
Marwar 21, 70, 71, 95, 114, 262
Medicine 184, 202, 214, 227, 299, 380
Meera Bai 126
Meerut 104, 171
Mehta, Sir Pherozeshah 246
Mewar 11, 33, 34, 57, 84, 95
Minto, Lord 254, 255
Mission, Cripps 282
Moderates 249, 250, 251, 252, 266
Modi, Narendra 370, 372, 377, 387,
Mookerjee, Dr Shyamaprasad 332, 334
Mountbatten, Louis 27, 290, 313-15, 319
Movement, Civil Disobedience 274,
    276, 321
Movement, Khilafat 273, 274
Movement, Non-cooperation 271, 273
Movies 4, 260, 303, 307-08, 344, 362,
    363-64, 369, 378, 382
Mukherjee, Jatindranath/Bagha Jatin 254
Mysore 103, 148-150, 224, 227-28, 299,
    304, 333

Naicker, E.V. Ramasamy 297, 298, 331
Naidu, Sarojini 285
Nampoodiripad, E.M.S. 331
Nana Sahib, Peshwa 167, 172, 174, 177
Nanda, Gulzarilal 348, 350
Naoroji, Dadabhai Sir 209-10, 246, 248
Narayan, Jayaprakash 331, 332, 353, 354
Navratna 39, 47
Nayudu, C.K. 302
Nehru, Jawaharlal 233, 272, 274-75, 292,
    312, 327-345
Nehru, Motilal 267, 272
Nil Darpan 213, 259
Non-Alignment 335, 336, 352
NRI (Non-Resident Indian) 371
Nur Jahan 56, 58, 60, 120, 386

Opium 15, 56, 87, 179, 208-212, 214-15,
    262, 387

Orientalists 183, 185, 186

Pact, Gandhi–Irwin 276
Painting 9, 15, 30, 33, 44, 55, 56, 63, 96,
    100, 102, 108, 112, 115, 122-25,
    153, 199-200, 298, 305-06, 310, 344
Pakistan 22, 26, 58, 80, 161-63, 281, 286-
    91, 313-19, 325, 334, 337, 339, 340,
    348-49, 352-53, 357, 373-74, 387
Pakistan, East 314, 352, 357
Pal, Bipin Chandra, 250, 253
Panipat, First Battle of 9,
Panipat, Second Battle of 30
Panipat, Third Battle of 91, 96, 98, 103, 151
Paramahansa, Ramakrishna 193-94
Parliament House 257, 290, 387
Parsis 37, 38, 261, 262, 301, 334
Partition, Bengal 249, 254, 256, 387
Partition, India 271, 288, 313-14, 319,
    333, 340, 387
Patel, Sardar Vallabhbhai 316-23, 328,
    337, 338
Patparganj, Battle of 153
Pax Britannica 158, 167, 226
Peacock Throne 62-66, 82, 87, 89, 127
Permanent Settlement 210-11
Plassey, Battle of 95, 133, 144, 386
Portuguese 138-142, 156, 191, 242, 317,
    321-22, 386
Prarthana Samaj 192

Queen Elizabeth I 40, 51
Queen Victoria 161, 172, 179, 228-29, 234

Radio 307, 317, 331, 344, 361
Rahim, Abdur 31, 47, 50, 126
Rahman, Mujibur 352
Rai, Lala Lajpat 250, 251, 252, 274, 332
Railways 166, 179, 208, 221, 222, 237,
    241, 355, 380
Rajagopalachari, C. 272, 286
Rajguru 278, 279
Rajputs 33, 37, 40, 43, 59, 61, 63, 70, 71,
    83-85, 95, 98, 102,-05, 113-15, 126,
    154, 177, 215, 309, 314, 318, 334
Ramachandran, M.G. 357, 358
Rana Pratap 33, 34, 59
Ranade, Mahadev Govind 192, 248
Rao, N.T. Rama 357
Rao, P.V. Narasimha 370, 371, 380
Rathore, Rana Jaswant Singh 70
Ray, Prafulla Chandra 199
Ray, Satyajit 180, 344
Red Fort 53, 62, 63, 69, 80, 90, 93, 121,
    132, 231, 281, 290, 386
Reforms, Montague-Chelmsford 266-67
Reforms, Morley-Minto 254-56
Religions, World Parliament of 194-95
Revolution, Industrial 2, 107, 179, 182,
    210-11, 392
Revolutionaries 253-54, 266, 267, 276,
    278, 330
Ripon, Lord 245-46
Rohillas 82, 90-91, 93, 96, 98-99, 102,
    105, 154, 386
Roopmati, Rani 32-33
Roy, Raja Ram Mohan 187-90, 227
Ruqaiya Sultan, Begum 61

Samarkand 7, 8, 10, 14, 64, 120
Sambhaji 76-77, 99-100
Samru, Begum 102, 104
Sanga, Rana 11, 12, 126, 386
Saraighat, Battle of 72
Saraswati, Dayanand 192-93, 252
Sardeshmukhi 76, 99
Sati 38, 106, 114-15, 126, 169, 183, 186,
    187, 201
Satyagraha 26, 266, 270-74, 285, 289
Science and Technology 299, 342, 382
Scindia, Mahadji 93-94, 96, 105, 151
Scripts 365-66
Seringapatam, Treaty of 150
Shah Jahan 62, 67-71, 83, 87, 92, 95, 116,
    119-27, 132, 164
Shah Shuja 61, 66

Shah, Muhammad 87-90, 123, 126, 161
Shah, Nadir 2, 65, 88, 89-91
Shah, Nawab Wajid Ali 167
Shahu 99-101, 103
Sharia 57, 63, 69, 325
Shastri, Lal Bahadur 349
Shivaji, Chhatrapati Maharaj 76-77, 99-
    101, 108, 143, 166, 251,
Singh, Bhagat 278, 279
Singh, Choudhary Charan 354, 355
Singh, Maharaja Duleep 162
Singh, Maharaja Ranjit 158-163
Singh, Manmohan 370, 371, 380
Singh, Raja Man 33, 44, 47, 50, 302
Singh, Raja Sawai Jai 119
Singh, V.P. 370
Singh, Veer Kunwar 177
Siraj-ud-Daulah 95, 143, 144
Sombre, David Ochterlony Dyce 104
Sorabji, Cornelia 203
Sports 45, 131, 238, 296, 301, 363, 377
States, princely 176, 221, 227, 256, 285,
    312, 314-16, 319-20, 322, 326, 387
Subsidiary Alliance 152, 154, 228
Sukhdev 278, 279
Sulah-i-kul 57
Sultan, Tipu 148-151, 386
Suri, Sherkhan/Sher Shah 15-24, 26, 41,
    43, 118, 294, 386
Surrender, Instrument of 385
Swadeshi 193, 250, 252, 254, 273
Swaraj 250, 252, 253, 272, 273, 275,
    289

Tagore, Dwarakanath 188-89
Tagore, Rabindranath 189, 204, 219, 250,
    259, 269, 305, 367
Tagore, Satyendranath 219, 220
Tahmasp, Shah 13, 70
Taj Mahal 58, 64-66, 80, 120, 127, 314

Tarabai 99, 101, 103
Tata, J.R.D 300, 341
Tata, Nusserwanji 262
Tavernier, Jean-Baptiste 78, 79
Tax, Salt 214, 221, 275, 276
Tea 212, 231, 235, 238, 262-63, 299
Tegh Bahadur, Guru 71
Terrorism 267, 374, 375
Tilak, Bal Gangadhar 243, 250-51, 260
Todarmal, Raja 42, 47, 51
Tope, Tantia 167, 172-74, 177
Tukaram, Sant 127, 192
Tulsidas, Goswami 126, 386
Tuzuk-e-Jahangiri 55, 125

Ulema 34, 49, 57
Uprising, (1857) 83, 94, 157-179, 195,
    218, 221, 223, 227, 240, 349, 387
USA, the 144, 252, 256, 263, 282, 300,
    307-08, 318, 324, 330, 335-39, 345,
    348, 352,-53, 368, 374, 379

Vajpayee, Atal Bihari 354, 370, 371, 374
Vidyasagar, Ishwar Chandra 190-91, 259
Vivekananda, Swami 194-94

War, First Anglo-Maratha 151
War, First Sikh 163
War, First World 252, 256, 263, 266,
    267, 291, 296, 300, 387
War, Second Anglo-Maratha 152
War, Second World 216, 277, 279, 281-
    83, 291, 330, 339, 345, 387,
Wellesley, Arthur 150, 153, 184
Widow Remarriage 38, 187, 191-93,
    201, 298

Zafar II, Bahadur Shah 94, 123, 130, 167,
    172, 173
Zedong, Mao 337, 345

Acknowledgements

We would like to thank Thomas Abraham at Hachette India for this unique opportunity to Make History Fun Again. Our editor, Vatsala Kaul Banerjee, for being a paragon of patience and working as hard as us on this book for so many years! We are truly grateful.

Thanks to our father, Balkrishna Garodia, for the enquiring and intellectual atmosphere at home, and fostering our interest in books, history, culture and science. To our beloved mother, Chandra Garodia, who was always our biggest cheerleader and who made all five of us believe we were limited only by our imaginations. We miss you every single day.

To our sisters – Aparna, Manjari and Meenakshi – for being rocks of encouragement and support. And also, hey guys, yes, we are *finally* done!

To our gorgeous nieces and nephews: Pia and Uma Geismar, Neil Saran, and Soham, Vedita and Vihana Kapadia, who have often been our first audience for newly chanced upon historical tidbits – whether they wanted to be or not! We hope this book will lead you to love history like we do.

> *Archana*: Thanks to my husband, Manoj Gupta, for his warm encouragement and for taking so many responsibilities off my back. Thanks to my sister-in-law, Nidhi Williams, who has been a pillar of support, and my nephew Justin Williams for acting as a guinea pig.

> *Shruti*: A big thanks to my friends in the USA, the UK and India – you know who you are – for patiently having 'The Book' as my inevitable companion during so many holidays and conversations for years.

We would like to acknowledge books that have been valuable sources: Eraly, Abraham (1997), *The Last Spring*, Delhi, Viking, Penguin Randomhouse India; Keay, John (2000), *A History of India*, Great Britain, HarperCollins Publishers; Sankrityayan, Rahul (1957), *Akbar*, Delhi, Kitab Mahal; Majumdar, R.C., Raychaudhuri, H.C. and Datta, K. (1950), *An Advanced History of India*, London, Macmillan and Co. Ltd.